Paradox in Public Relations

Paradox in Public Relations: A Contrarian Critique of Theory and Practice is a thought-provoking exploration of public relations, aiming to promote changes in meaning and perception by creating new meta-realities for public relations.

The term "Public Relations" was embraced by early practitioners primarily because it sounded more professional than the often-pejorative alternatives. This book argues for a reframing of some of the popular realities associated with modern-day public relations and uses psychological and organizational change theory to critique paradoxes in public relations theory and practice. By examining public relations through the lens of paradox, we can begin to identify the logical fallacies that have inhibited progress and innovation in public relations practice and theory. The book explores the paradoxical nature of key concepts, including public interest, relationship management, accountability, stewardship, loyalty, community, and ethics. It also recommends new conceptualizations for understanding the field.

This book will be of interest to media, communication, public relations, and advertising faculty and graduate students, particularly those interested in public relations theory and ethics. Scholars from other disciplines can also use this exploration of paradox in PR as a learning tool for identifying logical fallacies and inconsistencies.

Kevin L. Stoker is Professor and Director of the Hank Greenspun School of Journalism and Media Studies at the University of Nevada, Las Vegas. After eight years in professional journalism, he earned a Ph.D. from the University of Alabama and has since held faculty positions at the University of North Carolina-Greensboro, Georgia Southern University, Brigham Young University, and Texas Tech University.

Routledge New Directions in PR & Communication Research
Edited by Kevin Moloney

Current academic thinking about public relations (PR) and related communication is a lively, expanding marketplace of ideas and many scholars believe that it's time for its radical approach to be deepened. **Routledge New Directions in PR & Communication Research** is the forum of choice for this new thinking. Its key strength is its remit, publishing critical and challenging responses to continuities and fractures in contemporary PR thinking and practice, tracking its spread into new geographies and political economies. It questions its contested role in market-orientated, capitalist, liberal democracies around the world, and examines its invasion of all media spaces, old, new, and as yet unenvisaged.

The **New Directions** series has already published and commissioned diverse original work on topics such as:

- PR's influence on Israeli and Palestinian nation-building
- PR's origins in the history of ideas
- a Jungian approach to PR ethics and professionalism
- global perspectives on PR professional practice
- PR as an everyday language for everyone
- PR as emotional labor
- PR as communication in conflicted societies, and
- PR's relationships to cooperation, justice, and paradox.

We actively invite new contributions and offer academics a welcoming place for the publication of their analyses of a universal, persuasive mindset that lives comfortably in old and new media around the world.

Public Relations, Branding and Authenticity
Brand Communications in the Digital Age
Sian Rees

Paradox in Public Relations
A Contrarian Critique of Theory and Practice
Kevin L. Stoker

For more information about this series, please visit www.routledge.com/ Routledge-New-Directions-in-Public-Relations–Communication-Research/ book-series/RNDPRCR

Paradox in Public Relations

A Contrarian Critique of Theory
and Practice

Kevin L. Stoker

Routledge
Taylor & Francis Group

LONDON AND NEW YORK

First published 2020
by Routledge
2 Park Square, Milton Park, Abingdon, Oxon OX14 4RN

and by Routledge
605 Third Avenue, New York, NY 10017

Routledge is an imprint of the Taylor & Francis Group, an informa business

First issued in paperback 2021

British Library Cataloguing-in-Publication Data
A catalogue record for this book is available from the British Library

Library of Congress Cataloging-in-Publication Data
Names: Stoker, Kevin, author.
Title: Paradox in public relations: a contrarian critique of
theory and practice / Kevin L. Stoker.
Description: First Edition. | New York: Routledge, 2020. |
Series: Routledge new directions in PR & communication research |
Includes bibliographical references and index.
Identifiers: LCCN 2019056585 (print) | LCCN 2019056586 (ebook)
Subjects: LCSH: Public relations. |
Public relations—Moral and ethical aspects. | Organizational change.
Classification: LCC HD59 .S756 2020 (print) |
LCC HD59 (ebook) | DDC 659.2–dc23
LC record available at https://lccn.loc.gov/2019056585
LC ebook record available at https://lccn.loc.gov/2019056586

ISBN 13: 978-1-138-67194-2 (hbk)
ISBN 13: 978-1-03-223768-8 (pbk)
ISBN 13: 978-1-315-61665-0 (ebk)

DOI: 10.4324/9781315616650

Typeset in Bembo
by Newgen Publishing UK

Printed in the United Kingdom
by Henry Ling Limited

Contents

Acknowledgments

Several friends and colleagues have played an important role in helping me complete this book. I want to thank my long-time friend and co-author Dr. Brad Rawlins, Interim Director of the School of Media and Journalism at Arkansas State University. Brad was the first phone call I made after writing down my initial thoughts and ideas about paradoxes in public relations. We have spent a lot of time debating and discussing the concept of paradox and its implications for public relations theory and practice.

Dr. Carl Botan, now a Professor of Communication at George Mason University, also played a role in validating this kind of philosophical research in public relations. At an International Public Relations Research Conference in Miami he counseled me to investigate Alfred Korzybski's work on Bertrand Russell's Group Theory and Theory of Logical Types.

I've been fortunate to have the support of Dr. Rob Ulmer, Dean of the College of Urban Affairs at the University of Nevada, Las Vegas. He has listened to my ideas and provided advice and direction. My former dean in the College of Media and Communication at Texas Tech University, David D. Perlmutter, also served as a friend and mentor for this project.

My friends and colleagues at the University of Nevada, Las Vegas, and Texas Tech University showed a great deal of patience listening to my ideas about paradox and helping me develop more coherent arguments. In particular, I'd like to thank Dr. Weiwu Zhang, Dr. Eric Bucy, Dr. Rob Peaslee, Dr. Paul Bolls, Dr. Ben Burroughs, Dr. Gregory Borchard, Dr. Dave Nourse, Stephen Bates, and Ben Morse. I probably ruined several lunches talking about paradox.

I also have benefited from the pioneering work of public relations scholars, such as Dr. Dean Kruckeberg, Dr. Don Stacks, Dr. Don Wright, Dr. James Grunig, Dr. Robert Heath, Dr. John A. Ledingham, Dr. Stephen Bruning, Dr. Maureen Taylor, Dr. Michael Kent, Dr. Mary Ferguson, and Dr. Bey-Ling Sha. Their contributions to public relations research continue to create opportunities for dialog, discussion, debate, and deliberation—all critical to moving public relations forward.

Finally, I'd like to thank my wife, Tammie, whose support, encouragement, and prodding have proven invaluable in completing this project.

Introduction

Paradoxes in public relations have always fascinated me. The name "public relations" seems to describe two opposing ideas. Public involves a group of people who may have interpersonal relations in and among themselves, but how could the group, this abstract entity, have its own relations? The field used the term public relations to represent an organization's relations with the public, but that conception also raised questions as to how an organization made up of people working toward a common goal could relate with other organized and unorganized groups of people. Were relations interpersonal, inter-organizational, or interpersonal-inter-organizational? Once I began studying the characteristics of paradox, I discovered that public relations theory and practice were fraught with oppositional elements and contradictions. My co-author at the time, Dr. Bradley L. Rawlins, and I made a list of potential public relations paradoxes: Public relations v. private relations; information v. promotion; peripheral v. integral; social responsibility v. moral responsibility; managing relationships v. empowering relationships; the RACE (research, action planning, communication, and evaluation) formula v. the RERACE (research, evaluation, re-engineering, research, action planning, communication, and evaluation) formula; strategic communication v. dialogic communication; and Excellence Model v. Contingency Model. We also identified the paradox of positive publicity, which we defined as how the effects of communicating only positive publicity ultimately undermines the credibility of the communication channel used, as well as the communication itself. Although the validity of these public relations paradoxes may be debatable, it soon became obvious that paradox could provide new and innovative perspectives of public relations.

The first challenge then was to learn more about the nature of paradox and then apply it to public relations. Since ancient times, philosophers have wrestled with the concept of paradox. The Greek philosopher Heraclitus revealed the complexity of paradox when he said, "No man ever steps in the same river twice, for it's not the same river and he's not the same man" (Heraclitus quotes, n.d.). At one level of analysis, the person steps in the same river but when thinking about the person stepping into the river, we recognize that the water has flowed downstream and the person, too, has been changed by the flow of life and is not the same person. On the other hand, the person is the same one that first stepped in the river, and the river is the same one stepped in the first time. To understand paradoxes, we have to look beyond the obvious and delve deeper into meaning and language.

Danish philosopher and existentialist Soren Kierkegaard used paradox to explain one of the most perplexing of Bible stories. In his book, *Fear and Trembling*, he explored Abraham's paradox of faith that occurred when God commanded him to sacrifice his son. Obedience to God meant that Abraham must disobey universal moral law. To save his son, he would have to disobey God and deny his faith. An angel's intervention stopped the sacrifice but did not resolve the paradox. "The paradox of faith, then is this: that the single individual is higher than the universal, that the single individual…determines his relation to the universal by his relation to the absolute" (Kierkegaard, 1983, p. 70). In other words, a person's faith or relation to God trumped social obligations to a universal or binding moral law, even one based on logic and reason. Abraham's apparent blind faith defied moral law and also exemplified a pure faith that defied reason. The paradox of faith could not reasonably be explained. Kierkegaard accepted paradoxes as "unresolved contradictions" (Ricoeur, 1998, p. 15).

Contemporary scholars do not share Kierkegaard's pessimism, but they do share his passion for paradoxes that often defy logic and understanding. Cameron and Quinn (1988) defined paradox as involving "contradictory, mutually exclusive elements that are present and operate equally at the same time" (p. 2). When examined individually, these opposing ideas make sense but taken together, they become illogical and ridiculous. Van de Ven and Poole (1988), writing in the same book as Cameron and Quinn, defined paradox as "the simultaneous presence of two mutually exclusive assumptions or statements; taken singly, each is incontestably true, but taken together they are inconsistent" (p. 21).

The Oxford Dictionary defines paradox as, "A seemingly absurd or contradictory statement or proposition which when investigated may prove to be well founded and true" (Paradox, n.d.). Strictly speaking, for a paradox to exist, "some type of contradictory state of affairs or situation of opposition must be expressed in the very words used" (Kainz, 1988, p. 8). The liar paradox— "I always lie"–serves as an example of a statement that seems reasonable on one level but ridiculous and contradictory at another level. If the premise of statement is true, then the logical outcome of the statement is false. This is a common aspect of paradox. It is logically impossible and thus, "of no practical importance" (Watzlawick, Weakland, & Fisch, 2011, p. 62). Yet, the very pervasive nature of paradoxes in our personal and professional lives imbues them with profound importance. Paradoxes defy logic. They place us in the conundrum of accepting the fact that opposing statements or ideas can be illogical and true at the same time. To validate the existence of paradoxes is to expand the bounds of cognition and understanding. Ignoring paradoxes compounds their influence, leaving us trapped in a one-dimensional prison of our own making. We follow the rules down paths that initially may appear fruitful but ultimately magnify the negative effects of the paradox. Sometimes solutions are not found in following existing rules but in questioning the rules and asking whether the rules are "real" or valid (p. 27). Sometimes the most effective response is no response at all.

Paradoxical thinking has inspired theorists and researchers in fields ranging from psychotherapy to communication, business, and quantum physics. As a young man, Albert Einstein imagined what would happen if a workman fell from the scaffolding of a building and dropped an object, such as his watch or shoe. Though the man would be in motion, he might look at his watch and see that it is at rest, falling at the same speed as the man. Einstein's recognition of the paradox—that something could be at rest and in motion at the same time—inspired his revolutionary general theory of relativity (Cameron & Quinn, 1988; Berger, 2016). Einstein's colleague, John Archibald Wheeler, always pushed his students to think outside accepted frameworks. He reveled in "the profound and the paradoxical" (Folger, 2002, para. 7). Known for his research in quantum mechanics, Wheeler coined the term "black hole." Near the end of his life (he was 96 when he died in 2008), he focused on "ideas for ideas" and the nature of human existence. He wrestled with the paradox of whether human observation contributed to "the creation of reality" (para. 7). The universe, he contended, is the product of interaction between the observer and the observed. For example, light behaves as a particle and a wave depending on how it is observed. Wheeler surmised that through interacting with the universe, the observer gives meaning to the universe that would not exist without observation (Folger, 2002). Wheeler believed the infinite universe has no meaning absent the meaning given by the finite, insignificant human mind. Wheeler's observations made other physicists uncomfortable because he advocated that even objective reality was influenced by the subjective observer (Wheeler, 1975; Nesteruk, 2013).

In psychotherapy, the study of paradox has focused on pragmatics (language use and contexts) and its effects on human communication (Watzlawick et al., 2011). Of special interest is the effect of paradoxes on behavior disorders, such as schizophrenia. Watzlawick et al. defined paradox as a "contradiction that follows correct deduction from consistent premises" (p. 188). They identified three paradoxes. The first arise from logic and mathematics and are known as antinomies or logical contradictions that can be proved to be true. A common example is the statement "I always lie." It is stated as true but also the statement itself calls into question its validity. A second group occurs in language and is referred to as "*semantical antinomies* or *paradoxical definitions*" (p. 190). Semantic paradoxes arise from inconsistencies in levels of language (Ford & Backoff, 1988). They include the liar paradox, which arises from a statement by the Cretan, Epimenides, that "All Cretans are liars." The third type of paradox emerges out of ongoing human interactions and is known as pragmatic (behavioral) paradoxes. These paradoxes correspond with the theory of human communication and include paradoxical injunctions. In sum, the first type of paradox arises from logical syntax, the second from semantics, and the third from pragmatics (language use and contexts). The first two also lead to the emergence of prag-matic paradoxes (Watzlawick et al., 2011).

In organizational studies, researchers have discovered that pragmatic paradoxes are central to organizational development and change. Pragmatic paradoxes involve the ongoing process of human communication and are defined as "mutually exclusive alternatives that evolve over time" (Putnam, 1986, p. 153). Unlike logical paradoxes that emerge from contradictory statements that can be proved true or false, pragmatic paradoxes stem from communicative relationships (Putnam, 1986). The command to be spon-taneous is an example of a pragmatic paradox because it demands that a person be spontaneous when the act of spontaneity depends upon acting without mandate or direction. Pragmatic paradoxes are especially problematic in family and organizational relationships because the target of the injunc-tion has limited options for stepping away from the paradox. For example, a corporate executive might advise public relations to enter into a dialog with stakeholders but add that the organization has no plans to change its positions or alter its policy. To meet the demands of dialog, the practitioner must be open to change but to respond to the executive's injunction, the practitioner must not be willing to change anything. Resolving the paradoxical injunction would require the practitioner to step back and expose the illogic and incon-sistency of the situation.

The executive might respond by firing the practitioner or acknowledging the impossibility of the request. Recognition of paradoxes can lead to change. "Paradoxes reflect the underlying tensions that generate and energize organiza-tional change" (Ford & Backoff, 1988, p. 82). Groups are inherently paradoxical, and it is not unusual to find groups who, at the same time, desire change but do not want to change. This leads to inevitable conflict and tension (Smith & Berg, 1987). According to the force field analysis, the powers for change will always be met with an equal and opposite power that opposes change. Even when change occurs, organizational members, when faced with a crisis, revert back to old cause maps or strategic thinking in dealing with the problem (Weick & Bougon, 1986). In other words, the more things change, the more they might remain the same.

Prominent organizational theorist Karl Weick observed that organizational members and observers expect organizations to be "rational, accountable, orderly, predictable units that know what they're doing" (Weick, 1979, p. 243). However, when they inevitably encounter disorder, they overreact and assume the dissolution of the organization. Adopting rational approaches to dealing with the problems often pit those advocating change against those defending traditional approaches. They struggle to recognize that both sides are partially right and partially wrong. This tension allows organizations to be simultan-eously flexible and stable. Success depends on embracing the ambiguity of not knowing where the organization is going but knowing it is going somewhere. Searches for solutions will not provide much useful information "because of the inherent equivocality of situations" (p. 247). The goal is not to make the right judgment or avoid making a wrong one but to make a reasonable judgment and avoid an unreasonable judgment.

Rather than address the paradox, however, organizations and individuals tend to choose one alternative over the other. These either/or solutions often ease the tension or anxiety but ultimately exacerbate the problem (Lewis, 2000). Paradoxes consist of opposing, interrelated elements that make sense individually but are absurd and irrational when they appear at the same time. The logical approach is to choose the element that presents the most positive possible outcome. Thus, the falling person in Einstein's example finds comfort in seeing that the shoe is at rest while ignoring the fact that both will ultimately crash into the ground. Contractors continue to build new houses despite drop-offs in demand because to stop building would mean a reduction in revenue. It is a common principle of business that during successful times, one is laying the groundwork for failure in the future. Oil companies pump more oil, increasing supply and lowering the price of oil. Parents give into their child's demands and soon find that the child demands even more. Public relations scholars promote dialog and two-way symmetrical communication as normative and then lament the fact that one-way and asymmetric communication continue to dominate professional practice.

In each of these cases, the oppositional elements are interrelated, which means that any change of approach to dealing with one side produces intended and unintended changes in the alternative. This interrelationship helps explain why focusing on one element at the expense of the other can worsen the effects of the paradox. For example, an organization may respond to calls of more transparency by flooding stockholders and the media with more annual report information, causing the media and key stakeholders to perceive an attempt to provide more information as a strategy for obfuscation and misinformation. The interrelationship between the two poles means that any increase or decrease in focus on one aspect directly affects its antipode. This dynamic equilibrium forms the basis of a theory of paradox proposed by Smith and Lewis (2011). As organizational actors confront two interrelated, contradictory elements, they experience tension and mistakenly seek to relieve the tension by embracing one element or the other.

Other approaches to paradox place less emphasis on the interrelated nature of the oppositional elements. Elson (2010) incorporated media ecology research on symbols, language, and communication to uncover solutions to common communicative paradoxes. Elson (2010) defined paradox "as a state of affairs that our cognitive wordmaps represent as impossible or contrary to fact, but which is nevertheless the case" (p. 1). Despite the inability of language sometimes to explain phenomena that our minds view as contradictory and illogical, these phenomena can still be true if we employ a meta-communication to understand them. Some paradoxes, Elson continued, are solved by virtue of differences in *space*; what is true in one location may not be true at another. Others are solved based on changes over *time*, such as a person being shorter as a child but taller as an adult. A third set of paradoxes, which she called *levels paradoxes*, were analyzed and resolved by considering the *levels of abstraction* in language and communication. By applying research on levels of abstraction, Elson uncovered possible solutions to the liar paradox, the prediction paradox, and the prisoner's dilemma. She also applied levels of abstraction to double binds and humor (Elson, 2010).

The ability to grasp ordinality or levels of abstraction in language does more than just helping us get the joke. Korzybski (2000) argued that the social and cultural developments of civilizations depended upon their ability to grasp higher abstractions. "Now consciousness of abstracting in all cases gives us the semantic freedom of all levels and so helps evaluation and selection, thus removing the possibility of remaining animalistically fixed or blocked on any one level" (Korzybski, 2000, p. 441). Progress in civilizations, societies, organizations, and humans depend on bursting through levels of abstraction. Moving to higher levels of abstraction has enhanced our understanding of media and communication. Marshall McLuhan's (1964) famous statement, "the medium is the message," reflects a levels confusion in certain communication contexts (Strate, 2010). The medium exists at a higher level of abstraction than the message.

Confusing the levels of abstraction leads to paradoxes. I contend that confusion over levels of abstraction has stymied progress in public relations scholarship and practice. Instead of addressing the paradoxes created from confusing levels of abstraction, public relations scholars and practitioners have ignored them, particularly those paradoxes in public relations history (Brown, 2006). Public relations emerged from social movements aimed at winning converts, raising money, gaining legitimacy, and agitating and advocating for or against something (Lamme & Russell, 2010). In the 1890s, Progressive Era politicians, journalists, business leaders, and reformers employed publicity and propaganda to reform government, business, and society. They viewed publicity as a moral disinfectant for cleansing corporate and political corruption. By shining a light on society's ills, reformers hoped to improve the human condition. However, the success of publicity and propaganda campaigns in winning public support for America's involvement in World War I and later national Prohibition saddled publicity and propaganda with negative connotations (Stoker & Rawlins, 2005). By the 1920s, publicity had become a strategic weapon for influencing and engineering public opinion.

In response to publicity's semantic demise, professional publicists embraced public relations as the new name for promotional and publicity work. They emphasized the power of truthful information and ideas to advocate in the court of public opinion (Cutlip, 1994). They employed publicity to influence public opinion but, unlike their predecessors, they carefully selected clients worthy of representation (Bernays, 1928). These public relations counselors ostensibly served the public interest by introducing new ideas and information for public consumption. Subsequent public relations professionals and academics eventually distanced the field from these historical roots in advocacy and publicity and instead promoted dialog, management, and relationships. For the last half century, the dominant definition for public relations has been "the management function that establishes and maintains mutually beneficial relationships between an organization and the publics on whom its success or failure depends" (Broom & Sha, 2013, p. 5). This evolution of public relations theory and practice from advocacy, persuasion, and publicity to two–way symmetrical communication and dialog has stymied philosophical, theoretical, and practical progress in the field. Truthful disseminated information still qualifies as publicity and creating and maintaining a mutually beneficial relationship still serves organizational interests at the expense of some members of the public. Indeed, public relations can be sincere and strategic, mutual and self-serving, managed and unintended, and one–way and dialogic at the same time.

Korzybski (2000) could have identified public relations' paradoxes as the result of failing to distinguish between the map and the territory. The map is a description of the territory but not the territory itself. One does not explore the territory by walking on the map. Paradox serves as a spotlight identifying the misconceptions and fundamental discrepancies between the map and the territory. One may turn off the spotlight but "the misconceptions remain" (Elson, 2010, p. 161). Paradox serves as a learning tool for exposing logical and linguistic problems and fallacies in public relations theory and practice. "The study of paradox is useful as a way of overcoming the inherent tendency for researchers within a field to develop myopia in ways of thinking" (Gyrd-Jones, Merrilees, & Miller, 2013, p. 576). When faced with conflicting ideas, organizations tend to apply either/or thinking, addressing each opposing idea individually. "Paradox thinking is 'and' thinking. It is thinking that identifies pairs of opposites and determines how they are interdependent relative to a key goal" (Schroeder-Saulnier, 2014).

By confronting the clashing ideas and contradictions associated with paradoxes, public relations scholars and practitioners can develop a greater flexibility of thought and creativity (Cameron & Quinn, 1988). Paradoxes are important because they "reflect the underlying tensions that generate and energize organizational change" (Ford & Backoff, 1988, p. 82). In other words, these tensions, produced by clashing ideas and contradictions, play a critical role in organizational change and progress. They are inherent in paradigmatic shifts in thinking and theory (Kuhn, 1996). Paradox challenges and undermines the coherence, consistency, and parsimony of theoretical thinking (Van de Ven and Poole, 1988). For public relations to learn and change, it must stop ignoring and avoiding paradoxical tensions and embrace and learn from these paradoxes. Paradoxical tension serves as a catalyst for change. By applying paradoxical thinking in public relations scholarship and practice, the field may begin to adopt definitions that are truly new and innovative.

Westenholz (1993) argued that individuals tend to get caught up in their typical frame of reference and respond to problems compatible with that frame. They fail to seek information outside the frame because the existing frame "entails a spontaneous self-referential and self-production process" (p. 38). In other words, the frames we use to represent reality tend to reinforce that perception of reality. If we view public relations as a management function that builds relationships, then we tend to see only those practices that reinforce that reality. These frames provide an unambiguous representation of a reality that is actually chaotic and unstable.

> As social beings, we are creating these pictures to defend our identity against a chaotic world. Without this defence we would be unable to deal with the world. At the same time, however, the pictures become a prison into which we are locked, so that we cannot view the world "afresh."
>
> (p. 39)

To break out of the self-imposed mental prison, individuals need a new way of making sense of the world. To see the world from a different perspective requires moving to a higher level of abstraction or changing the rules guiding our actions. Westenholz (1993) does not suggest abandoning the old frames but simply placing new meanings and references on top of the old frame. Again, paradoxes constitute either-and thinking in which the old and new frames coexist. The goal is to establish a new relationship with the situation and then recognize the power of contraries in providing new solutions to old paradoxical problems. By recognizing that the situation may not be what it seems to be, we open up possibilities for new understandings and perspectives. More important, we create conditions for progress and change.

In this book, I plan to use paradox research and theory to challenge popular conceptions of public relations on such topics as the field's obligation to the public interest, the recent focus on public relationships and relationship management, and the current obsession with dialog and symmetry. I also will examine public relations paradoxes associated with accountability, loyalty, and community. Paradox research comes from a variety of disciplines, including philosophy, psychotherapy, communication, business management, and others. By applying paradox research to public relations, I will show that popular assumptions and paradigms have inhibited progress in the field because they have failed to consider opposing perspectives. By their nature, paradoxes produce tensions and oftentimes the solution to the paradox lies in what appears as the negative of the two opposing elements. The natural tendency is to focus on the most favorable alternative, but, in studying public relations paradoxes, I will show that the least acceptable option can free the field from logical fallacies that stymie progress and change. Of particular interest will be the theories and metaphors that guide contemporary scholarship in public relations research and practice. These theories and metaphors often place unrealistic expectations on practitioners and send contradictory messages to the public as to the true nature of public relations. The ability to recognize paradoxes will help public relations scholars and practitioners discard and revise some metaphors that limit progress and change and adopt new linguistic frameworks that enable reorientation and reinvention. The first step is to take a closer look at the theories and concepts associated with paradox and then use them as a lens through which to examine public relations theory and practice.

Chapter 1 introduces research on several theories related to the concept of paradox. Though some research often refers to paradox as a theory, most scholars view paradox more as a conceptual framework of analysis made up of several theories. Paradox allows researchers to see beyond the logical, rational framework of ordinary thinking and peer deeper into the dialectical and contradictory nature of human interaction and meaning. As nineteenth century Danish philosopher Soren Kierkegaard explained, the capacity to embrace paradox reflects a passion for wisdom. "But one must not think ill of the paradox, for the paradox is the passion of thought, and the thinker without the paradox is like the lover without passion: a mediocre fellow" (Kierkegaard, 1985, p. 205; see also Ree & Chamberlain, 1998, p. 4). Kierkegaard considered paradoxes the "essential truth of the world" (Ree & Chamberlain, 1998, p. 4). To understand the nature of paradoxes is to peel back the layers of abstraction in language and begin to discover the logical fallacies and contradictions that undermine long-term progress, innovation, and change.

The paradox of the public interest provides the focus for Chapter 2, particularly the historical and contemporary interpretation of the concept by public relations practitioners and scholars. In the modern era of public relations, practitioners and scholars have alternated back and forth between the conflicting conceptions of the public espoused by Walter Lippmann and John Dewey. Those taking a Lippmann-like approach to public relations have viewed the public as a passive and uninformed group that needs help from intellectual elites to shape meanings for them. Edward Bernays liberally borrowed from Lippmann's philosophy of public opinion and positioned professional public relations counselors as ethical advocates serving private and public interests in the court of public opinion (Stoker, 2014). Other practitioners and scholars proposed an alternative view that framed practitioners as facilitators who allowed the public to determine their own interests. Viewing the conflict through the lens of paradox proposes a solution that incorporates Lippmann *and* Dewey, rather than choosing one frame of reference or the other.

Chapter 3 explores the paradox of managing a phenomenon that cannot be managed without manipulation and coercion. Management and relationships have evolved into two of the most dominant metaphors guiding public relations theory and practice. Contemporary scholarship has combined these two metaphors and added the expectation that practitioners manage the prescribed mutually beneficial relationships. However, *relationship management* assumes that practitioners have the power to manage the perceptions of the parties in a relationship. Based on the mathematical Theory of Logical Types, relationship management breaches the levels of abstraction in language, combining two terms that classify a set of activities that exist at two different levels of ordinality. The result is a paradox. Relationship management places practitioners in double bind, expecting them to manage the perceptions and preferences of others while undermining the freedom and choice necessary in a healthy, long-term relationship.

The dominant frame for public relations communication will be the focus of Chapter 4. Since the 1980s, prominent scholars have promoted two-way symmetrical communication as the most ethical process of communicative exchange but in the late 1990s, other scholars proposed relationship-centered dialog as the most ethical form of public relations. Other types of communication, especially those classified as one-way strategic and persuasive, are morally suspect, and practitioners of these forms of communication—press agents, publicists, and propagandists—are considered relics of a bygone era. This professional class system emerged with the best of intentions; scholars wanted public relations to be more accountable and adaptive to society and the public. When confronted with competing philosophies of dissemination and dialog, public relations scholars chose the more positive and popular of the alternatives. Of course, dialog should serve as the normative approach to public relations communication because it requires give and take by both parties. Contingency Theory reflects a dialectic approach to public relations and argues that the type of communication depends on a variety of factors that fall somewhere along a continuum between advocacy and accommodation. But Contingency Theory introduces its own set of paradoxes, not the least of which is the high number of contingent variables that undermine its explanatory power. I propose an alternative frame that highlights the value of differences and the particularly unique human characteristics of recognition and reconciliation.

In Chapter 5, the accountability paradox is explored. When faced with calls for more accountability for their actions, organizations rely on public relations practitioners to respond and provide a defense. The use of public relations to deal with direct agent-accountant relationships or social accountability reinforces the perception that public relations is a self-serving strategy for deflecting criticism and avoiding accountability. In some ways, legislation calling for greater accountability has paradoxically caused organizations to be less responsive and transparent. Even if they do meet their legal obligations, the public gives them little credit because they were forced to be accountable. Public relations can help organizations resolve these paradoxes by adopting an *ideal accountability* in which organizations (and practitioners) hold themselves accountable. This kind of ideal accountability constitutes second-order change and reframes public relations practitioners as "ideal accountants" who hold themselves and their organizations responsible to core values and ideals. This aligns accountability with moral autonomy, responsibility, and stewardship. This reframing is consistent with successful crisis management strategies in which organizations look inward to improve processes and approach crises as opportunities for re-engineering and renewal.

Chapter 6 deals with the paradox of public relations loyalty and the potential conflicts between private and public loyalties. The field may advocate a philosophy that broader loyalties to the public take precedence over narrower loyalties to colleagues and the organization. Practitioners can resolve the paradox by choosing loyalties that have universal value. In other words, the object of loyalty must be worthy of the practitioner's loyalty as well as the public's loyalty. This *loyalty to loyalty* allows practitioners to subjugate their interests to the interests of the organizations because those interests are based on universal ideals and values. Once one chooses an object of loyalty, one must remain vigilant, seeking truth as to the organization's commitment to its values, especially in times of deterioration and crisis. I provide a formula by which practitioners can determine when their loyalty crosses the line from virtue to vice and continued loyalty undermines loyalty to loyalty.

The paradox of being a part of and separate from a community is the focus of Chapter 7. In public relations, community is often viewed as a means to accomplishing the organization's ends. According to Group Theory, classifying the community as another public or as another stakeholder places the organization outside the community and undermines its relationship with its neighbors, friends, and family. The paradox for public relations is that the more organizations use their communities to achieve self-serving goals, even if those goals are mutually beneficial, the more likely they are to alienate themselves from their communities. Change occurs as public relations practitioners reframe their relationship with their communities to include themselves and their organizations. Thus, community relations and organizational relations unite in a community of interpretation and inquiry. Rather than being *morally detached* from their communities, as Josiah Royce labeled this phenomenon, organizations morally attach themselves through interpreting community issues and problems as their issues and problems. The individual or organization retains its status as an I while also embracing its bond as a We.

Works cited

Berger, A. (2016, June 15). All in Einstein's head. *Discover*. Retrieved March 31, 2017 from discovermagazine.com.

Bernays, E. (1928). This Business of Propaganda. *Independent, 121*, 198–199.

Broom, G. M. & Sha, B. L. (2013). *Cutlip and Center's effective public relations* (11th Ed.). New York: Pearson.

Brown, R. E. (2006). Myth of symmetry: Public relations as cultural styles. *Public Relations Review 32*, 206–212.

Cameron, K. S., & Quinn, R. E. (1988). Organizational paradox and transformation. In R. E. Quinn, & K. S. Cameron, (Eds.), *Paradox and transformation: Toward a theory of change in organization and management* (pp. 1–18). Cambridge, MA: Ballinger Publishing Company.

Cutlip, S. (1994). *The Unseen Power: Public Relations. A History.* Hillsdale, NJ: Lawrence Erlbaum Associates.

Elson, L. G. (2010). *Paradox lost.* Cresskill, NJ: Hampton Press.

Folger, T. (2002, June 1). Does the universe exist if we're not looking?. *Discover*. Retrieved November 8, 2019 from discovermagazine.com.

Ford, J. D., & Backoff, R. W. (1988). Organizational change in and out of dualities and paradox. In R. E. Quinn, & K. S. Cameron (Eds.), *Paradox and transformation: Toward a theory of change in organization and management* (pp. 81–121). Cambridge, MA: Ballinger Publishing Company.

Gyrd-Jones, R., Merrilees, B., & Miller, D. (2013). Revisiting the complexities of corporate branding: Issues, paradoxes, solutions. *Journal of Brand Management, 20* (7), 571–589.

Heraclitus quotes. (n.d.). *Goodreads.* Retrieved November 8, 2019 from goodreads.com.

Kainz, H. P. (1988). *Paradox, dialectic, and system: A contemporary reconstruction of the Hegelian problematic.* University Park, PA: The Pennsylvania State University Press.

Kierkegaard, S. (1983). *Fear and trembling* (H. V. Hong & E. H. Hong, Eds. & Trans.). Princeton, NJ: Princeton University Press.

Kierkegaard, S. (1985). *Philosophical fragments* (H.V. Hong & E. H. Hong, Eds. & Trans.). Princeton, NJ: Princeton University Press.

Korzybski, A. (2000). *Science and sanity: An introduction to non-Aristotelian systems of general semantics.* Brooklyn, NY: International Non-Aristotelian Library Publishing Company.

Kuhn, T. S. (1996). *The structure of scientific revolutions* (3rd Ed.). Chicago, IL: University of Chicago Press.

Lamme, M. & Russell, K. (2010). Removing the spin: Toward a new theory of public relations history. *Journalism Communication Monographs, 11* (4), 281–362.

Lewis, M. (2000). Exploring paradox: Toward a more comprehensive guide. *Academy of Management Review 25* (4), 760–776.

McLuhan, M. (1964). *Understanding media: The extensions of man.* New York: McGraw-Hill.

Nesteruk, A.V. (2013). A "participatory universe" of J. A.Wheeler as an intentional correlate of embodied subjects and an example of purposiveness in physics. *Journal of Siberian Federal University. Humanities & Social Sciences, 6* (3), 415–437.

Oakley, T. (2014). The ups and downs of PR for Apple. The Marketing Agenda. Retrieved March 21, 2017 from themarketingagenda.com.

Paradox. (n.d.). *Oxford Dictionary.* Retrieved March 28, 2017 from en.oxforddictionaries.com.

Putnam, L. (1986). Contradictions and paradoxes in organizations. In L. Thayer (Ed.), *Organization communications: Emerging perspectives* (pp. 151–167). Norwood, NJ: Ablex.

Rawlins, B. L. (2009). Give the emperor a new mirror: Toward developing a stakeholder measurement of organizational transparency. *Journal of Public Relations Research, 21,* 71–99.

Ree, J. & Chamberlain, J. (1998). Introduction. In J. Ree, & J. Chamberlain (Eds.), *Kierkegaard: A critical reader* (pp. 1–8). Malden, MA: Blackwell Publishers.

Ricoeur, P. (1998). Philosophy after Kierkegaard. In J. Ree, & J. Chamberlain (Eds.), *Kierkegaard: A critical reader* (pp. 9–25). Malden, MA: Blackwell Publishers.

Schroeder-Saulnier, D. (2014). *The power of paradox: Harness the energy of competing ideas to uncover radically innovative solutions.* Pompton, NJ: Career Press.

Sherman, E. (2014, May 21). Steve Jobs' Rules for Public Relations. *Slate.* Retrieved March 21, 2017 from slate.com.

Smith, K. & Berg, D. (1987). *Paradoxes of group life.* San Francisco: Josey-Bass.

Smith, W. K. & Lewis, M.W. (2011). Toward a theory of paradox: A dynamic equilibrium model of organizing. *Academy of Management Review, 36* (2), 381–403.

Stoker, K. (2014). Defining public in public relations: How the 1920s debate over public opinion influence early philosophies of public relations. In B. St. John, M. O. Lamme, & J. L'Etang (Eds.), *Pathways to public relations: Histories of practice and profession* (pp. 340–351). London: Routledge.

Stoker, K. & Rawlins, V. L. (2005). The "light" of publicity in the Progressive Era: From searchlight to flashlight. *Journalism History, 30* (4), 177–188.

Strate, L. (2010). An introduction to Paradox Lost. In L. Elson, *Paradox Lost: A cross-contextual definition of levels of abstraction*. Cresskill, NJ: Hampton Press.

Turney, M. (2012). Still seeking a definition after all these years. Online readings in public relations. Retrieved March 21, 2017 from nku.edu.

Van de Ven, A. H., & Poole, M. S. (1988). Paradoxical requirements for a theory of organizational change. In R. E. Quinn, & K. S. Cameron (Eds.), *Paradox and transformation: Toward a theory of change in organization and management* (pp. 19–63). Cambridge, MA: Ballinger Publishing Company.

Watzlawick, P., Weakland, J. H., & Fisch, R. (2011). *Change: Principles of problem formation and problem resolution*. New York: W.W. Norton.

Weick, K. E. (1979). *The social psychology of organizing*. Reading, MA: Addison-Wesley Publishing.

Weick, K. E. & Bougon, M. G. (1986). Organizations as cognitive maps: Charting ways to success and failure. In *The thinking organization*. H. P. Sims, Jr., D. A. Gioia & Associates (Eds.). San Francisco, CA: Jossey-Bass Publishers.

Westenholz, A. (1993). Paradoxical thinking and change in frames of reference. *Organizational Studies, 14*, 37–58.

Wheeler, J. A. (1975). The universe as home for man. In O. Gingerich (Ed.), *The nature of scientific discovery* (pp. 261–296). Washington: Smithsonian Institution Press.

1   Paradox in public relations

In the last 20 years, Apple has revolutionized the consumer electronics industry with innovative products, such as the iPad and iPhone. The company's public relations staff aggressively promotes new products by creating buzz around the impending release of new technology and then producing dramatic media events for product launches. Outside these bursts of promotion and publicity, the company's public relations activities tend to be more reactive and reserved. When faced with a crisis, Apple clams up and relies on loyalists to speak for the company (Oakley, 2014). In identifying Apple's paradoxical approach to public relations, Oakley suggested Apple should deal more directly and forthrightly to criticism. As a technology company, however, Apple owes much of its success to its organizational culture of secrecy. "Secrecy is part of the company's strategy to minimize theft of proprietary information or intellectual property" (Meyer, 2019, para. 7). This strategic management approach may conflict with expectations for corporate transparency but it is embedded in the company's mission and values. Apple's philosophy of public relations is paradoxical—it violates some norms while adhering to others (Oakley, 2014).

And yet this against-the-grain approach has contributed to Apple's successes in innovation, marketing, and public relations (Craig, 2016). Although the corporate culture depends on secrecy, Apple has a knack for making complex technology that communicates to its users that the company has their best interests in mind. Its technology is known for being simple and easy to use. It might be simplistic to say but, through its technology, Apple lets its engineers and designers do the talking to consumers. Apple uses the same strategy in media relations, creating press releases that a fourth grader could understand. It also avoids overwhelming reporters with information about every new product, software update, or personnel change, and instead only contacts reporters on major stories. Any time the company releases a new innovation, it takes the time to show a limited number of reporters and analysts how to use the products and gives them access to 24/7 tech support. In the meantime, Apple's public relations refuse to comment on issues unrelated to the company's core mission. By focusing on a small group of influential reporters, giving them exclusive access to its people and new products, Apple has paradoxically increased excitement for its new products and magnified the amount of media interest in its innovations (Craig, 2016).

Sometimes Apple's behavior has raised ethical concerns, such as when it limited access to reporters it did not like. Pundits and scholars have demanded more corporate transparency, but Apple remains secretive and goes to great lengths to restrict the flow of information out of the company. Instead, the company relies on a select group of reporters and media outlets and strategically leaks information and some disinformation to its media contacts (Sherman, 2014). Apple's example shows that, at some level of communication, a company can violate public relations norms of dialog and transparency and still maintain a positive reputation among key publics and stakeholders. It also reveals the complexity of public relations as a discipline and the difficult task facing practitioners and scholars who want to establish some basic rules and guidelines for professional practice.

Public relations is inherently paradoxical. At one level of analysis, Apple defies the common logic of public relations practice. At another level of abstraction, however, Apple does respond directly to criticism. Apple's engineers have long communicated with consumers, listening to customer criticism and complaints, and they react by going to great lengths to resolve problems. Instead of responding to the media, as recommended by Oakley (2014), the company responds to its customers, who have come to trust the company to fix the inevitable glitches in new technology. Thus, a company known for its secrecy is also known for its responsiveness. Indeed, the technology itself—the customer friendly iPhone and iPads—communicates a message of sincerity and authenticity that bypasses traditional media channels and speaks directly to the consumer.

The Apple example provides an entrée into an examination of paradox in public relations. Apple may not do a good job of communicating *about* its technology but has proven very effective at communicating *through* its technology. Telling Apple's story through the media exists at a higher level of abstraction than telling Apple's story through its technology. Each level of abstraction changes meanings, turning a positive at one level into a negative at the next level: Thus, the paradoxical nature of Apple's public relations. The messages that come across as secretive and unresponsive at a higher level of abstraction can come across as insider knowledge or a personal message at a lower level of abstraction. A wink and a nod to the knowing listener may send one message and go completely unnoticed by an outsider receiving another message. Paradoxes occur when we confuse levels of abstraction. Paradoxes are oppositional, contradictory, or contrary phenomena that, when examined individually, seem logical, but, when occurring simultaneously, appear illogical, false, and inconsistent. They are cognitive creations that befuddle understanding but, through meta-analysis and ordinality or levels of abstraction in communication, they can be better understood, accepted, and, in some cases, resolved. The ability of paradox to expose flaws in logic and language serves to facilitate learning and provide a catalyst for change. "The study of paradox is useful as a way of overcoming the inherent tendency for researchers within a field to develop myopia in ways of thinking"

(Gyrd-Jones, Merrilees, & Miller, 2013, p. 576). The tendency to build on existing knowledge causes scholars to rely too much on the consistency of results rather than inconsistent outliers and anomalies. "It is the outlier data in the form of tensions and paradoxes in theory development that challenge our way of conceptualizing phenomena under study" (p. 576). Instead of avoiding the tension, paradoxes inspire us to embrace it and view tensions as opportunities to re-evaluate and reassess existing theories. Paradoxical tensions can enable innovation and creativity and ultimately produce new frames and theories.

Some organizational researchers, such as Smith and Lewis (2011), have tried to develop a unique paradox theory, and their dynamic equilibrium model proved helpful in evaluating the paradox of loyalty in public relations. For the most part, however, this study pulls from multiple disciplines to illuminate paradoxes in public relations and uncover alternative approaches to resolving them. Of particular interest are the paradoxes resulting from confusing levels of abstraction in language and communication. The logical fallacies that plague public relations theory and practice arise from levels confusion, and resolving them depends on having an understanding of the ordinal nature of language.

Levels of abstraction are based on two theories—Group Theory and the Theory of Logical Types—developed by mathematicians Bertrand Russell and Alfred North Whitehead (1992) in their monumental three-volume work, *Principia Mathematica,* first published in 1927. The world and our perceptions are organized in levels of abstraction. An object exists at a higher level of abstraction than its molecular structure. A word exists at a higher level of abstraction than what it represents. These semantic levels were explained by Alfred Korzybski (2000) in his 1933 book *Science and Sanity.* At the lowest level was identification, the concrete identity of an object. Description *about* what was identified existed at a higher level and inference *about* that description existed at an even higher level. Evaluation of or *about* the inferences was at an even higher level. Note the importance of *about* in moving from one level of abstraction to another. Awareness of levels of abstraction serves as the first step to solving the inevitable confusion between and among levels. Advertising's power to seduce us comes from its appeal to our inferences and emotions, which reside at higher levels of abstraction (Elson, 2010).

Bertrand Russell is often credited with the development of Group Theory, which is considered "one of the most imaginative branches of mathematics" and has played "a powerful role in quantum and relativity theory" (Watzlawick, Bavelas, & Jackson, 2011, p. 5). Group Theory and the Theory of Logical Types were applied to psychotherapy and communication by anthropologist, psychologist, and social scientist Gregory Bateson. Indeed, Bateson (2000) referred to the Theory of Logical Types as basically a communication theory. Further examination will show that it also helps to expose the paradoxes in public relations.

Group Theory

Public in public relations is generally defined as a group of people who share something in common. The field generally looks at publics as targets for their messages. Indeed, the index of a public relations theory book recommends that readers looking for a definition of public should "see audience; target public" (Botan & Hazelton, 1989, p. 350). Public relations treats publics as key groups of people critical to an organization's success. The field has long wrestled with the question as to whether publics serve as a means to achieving organizational ends or as ends in and of themselves. Indeed, Botan and Hazelton's main reference to audiences occurs in a chapter on theoretical models for strategic public relations campaigns. Other public relations theories dealing with publics tend to identify publics by their willingness to act or not to act. In other words, they are categorized based on their likelihood to take action or susceptibility to be persuaded to act (Grunig, 2005).

A different approach to thinking about groups and publics comes from communication research in psychotherapy. Watzlawick, et al. (2011, pp. 5–7) introduced the following basic properties of Group Theory: 1) Members share one common characteristic and changes occur among members within the group, but they cannot place themselves outside the group; 2) members can be combined in various sequences but still produce the same outcome; 3) the combination of an identity member with any other member maintains the other member's identity; 4) every member has an opposite and combining a member with its opposite produces the identity member (p. 7). Group Theory helps explain the interdependence between stability and change, control and flexibility, independence and dependence, and expansion and contraction. It is important to note, however, that Group Theory cannot explain changes that occur in the system or frame itself. In organizations, the paradox of stability and change means that the forces for change will be met with an equal resistance to change. For every action taken to bring about change, there will be an opposite reaction to produce the identity member. Indeed, one study contended that public relations practitioners, as boundary spanners, help organizations to manage the complexity and tensions surrounding persistence and change (Harter & Krone, 2001).

Based on Group Theory, groups consist of collections of things that share common characteristics, including actions, rules, events, or numbers. Those things united by a specific characteristic are known as members, and the group within which they reside is designated as a class. Anything describing all of a class or collection is not a member of the collection or class. For example, a community represents a group of individuals but a community is not an individual. In the traditional sense, it is a designation representing a class of individuals living within a common geographic boundary. An ethics code may consist of a list of values but the code is not a value. "The grouping of 'things' (in the widest sense) is the most basic and necessary element of our perception and conception of reality" (Watzlawick et al., 2011, p. 6).

Watzlawick and his colleagues applied Group Theory to expand our understanding of human communication and behavior. For example, the group of activities required for most people to fall asleep are a comfortable bed, cool temperatures, and a relaxed state of mind. However, the insomniac may create the perfect conditions and still not fall asleep. Falling asleep is a spontaneous act.

Insomniacs may recognize this fact but the more they try to act spontaneously, the more likely they increase their anxiety and fail to fall asleep. To resolve the paradox, therapists may counsel insomniacs to focus on the opposite side of the paradox and try to not fall asleep. In other words, the solution to the paradox is not in simply trying to employ typical sleep strategies but to change one's whole approach to sleep. The solution to the paradox lies in reframing the insomniac's activities to include the act of not falling asleep.

In an organization, employees qualify as a group whose members share a common denominator, namely employment at a particular organization. The organization may shift its people from department to department, organizing them into different work teams, but these internal changes produce no change in the group itself. No matter how many ways the organization rearranges its members, the outcome is still the same. If an employee moves from one department to another, the previous department loses one member while the other gains a member. The loss in one department is offset by the gain in another. The net gain for the group is zero or the member's identity member. In simple addition, the identity member is zero, meaning no matter how many times you add zero to the number, you get the same number. In multiplication, the identity member is one, meaning the multiplication of the number by one always equals the same number. Every member of the organization also has an opposite, and the combination with that opposite is the identity member. As examples, Watzlawick et al. (2011) suggested that in a group of sounds the identity member is silence. In a group of moving parts, the identity member is stationary or immobile.

Group Theory has profound implications for public relations. The field often organizes its stakeholders into publics and then applies interpersonal constructs to describe relationships between groups. The public, however, is an abstract designation, a name for a class of individuals with a common characteristic. The public cannot be a member of itself. Therefore, cultivating relationships with a public constitutes the cultivation of a relationship with an abstraction that cannot, by any logical means possible, enjoy an interpersonal relationship with organizational members. Totalitarian governments apply this kind of thinking in making The State the focus of relationships, thus rendering the individual as a meaningless cog in State machinations. Everything revolves around the state or class, rather than around individual members.

Public relations has long relied on Systems Theory to explain the relationship between organizations and their environments. Though not incompatible with Systems Theory, Group Theory provides a different perspective for understanding what occurs when organizations adjust and adapt to their environment. According to Systems Theory, the system's goal is to maintain its steady state or homeostasis. The logical action when faced with economic downturns is for a company to retract and restructure. Most often organizations cut costs and become more conservative. However, if applying paradoxical thinking, both options are on the table (Schroeder-Saulnier, 2014). Logical one-sided solutions often fail because they ignore the fact that every member of a group has its opposite. Too much emphasis on retraction over its opposite exaggerates the effects of the very problem one may be trying to solve (Schneider, 1990). Handy (1994) argued that the best time for organizations to contract or re-engineer is at the height of an economic boom rather than during a decline. At the very apex of success, organizations sow the seeds for their demise. Thus, at the top of the S curve, as Handy describes it, organizations should retract and change while at the bottom of the curve, the economic downturns, they should expand and press forward.

A parallel in public relations is corporate social responsibility (CSR). If serving the community is not part of the organization's DNA, the public will accurately interpret its CSR initiatives as insincere and self-serving, thus defeating the very purpose of its CSR strategy. Group Theory helps explain the paradox that the more things change, the more they stay the same. "What Group Theory apparently cannot give us is a model for those types of change which transcend a given system or frame of reference" (Watzlawick et al., 2011, p. 8). Group Theory explains first-order change or change in the group or system, but to understand systems-level changes or second-order, we need another theory that "begins with a collection of 'things' which are united by a specific characteristic common to all of them" (p. 8). That theory is known as the Theory of Logical Types, which goes a step further and incorporates changes in the system itself (Watzlawick et al., 2011).

Theory of Logical Types

The Theory of Logical Types expands on Group Theory by focusing in on the distinction between a class or group and its members.

> The class cannot be a member of itself nor can one of the members be the class, since the term used for the class is of a different level of abstraction—a different Logical Type—from terms used for members.
>
> (Bateson, 2000, p. 202)

Formal logic tries to keep a separation between the levels of abstraction, but the reality of human communication is that people continually breach the discontinuity between levels and these breaches generate paradoxes. Bateson considered the Theory of Logical Types a communication theory because it explained how language and meaning changed from one level of abstraction to another.

Some examples will help to explain how the theory works. The Theory of Logical Types compares to the gears on a car with a standard transmission. In first gear, the car can move faster or slower but is limited in the amount of acceleration and deceleration available. By shifting to a higher gear, one enters a new level with additional options for acceleration and deceleration. Another example is a restaurant menu. The items on the menu are names of certain classes of foods, giving the customer information regarding the logical type of food made to order. As Bateson (2000) noted, the name of something is not the thing named. Thus, on the menu, one might see the name, cheeseburger, describing a particular food that generally consists of a bun, a meat patty, cheese, tomato, and condiments. As ridiculous as it may sound, if customers ate a "hamburger," they would have to eat the actual menu. Hamburger is a name and description, not the identity of the actual food item. The description of the food is not the food—it is simply a name describing a class of foods. A paradox results when a person fails to distinguish between the levels, eating the menu, not the food item, mistaking the class for one of its members.

Logical typing also applies to learning. Bateson (2000) applied logical typing to the process of learning and the role it plays in communication and change. Learning denotes change, Bateson wrote, change denotes process, meaning the very processes of learning "are subject to 'change'" (p. 283). Bateson's use of logical typing to identify various levels of learning stands out as one of his most significant contributions (Watzlawick & Jackson, 2010). At the lowest level, change occurs when we learn to correct errors or choose between alternatives. At the next level, change occurs in the learning process as we learn from the choices we made at the first level. The experience with learning increases knowledge as well as increasing the ability to acquire knowledge. In other words, we learn to learn. Bateson (2000) called this type of learning to learn, "deutero-learning" (p. 293). Deutero learning is at a higher more abstract logical type than first-order learning. At the higher level, an individual has interpreted his or her emotions, relationships, and experiences and created "second-order premises *about* the world" that changes the frame in which the individual views "objective reality" (Watzlawick & Jackson, 2010, p. 61).

Bateson's deutero learning shows that the Theory of Logical Types is effective in understanding a wide range of communication phenomena. In particular, it helps to resolve paradoxes based on breaches between levels of abstraction, such as "all Cretans are liars." Such statements are self-referential in that they assert their own falseness (Chapman, 2015). "Such statements are not provable and create circular confusion in the minds of those who encounter them" (p. 68). Using the Theory of Logical Types, however, the Cretan making the statement is not a member of the class of Cretans referred to in the statement; therefore he or she can make a true statement about a separate class of people. Citing Watzlawick et al. (2011), Chapman (2015) explained,

> Errors in logical typing normally occur either because a particular property has been incorrectly ascribed to a class instead of a member (or vice versa), or by treating class and member as if they are one on the same level of abstraction.
>
> (p. 68)

Bateson (2000) believed that extreme breaches between levels of abstraction or logical types led to schizophrenia, a breakdown in a person's thinking, feeling, and acting and were generally associated with the inability distinguish between the imaginary and real. Persons with schizophrenia are often caught in *double binds* in which they cannot move from one logical type to another. They tend toward literal interpretations of communication. Bateson was fascinated by how healthy people can deal with paradoxes and move from one logical type to another. In play, even animals can distinguish between the contexts in which actions occur, such as simulating fighting while actually playing. In human communication, the person who fails to get the joke is often unable to move from one level of abstraction to another. Others struggle to know what type of communication is appropriate in one context but not another. Anyone who has played pickup basketball knows that driving to the basket is not the same as driving a vehicle. A television series storyline ripped from the pages of today's headlines does not involve any tearing of paper.

The Theory of Logical Types explains this dual nature of first-order change—change within the system versus second-order change in the system itself. Watzlawick et al. (2011) noted that opposites, such as persistence and change, exist simultaneously. Change within the system fails to explain systemic change. First-order level change occurs among members of the group while change in logical typing takes place in the very rules and properties that govern class membership. To actually change a group, one has to change the meta aspect or type of the group, including the rules, norms, and values that define the group. First-order change is based on common sense while second-order change often falls outside logic and appears illogical. To bring about second-order change, one has to move to a meta-level of analysis. It means questioning existing frames or at least looking outside those frames for counterintuitive solutions. This may sound easy, but it is very difficult to do. As Kuhn (1996) noted in *The Nature of Scientific Revolutions*, existing paradigms resist change despite the fact that the competing theory may better deal with the theoretical problems and anomalies. Though a relatively new discipline, public relations has developed several competing theories and models, and, regardless of valid or invalid criticism and questions, their adherents continue to train graduate students who propound these theories without ever questioning their basic assumptions. This both enables and disables theoretical progress in the field.

A common blunder in crisis communication provides an example. Organizations sometimes justify unjust or inappropriate behavior by citing company policy that mandated that type of behavior. In spring 2017, United Airlines, known for encouraging the public to fly the friendly skies, took actions in direct conflict to that mission. First, staff members refused to allow an employee's two daughters to board a plane because they failed to meet the dress code for company fliers. Second, the airline forcibly removed a man from a plane after he and three others were randomly selected to be taken off the plane to make room for four United employees. The ensuing public relations fiasco was magnified by United's justification that it had followed policy but felt bad about the event and was sorry to have had to "re-accommodate these customers" ("4 statements by United," 2017, para. 5). In other words, the airline was sorry for the problems resulting from following its policy. The company never questioned the justice or injustice of the policy. United's executive team failed to recognize that a public relations crisis occurred because the policy was flawed and unjust. The media quickly picked up on the paradox exposed by policies that conflicted with United's friendly skies mission. The company's past experiences enforcing the policies had provided zero learning, a specific response not subject to correction (Bateson, 2000). Higher level learning might have exposed the unjust policy and averted the crisis.

Thus, the first step to solving levels paradoxes requires a greater awareness of abstraction (Korzybski, 1994). The second step is to move to a higher level and reframe our perception of the situation (Watzlawick, et al., 2011). By reframing at a higher level, one can reinterpret the meaning of the situation and escape from the paradoxical discontinuity or disturbance. For example, teacher serves as a name for a group of persons who mentor and teach another group of persons, typically given the name of students. Professors want their students to share in the responsibility for their education, but no matter how much professors want this relationship, it is logically impossible when both are not members of the same class. The only way to change the relationship is to move to a higher level of abstraction in terms of the nature of the class or group. The rules dictate that professors teach and students learn. To bring about a new relationship, professors must change the rules, and thereby change the nature of the group. By reframing their relationship with the students, describing them as fellow learners and scholars, they expand the group to now include themselves and their students. Learning is now the common denominator for the group. The rules that created the discontinuity between the class of teachers and the class of students have been changed to create a class of learners and scholars. This kind of problem formation and problem resolution reflects second-order change, requiring a jump from one level of analysis to another. Second-order change generally comes from outside the system and can often appear paradoxical and illogical because it changes the rules of the game rather than the relationship among the players. Thus, John Keating's colleague in *Dead Poets Society* warns him against empowering his students to think for themselves because every aspect of their lives, including their school, has been chosen for them.

Paradoxes arise when we confuse the discontinuities between members and class. Dictators often demand that their people comply, not only in their acts but in their thoughts, values, outlooks, and motives. It is an impossible demand because these desires are not produced through coercion but are products of free will. A mother wants her child to want to read but the reality is that she is trying to impose an action that can only result from a spontaneous desire on the part of the child (Watzlawick, et al., 2011). Public relations practitioners want stakeholders to engage in relationships with their organizations and enact persuasive communicative strategies to achieve that goal. In reality, however, practitioners have no power over the public's choice to engage and reciprocate or even define their interaction as a relationship. The same can be said about wanting to build mutually beneficial relationships. The very act of desiring those relationships calls into question their mutuality. We want two-way communication but the statement itself is one-way. It becomes a self-reflexive paradox akin to the liar paradox or the Cretan paradox. It violates "the central axiom of the Theory of Logical Types, i.e. that whatever involves all of a collection (class) cannot be one of the collection (a member). The result is a paradox" (Watzlawick et al., 2011, p. 65).

The very recognition of paradoxes can lead to change (Ford & Backoff, 1988). Thus, the first step is to use paradox to promote progress and change in public relations. It moves beyond zero learning to deutero learning—learning from what paradoxes teach us about public relations. The very process of applying paradox to public relations creates the condition for learning and thus change. As a largely communicative activity, public relations is inherently paradoxical, but scholars and practitioners have generally ignored or overlooked paradoxes. They have applied convergent thinking in an effort to solve divergent problems. Convergent thinkers see problems as distinct, precise, quantifiable, and logical and subject to empirical investigation. Divergent thinkers see problems as more complex and difficult to explain or quantify. They recognize that no simple predictable solutions exist (Westenholz, 1993). The world of logic is often insufficient in understanding the world of phenomena (Bateson, 2000). The one problem that computers cannot solve is that of the self-referential paradox as already identified in the liar paradox and Cretan paradox (Bhatia, 2014).

In the next chapter, the self-referential frame inspired early public relations practitioners and scholars to emphasize the field's obligation to the public interest. They advocated that public relations served the public interest because they wanted legitimacy and public approval for their work on behalf of private interests. They wanted a convergent solution to a divergent problem. But resolving the paradox of the public interest is not that easy, especially when practitioners and scholars refuse to admit the existence of the public interest paradox. The paradox of the public interest in public relations, however, does exist and the best way to solve the paradox may come as a surprise.

Works cited

4 statements by United on passenger's removal from flight (2017, April 14). Associated Press. Retrieved April 15, 2017 from apnews.com.

Bateson, G. (2000). *Steps to an ecology of mind*. Chicago: University of Chicago Press.

Bhatia, A. (2014, February 5). The question that computers never can answer. *Wired*. Retrieved April 12, 2017 from wired.com.

Botan, C. & Hazelton, V. (1989). *Public relations theory*. Mahwah, NJ: Lawrence Erlbaum Associates.

Chapman, K. (2015). *Complexity and creative capacity: Rethinking knowledge transfer, adaptive management and wicked environmental problems*. London: Taylor & Francis.

Craig, C. (2016, July 27). What I learned from 10 years of doing PR for Apple. *Harvard Business Review*. Retrieved March 21, 2017 from hbr.org.

Elson, L. G. (2010). *Paradox lost*. Cresskill, NJ: Hampton Press

Ford, J. D. & Backoff, R. W. (1988). Organizational change in and out of dualities and paradox. In R. E. Quinn & K. S. Cameron (Eds.), *Paradox and transformation: Toward a theory of change in organization and management* (pp. 81–121). Cambridge, MA: Ballinger Publishing Company.

Grunig, J. (2005). Situational theory of publics. In Heath, R. L. (Ed.), *Encyclopedia of public relations* (vol. 2, pp. 778–780). Thousand Oaks, CA: Sage.

Gyrd-Jones, R., Merrilees, B., & Miller, D. (2013). Revisiting the complexities of corporate branding: Issues, paradoxes, solutions. *Journal of Brand Management, 20* (7), 571–589.

Handy, C. (1994). *The age of paradox.* Boston: Harvard Business School Press.

Harter, L. M. & Krone, K. J. (2001). The boundary-spanning role of a cooperative support organization: Managing the paradox of stability and change in non-traditional organizations. *Journal of Applied Communication Research, 29* (3), 248–277.

Korzybski, A. (1994). *Science and sanity: An introduction to non-Aristotelian systems of general semantics* (5th Ed.). New York: Institute of General Semantics.

Korzybski, A. (2000). *Science and sanity: An introduction to non-Aristotelian systems of general semantics.* Brooklyn, NY: International Non-Aristotelian Library Publishing Company.

Kuhn, T. S. (1996). *The structure of scientific revolutions* (3rd Ed.). Chicago: University of Chicago Press.

Meyer, P. (2019, February 15). Apple Inc.'s organizational culture & its characteristics (an analysis). Panmore Institute. Retrieved from http:www.panmore.com.

Oakley, T. (2014). The ups and downs of PR for Apple. *The Marketing Agenda.* Retrieved March 21, 2017 from themarketingagenda.com.

Schneider, K. J. (1990). *The paradoxical self: Toward an understanding of our contradictory nature.* New York: Plenum Press. https://doi.org/10.1177/0022167814537889.

Schroeder-Saulnier, D. (2014). *The power of paradox: Harness the energy of competing ideas to uncover radically innovative solutions.* Pompton, NJ: Career Press.

Sherman, E. (2014, May 21). Steve Jobs' Rules for Public Relations. *Slate.* Retrieved March 21, 2017 from slate.com.

Smith, W. K. & Lewis, M. W. (2011). Toward a theory of paradox: A dynamic equilibrium model of organizing. *Academy of Management Review, 36* (2), 381–403.

Watzlawick, P., Bavelas, J. B., & Jackson, D. D. (2011). *Pragmatics of human communication: A study of interactional patterns pathologies and paradoxes.* New York: Norton Paperback.

Watzlawick, P. & Jackson, D. D. (2010). On human communication. *Journal of Systemic Therapies, 29* (2), 53–68.

Westenholz, A. (1993). Paradoxical thinking and change in frames of reference. *Organizational Studies, 14,* 37–58.

Whitehead, A. N. & Russell, B. (1992). *Principia mathematica* (Orig. pub. 1927). Cambridge, England: Cambridge University Press.

2 The public interest paradox

To say something is in the public interest, political theorist R. E. Flathman (1966) argued, requires justification as to why it is in the public interest. Since the Progressive Era of the early 1900s, publicists and public relations practitioners have tried to explain how public relations serves the public interest. As early advocates of publicity's power to rally public opinion in support of social and political change, Progressives determined what was in the public interest and then communicated that knowledge to the public. Progressives represented the middle class in advocating for women's rights, civic association, and social solidarity. They sought to find a middle ground between the extremes of individualism and socialism (McGerr, 2003). The public interest embodied middle-class values of "moderation, harmony, cooperation, and good will" and thus stood paramount to all other interests (Sorauf, 1957, p. 634). For moral crusaders and social reformers, the public interest served as inspiration because it represented higher moral laws (Sorauf, 1957). The public interest also justified the use of any means or messages to achieve their private and group interests, including coercion, propaganda, and legislative action. After World War I, the younger generation—the new middle-class culture—rejected the Progressives' paternalism and placed a higher value on individual freedom and expression (McGerr, 2003). Publicity's connotative definition also changed after the war, transforming from something considered inherently in the public interest into a weapon used by private interests to influence and manipulate public opinion (Stoker & Rawlins, 2005).

With the terms publicity and propaganda out of public favor in the 1920s, publicists sought to rebrand their occupation to include more than just publicity. They promoted a new class of actions that included advising organizations on how to improve their relations with the public. Public relations provided that rebranding. It better described their professional role as mediators between organizations and the public. Unlike publicists and press agents, public relations counselors served the client's private interests and the public interest at the same time. They contributed to the marketplace of ideas by pleading their cases in the court of public opinion. Acting behind the scenes, public relations professionals adhered to the highest ethical standards, including acting in the public interest, to influence public opinion (Bernays, 1928a).

Public relations scholars and practitioners continue to emphasize ethics and serving the public interest—although it is now identified with corporate social responsibility or a by-product of mutually beneficial relationships. Practitioners have founded professional associations and adopted codes of ethics. They have failed, however, to address the paradox of the public interest, which manifests itself every time practitioners try to define or justify what they do. In 2011, Canadian academics and professionals developed their own definition of public relations, and chose from a pre-selected list of possibilities. The most popular definition defined "strategic public relations" as "the strategic management of relationships between an organization and its diverse publics, through the use of communication, to achieve mutual understanding, realize organizational goals, and serve the public interest" (Moran, 2011, para. 2). Once the definition was made public, practitioner Caroline Kealey questioned the inclusion of serving the public interest. Public relations should act in the public interest but she questioned whether it was "intrinsic to the core definition of the function" (Kealey, quoted in Moran, 2011, para. 5). Including the public interest in the definition, she wrote, smelled "of doing PR on the PR function which I think does more to muddy than to clarify the nature of the discipline, which is already subject to significant confusion" (Kealey, quoted in Moran 2011, para. 5).

Kealey intuitively recognized the paradox created by confusing the levels of abstraction in language. The definition of public relations should identify *what* public relations is and not *why* it is what it is (Watzlawick, Bavelas, & Jackson, 2011). Practitioners may realize organizational goals by strategically managing relationships, but they cannot control whether they achieve mutual understandings with the public, achieve organizational goals, or serve the public interest. Terry Flynn, the leading proponent of the new Canadian definition, admitted that acting in the public interest was more aspirational than denotative of public relations practice. His response actually supported Kealey's criticism because it described how the field wants to be perceived rather than what the field is. In other words, Flynn reinforced the paradox resulting from a breach in language's levels of abstraction. In hopes of justifying the morality of public relations, he confused the concrete denotative with the more abstract connotative. Flynn fell victim to the paradox that has afflicted public relations since the Progressive Era.

If there is a foundational paradox in public relations, it is the paradox of the public interest. How can public relations practitioners serve private interests and public interests at the same time? In this chapter, I will first provide a brief review of the major perspective of the public interest. Second, I will analyze the historical evolution of the public relations interpretation of the public interest from the Progressive Era through the modern era. In particular, I hope to iden- tify how observers inside and outside public relations described and defended the field's relationship with the public interest. Throughout this analysis, I will employ concepts from paradox research to critique these interpretations. Finally, I will argue that the resolution to the paradox of the public interest requires the field to embrace its history, accepts its role as a partisan, and recognize that public relations at the denotative (identification) level does not serve the public interest. Then I will propose a counterintuitive approach to serving the public interest through the responsible representation of private interests and the recognition of the public's right to serve its own interests.

Public interest theory

Based on the literature at the time, Cochran (1974) identified four perspectives associated with the public interest: normative, abolitionist, process or proceduralist, and consensualist. Normative theory views the public interest as an ethical standard by which we evaluate public policies and actions. A public action is judged by whether it serves the common good and strengthens communal associations. A leading advocate of normative theory, Cassinelli (1962), argued that the word "public" provided the public interest with its ethical value and universalized its application to every member of the political community. "The word 'interest' indicates the evaluational meaning of the standard; it refers to something we would be 'interested in,' even though we may not be, and it could be replaced by 'profit,' 'welfare,' or 'benefit.'" (p. 46). Cassinelli argued that the public interest represented the highest ethical standard of political affairs and gave meaning to political rights and duties. When public relations scholars and practitioners refer to the public interest, they generally describe it as an ethical standard for the profit and benefit of common good.

By the 1970s, the normative theory had few adherents in philosophy and political science. Public relations educators also lost interest in the concept as an ethical standard—although practitioners continued to cite their professional obligation to the public interest. Some scholars questioned whether a public interest even existed. Abolitionist theorists argued that there was no public interest but only group interests that competed for dominance and influence. The proceduralists defined the public interest as simply a part of the democratic process. The public interest was the sum of interests, resulting from a clash of interests or a reconciliation of interests. Consensualists, on the other hand, recognized that, despite its flaws and ambiguity, the public interest had value because it recognized overlooked interests and gave more weight to broader interests than narrower interests (Cochran, 1974).

More recently, Bozeman (2007) narrowed Cochran's four theories down to two—the liberal model and the communal model. The liberal model reflects a more individualistic and utilitarian approach in which individuals make subjective decisions about what is in the public interest. Borrowing from utilitarianism, the liberal model measures the public interest by ranking good consequences over bad or by determining what action serves the greater good. The public interest in the communal model is socially constructed and focuses on identifying an objective common good. The communal model takes into consideration community values and formal principles in determining the public interest. Contemporary public relations scholars predominantly employ the communal theory, emphasizing the use of dialog or symmetrical communication to build mutually beneficial relationships.

Public relations and the public interest

Historically, however, public relations practitioners adopted the liberal model of the public interest, emphasizing the role of publicity in the democratic process. In the late 1800s, social reformers sought to inform the public and promote social reform through publicity and public events. They believed that by bringing attention to social ills, such as slavery, prohibition, women's suffrage, and public health, they could inspire public action and reform society. In reviewing newspaper and magazine articles from the 1870s, Russell and Bishop (2009) found that publicity was defined as making something public or reporting business information to government. By the 1890s, Progressive reformers in business and politics associated publicity with moral reform and public improvement (Stoker & Rawlins, 2005). As with the liberal model and normative theory of the public interest, "public" provided publicity with its ethical value. Stoker and Rawlins examined popular literature from the 1890s up until and beyond World War I and found that early proponents of publicity believed that making things known to the public could serve as a catalyst for reform, change, and improvement. Whereas society had long relied on interpersonal communication to initiate social and political improvement, the industrial age used mass communication to promote progress and change. One of the leading advocates for this viewpoint was Henry C. Adams, a professor of political economy at the University of Michigan. In 1902, Adams defined publicity as making public those things that affect the community (Adams, 1902). He wanted the government to set standards of publicity to hold corporations more accountable to the public. Publicity would fill the vacuum created by the loss of the local marketplace in which "personal relations between producer and consumer ... exercised a powerful moral restraint on business conduct" (p. 897). The "colossal" growth of business and industry had separated the producer from the consumer, decreasing accountability and transparency. In other words, the interpersonal relationship with the individual members of the public had been replaced by abstract organizational relationships with the masses. Publicity served to allay suspicions and increase public confidence because publicity was at once personal and public. With more publicity, Adams argued, public opinion would control corporate power.

The Progressives considered corporate monopolies a threat to the public interest. Politicians, joined by crusading journalists and activists, began looking for ways to regulate corporations. Corporations hired publicists to help them respond and defend against scrutiny and regulation from Progressive politicians, such as President Theodore Roosevelt (Russell and Bishop, 2009). "To the Populists and Progressives, support of the public interest involved the regulation and control of business and capital, the vested interests opposing the public interest of the rest of American society" (Sorauf, 1957, p. 620). The Progressives targeted "quasi-public interest" organizations, such as the railroads, utilities, and oil companies, that received special protections from the government. "[F]irst of all comes the public relation, and the policy of railroad management must be settled by what will serve the public best, not what will be of most advantage to private stockholders" (Bridgeman, 1905, pp. 460–461). These corporations employed publicists to win back public support and avoid government regulation (Cutlip, 1994). Publicists ostensibly served the public interest by helping these corporations to inform the public.

Public relations pioneer Ivy Lee advocated this approach. In claiming that his work served the public interest, Lee adopted the metaphor of the legal system and applied it to publicity. Ivy Lee argued in the court of public opinion and served as a spokesman for the defense and the prosecution. In other words, he set the stage for future public relations scripts in which practitioners mediated between organizations and the public. In 1906, he defined publicity as supplying factual information to the press and public "concerning subjects which it is of value and interest to the public to know about" (Cutlip, 1994, p. 45; Lee, quoted in Ewen, 1996, p. 77). Lee interpreted the public interest as part of the democratic ideal of an informed public. For democracy to succeed, the public needed to be informed and motivated to act (Hiebert, 1966). In the preface of Lee's biography, Hiebert claimed that without public relations, "democracy could not succeed in a mass society" (p. 7). One of Ivy Lee's major contributions to the field, according to a contemporary public relations textbook, was his contention that "business and industry should align themselves with the public interest" (Wilcox et al., 2011, p. 70). Lee's principles of providing accurate information in the public interest profoundly influenced later practitioners, who viewed him as the father of public relations (Hicks, 1953; Stephenson, 1971).[1] Despite this emphasis on democracy and the search for truth, Lee was first and foremost an advocate for the private interests of his clients. His clients and contacts appreciated his personal integrity and listened to his counsel, but his primary objective was to service the client's interests (Hallahan, 2002).

Based on Lee's principles, publicists worked with the press to bring valuable information to the public. Albert Shaw (1909), editor of the *Review of Reviews*, viewed publicity as a service to newspapers, helping them fulfill their role of serving the public interest. Properly governed and regulated, publicity made up for newspapers' shortcomings. Shaw argued that publicity was more effective than advertising in conveying the type of good stories that journalists refused to tell or did not tell well. Shaw failed to mention that publicists and their clients did not have to pay for publicity, and their alleged service to newspapers directly benefited them more than it did the press. Publicists exploited newspaper credibility to promote positive news about their clients. As one Progressive writer explained it, bad news had wings but good news needed a little help. Journalists were sometimes labeled as publicists (Stoker & Rawlins, 2005), but their job to make things known to the public rarely entailed purposeful and strategic promotion of private interests. Broadly speaking, publicity meant "publication, making things known in some sort of public way—in a way that is accessible to all men or the great majority of men" (Burke, 1910, p. 198). Professional publicists should not to be confused with promoters and press agents. Publicity and press agentry "developed separately and for different reasons" (Russell & Bishop, 2009, p. 98).

Like journalism, publicity represented a truthful account of the actual conditions, habits, and acts of individuals, institutions, and nations (Burke, 1910). By bringing to light information for the betterment and advancement of the community, publicity served the public interest. Social reformers perceived the public as educated, intelligent, and moral, fully capable of acting to correct social evils (Burke, 1910). The effectiveness of publicity, Vance (1907) argued, depended on whether it resonated with the public and served a good cause. When running for President in 1913, Progressive Democrat Woodrow Wilson argued that the good cause served by publicity stemmed from its power to purify politics and expose corruption in business and government. For the popular will to substitute for the "rule of guardians," the doors of government needed to be opened to "let in the light on all affairs which the people have a right to know" (Wilson, 1913, p. 111). President Wilson demanded greater public scrutiny of the political process as well as business. Popular government depended on opening doors and shining light on the private machinations of government and business. The public had a right to know, and government and business had a responsibility to inform them about the processes of politics and capital (Wilson, 1913).

Russell and Bishop (2009), who studied the role of publicity in the late 1800s, discovered that the rise of corporate publicity corresponded with Progressive leaders, such as Presidents Theodore Roosevelt and Woodrow Wilson, demanding more accountability and transparency. Russell and Bishop called into question the long-held assumption that corporate publicity primarily developed as a reaction to journalistic muckraking. However, it should be noted that "the Progressive mind was characteristically a journalistic mind, and that its characteristic contribution was that of the socially responsible reporter-reformer" (Hofstadter, 1955, p. 186). In other words, corporations felt pressure from social forces that included Progressive politicians and journalists. Paradoxically, the Progressives' high-minded views of publicity contributed to the concept's evolution from the process of making things known for the public good to making things known that benefited private interests. The professional practice of publicist grew out of a strategic need to use publicity's power to influence public opinion and behavior.

President Wilson tapped into this power when he needed public support for total war. Having campaigned for re-election in 1916 on the platform that he had kept America out of the European war, President Wilson needed to persuade the public in April 1917 to support America's involvement in the war. President Wilson appointed former Denver newspaper editor George Creel to rally public support using all means of publicity available. The Committee on Public Information, or Creel Committee, touched every aspect of public life, including schools, theaters, magazines, and newspapers, to influence public opinion. The press voluntarily embraced government propaganda and self-censorship and carefully filtered out many of the horrors of war. Ironically, the public interest was not served by what publicity uncovered but what it covered and covered up. The Creel Committee invoked the public interest to serve the private interests of the Wilson administration. After the war, the committee's success at winning the hearts and minds of the press and the public raised serious concerns about the government's use of publicity to influence its own people. The subsequent public backlash accelerated publicity's connotative transformation from moral disinfectant to strategic weapon. After the war, Congress "wiped out the existence" of the Committee, causing Creel (1920) to write a defense of the committee's work in a book aptly called, *How We Advertised America: The first telling of the amazing story of the Committee on Public Information that carried the gospel of Americanism to every corner of the globe.*

The Creel Committee showed how trained publicists could mobilize and influence public opinion. The name "publicity," and to some extent the title "publicists," never completely recovered from these connotative changes (Stoker & Rawlins, 2005). Former members of the Creel Committee set up publicity bureaus and marketed publicity to corporate clients. Their experiences during the war had taught them that publicity could be weaponized in the court of public opinion (Cutlip, 1994). Some journalists condemned the growing influence of publicists while others joined their ranks. Whereas publicity had once served the public interest because it exposed government and corporate ills and corruption, it now ostensibly served the public interest by showing the good things government and corporations did. Brownell (1922) justified private interest publicity by claiming that the press reported more bad news than good news. Publicists served the public interest by telling stories advertising could not tell and journalists would not tell or could not tell well.

The literal meaning of publicity did not change, but the connotative meaning was forever altered. At a higher level of abstraction, publicity acquired a more sinister, pejorative meaning. Where once its virtue rested in its power to inform individuals and individual action, "the foundation stone of popular government" (Burke, 1910, p. 209), its value now stemmed from its power to influence public opinion. The focus shifted from information made public to benefit the common good to information made public to benefit the communicator. Publicity no longer inspired public action on behalf of the public welfare but persuaded the public to act in the interests of a particular cause or organization. The public interest of publicity did not arise from correcting social ills but in promoting commerce, and the Adam Smith-inspired doctrine that individuals pursuing their self-interest ultimately promote the common interest.

The democratic role of publicists also changed. They no longer played a critical role in democracy but were now considered by-products of democracy (Publicity, public opinion, and the wily press agent, 1920). "The press-agent, the director of public information, the public relations adviser, are each in their degree engaged in making public opinion for the causes they represent" (p. 61). The ethics of their work was still judged by the cause they represented, but the primary benefactor of that cause was the client, not the public. If the client's cause was good, then the methods of publicity could be excused (Publicity, public opinion, and the wily press agent, 1920). Democracy was not so much about an informed public as it was about informing the public as to what they should know and think. The public interest now shifted from publicity that inspired the public to act in their own interests to public relations that influenced public opinion and served private and public interests. The responsibility for the public interest now rested on the shoulders of public relations experts whose relations with the public required the public interest as an ethical standard.

Publicity lost its connotative connection to social and moral reform (Stoker & Rawlins, 2005). It was no longer a moral disinfectant for public improvement, but a strategic weapon for engineering and manufacturing consent (Bernays, 1947). Publicity also changed from being something provided by newspapers and magazines to the public to something that government and business provided to newspapers and magazines for the public (Russell & Bishop, 2009). These changes in the nature of publicity opened the door for a new kind of publicist, an expert who could bridge the chasm between organizations and the public.

The public relations counselor and the public interest

Ironically, the theorist behind this new philosophy of molding and shaping public opinion was a prominent editorial writer and editor for the *New York World*. During World War I, Walter Lippmann "learned how easy it was to manipulate public opinion" (Steel, 1997, p. xii). Lippmann served as special representative for the White House in military intelligence during the war and was a close confidant of President Wilson after the war. As editor of *The New Republic* and an editorial writer for the *New York World*, Lippmann knew the press often did a poor job reporting on major events, especially what he considered the good news about world events. He also knew that stereotypes and prejudices powerfully shaped the public's interpretation of events. He also laid partial blame on the press for the public's rejection of President Wilson's peace plan and America's shift toward nationalism and isolationism.

In his 1922 book, *Public Opinion,* Lippmann (1922[1997]) questioned the democratic ideal of an informed public. Without first-hand experience, he argued, people could not form an accurate mental image or interpretation of an event. Instead they reacted to a pseudo environment inserted between them and the actual environment, which Lippmann claimed was far too complex for direct experience anyway. Individuals then faced the paradoxical situation of thinking their behavior is based on the real environment rather than the pseudo environment constructed in their minds. The public responded to events based on the pictures inside their heads and not the actual event itself.

In Lippmann's view, public opinion resulted from the confluence of the casual fact, the creative mind, and the will to believe. To provide the public with a more clear and accurate representation of the world, Lippmann (1922[1997]) proposed establishing a group of experts to make "the unseen facts intelligible to those who have to make decisions" (p. 19). These experts could manage public opinion for the public and make sense of issues and events that the public needed to know. The experts would act in the public interest, shaping the pictures inside the public's heads and thus influencing and directing public opinion. In some ways, Lippmann had substituted a new rule of guardians for the popular will. Underlying Lippmann's philosophy was the need for highly skilled independent observers who could understand the needs of the people and organizations at the same time.

Lippmann's theory of public opinion resonated with Edward Bernays, who embraced the idea of experts organizing intelligence for the public. A veteran of the Creel Committee and the self-appointed spokesman for the new public relations industry, Bernays quoted liberally from Lippmann's work in his 1923 book, *Crystallizing Public Opinion* (Bernays, 1923[1962]). For Bernays, Lippmann's conception of independent experts organizing and shaping public opinion gave public relations its *raison d'être*. The new publicist would do more than just make things known; the public relations counsel would make sense of things for the public while at the same time skewing interpretations in the client's favor. Bernays (1928b) preferred using the name "public relations counsel" over terms such as publicist or "publicity director" because he liked the comparison to the legal profession. In the court of public opinion, the public relations counsel acted as an advocate, pleading a case before the public with hopes that the public would "accede to opinion and judgment" (p. 199). Unlike attorneys, however, the public relations counsel must represent good causes or, as Bernays described it, those clients acceptable to the higher court of public opinion. "It is one of the manifestations of democracy that anyone may try to convince others and to assume leadership on behalf of his own thesis" (Bernays, 1928a, p. 959). As a by-product of democracy, public relations served the public interest.

Unlike Progressive reformers, Bernays did not ascribe publicity with any inherent social value but instead imbued the "special pleader" with social motives (Bernays, 1928a, p. 960). Bernays acknowledged that some might manipulate public opinion for nefarious purposes, but he believed that the very act of people trying to persuade the public improved the public's ability to discern between good and bad publicity. Despite this belief, he still recognized that the success of public relations depended on the ethics and integrity of professional persuaders and their commitment to serve the public interest. "He who seeks to manipulate public opinion must always heed it" (p. 971).

To heed public opinion, the special pleaders needed to learn "what others think they know" and understand the motivations behind their behavior (Lippmann, 1922[1997], p. 9). This allowed public relations counselors to align the interests of the client organization with the interests of the public. The practitioner would mediate between an organization and the public, organizing intelligence about the client for the public and organizing intelligence about the public for the client. "*This is always predicated on the relationship being on an entirely ethical basis*" (Bernays, 1928b, p. 199). In other words, the ethics of public relations depended on the morality of the practitioner, who should never put "his duty to the groups he represents above his duty to society" (p. 199).

Bernays' logic was consistent with the normative theory of the public interest advocated by Walter Lippmann. The disinterested professional, acting rationally and benevolently, could more effectively determine what was in the best interests of the public (Lippmann, 1955; Bozeman, 2007). As expert professionals, practitioners ignored the whims of special interests and organized intelligence for the public. They acted as mediators between the public and their client organizations. If they knew how the public perceived the world, they could change the pictures inside their heads. Their role was to inform, influence, educate, and enlighten the public. They solicited public input, not so much to make their messages more persuasive—though that was a consideration—but to change public perception of their interests. Like legal advocates in a court of law, public relations counsels wanted the jury to accept their version of the story and their framing of the facts, but unlike legal counsel, public relations could reject "socially unsound" clients (Bernays, 1928b, pp. 198). Of course, the desired frame portrayed socially sound clients in the best possible light. They were professional persuaders, employing propaganda for the private interests of their clients.

Nearly a decade after leaving the Creel Committee, Bernays, along with his wife, Doris Fleischman, was so confident in his abilities in public relations that he took on the challenge of rehabilitating propaganda's tattered reputation. He wrote a book, aptly titled *Propaganda*, and tried to persuade the public that, despite its partisan nature, propaganda "serves to focus and realize the desires of the masses" (Bernays 1928[2005], p. 57). Bernays (1928b) claimed that propaganda more aptly described public relations than publicity. Approaching propaganda as a social scientist, Bernays defined it as the method for manipulating the mechanism controlling the public mind. In other words, the public relations counsel used propaganda to influence public judgments and actions. He argued that the "special pleader, [the practitioner] is not disassociated from the client in the public's mind" (p. 199), and part of the pleader's job was to discover the public mind and align with it. Indeed, public relations and propaganda were much more effective if consistent with public interests. Bernays saw nothing untoward about tapping into public opinion before advocating on behalf of a client in the court of public opinion. In a courtroom, the judge and jury provide a balance of power between legal adversaries, but in the court of public opinion, the public served this role. However, the public relations counsel still had the moral responsibility to balance the interests of the client and the public. Practitioners should represent honorable clients and then clearly identify the source of propaganda on behalf of those clients.

Aligning public relations with propaganda did not set well with historian Scott Cutlip (1994), who believed Bernays' book undermined the field in the eyes of the public and aided the field's critics. Stated another way, Bernays' book on propaganda was bad public relations for public relations. But Bernays had intuitively recognized that the paradox of the public interest demanded that the field be upfront about using social scientific methods to shape public opinion. In a 1936 speech published as part of *Vital Speeches of the Day*, Bernays (1936) defended his description of propaganda as part of public relations practice. In the court of public opinion, he wrote, winning ideas were those in the public interest. "Propaganda is an attempt to give currency to an idea by finding the common denominator between the idea and the public interest and stating it. It is bringing an old or new idea to acceptance by the public" (p. 744). If an organization's message won public favor, it was in the public interest and in the financial interests of the capitalistic system. Bernays simply stated the truth. Unlike publicity, propaganda was about influencing and changing public opinion to align with partisan interests. The use of the word "propaganda" rather than "publicity" indicated that the idea of making things known had been replaced by propaganda's goal of creating the desired picture inside the people's heads.

The public and the public interest

In contrast, philosopher John Dewey believed the public should be creating their own pictures inside their heads. Dewey argued that the public discovered and expressed their own interests through the democratic process of communal life (Dewey, 1927). Dewey put more trust in the public's capacity for action than he did in experts or authorities. "The world has suffered more from leaders and authorities than from the masses" (p. 208). Publics organize through participation in groups and across groups. The public "arrives at decisions, makes terms and executes resolves ... through the medium of individuals" (p. 75). Those individuals could be elected legislators and executives or even citizen voters who express their will as representatives of the public interest. The role of those individuals, however, was not to make sense of the world for the public but to inform, educate, and enlighten the public so that the public could determine its own interests. The problem in the machine age, as Dewey described it, was that society had become so complex that the public struggled to identify and distinguish itself. The sheer number of publics and public issues limited the public's resources and capacity for pulling together a common public interest. The only way for the public to overcome the problems of democracy was more democracy—more opportunities for the public to define and express its interests.

More democracy, according to Dewey, meant more communication and publicity. "There can be no public without full publicity in respect to all consequences which concern it," Dewey wrote in 1927. "Whatever obstructs and restricts publicity, limits and distorts public opinion and checks and distorts thinking on social affairs. Without freedom of expression, not even methods of social inquiry can be developed" (p. 167). Unlike Bernays' public relations counsel, Dewey's publicist would not serve as a mediator between client organizations and the public but as a facilitator (Stoker, 2014). The role of public relations practitioners was not to determine the public interest but to facilitate the direct flow of information and increase opportunities for communication. With more information and communication, the public could identify and define its own interests. Any obstruction or distortion of that communication retarded the public's ability to learn, inquire, and ultimately determine its interests. The same is true for information from the public flowing back to the organization. To identify their shared interests, organizations needed access to public information. The public interest then depended on individuals taking part in free and open communication that enabled the discovery of shared meanings and common interests.

Citing Dewey (1927), Bozeman (2007) noted that the public interest applied when individual or group action affected individuals or groups unaffiliated with that action. This public exists outside the group or stakeholder domain. One must move up two levels of abstraction and evaluate how the organization's concrete actions and the affiliated public's description of those actions are in the interests of the unaffiliated public. The outside group consists of everybody else and becomes what Dewey called "The Public" (Dewey, 1927, p. 35; Bozeman, 2007, p. 89). Public relations serves the immediate interests of the organization and possibly some stakeholders, but it cannot make a determination about the public interest until after a public evaluation over which it has little to no control. That determination has to be made by The Public, groups of people indirectly affected by public relations activities. Whether an organization's actions serve the public interest is outside the control of the organization or even its affiliated groups. Instead, the public interest is determined by The Public, which provides a more objective evaluation of whether it has reaped any benefits.

Based on Dewey's pragmatic idealism, Bozeman (2007) defined the public interest as the outcome of social inquiry that promotes the health and survival of the public. In other words, Dewey recognized the paradox of the public interest. The public interest was a work in progress, socially constructed through communal action. Dewey's work added "a method of democratic social inquiry modeled after the ideal workings of the scientific community, and a focus on the key role of deliberation, social learning, and interest transformation in this process" (p. 10). Dewey's philosophy reconciled "the need to preserve public value ideals and to enable practical application" (p. 10). In other words, Dewey's focus on discussion and participation enables people to recognize their shared interests while at the same time allowing them to judge special interests and expose private interests posing as public interests.

The economic collapse of 1929 exposed the public charade of private interests. The unrestrained focus on speculation and profit undermined the public's faith in business and industry. As Milton Wright wrote in his 1935 book on strategic communication, publicity was all about winning over the public. Despite efforts by prominent practitioners to change public perceptions, the popular press and trade publication continued to invoke the terms publicity and propaganda when referring to public relations practice. *Forbes* defined public relations as "the job of putting across the desired image" (The public is not damned, 1939, p. 84) and identified four ways public relations helped business fulfill its social obligations: poor propaganda, good propaganda, inquiry, and action. Poor propaganda lacked conviction while good propaganda dealt with information in which the public was interested. Good propaganda sparked public inquiry because it was tailored to the interests of the public. The "action" part of propaganda referred to the organization's need to change if it found itself out of line with the public (p. 114).

Although *Forbes* aptly described the professional role of public relations as helping business fulfill its social obligations, the magazine also aligned the field with the dark art of propaganda. Other evaluations of the field were not so balanced. In response, public relations educators advocated professionalism and distanced the field from one-way forms of communication, such as propaganda and publicity. Rex Harlow taught public relations at Stanford University and helped found one of the professional associations that evolved into the Public Relations Society of America. Harlow's approach to public relations was ahead of its time and foreshadowed the field's emphasis on dialog and relationships. It also reflected elements of John Dewey's pragmatic idealism (Stoker, 2014).

Referring to university public relations practice, Harlow (1937) advocated the cultivation of continuous interactions between educational institutions and the public. All parties shared in the costs and benefits of these interactions. Self-interests and private interests were intertwined. Universities engaged the public because the public paid the bills and, as public institutions, they were accountable to the public. Later Harlow (1942) argued that business also was obligated to interact with the public. No business, he wrote, can only focus on producing and marketing a product. It must also consider the social effect of its enterprise. The measurement of that social effect, Harlow wrote, was whether it contributed to the public interest. "After all," he continued, "each individual, each business, is responsible for what it does. Public relations representing an enterprise should interpret that enterprise in an authoritative and responsible fashion" (p. 26). The determination of service to the public interest and social effect depended on a Dewey-like unaffiliated group evaluation of whether the actions were socially responsible. Public relations served the self-interests of the organization by communicating in an authoritative and responsible fashion, but the public determined whether that communication served the public interest. Harlow intuitively recognized the levels of abstraction in communication. He claimed that private and public interests were connected and disconnected at the same time. Harlow solved the paradox by urging practitioners to focus on what they could control—communicating responsibly—and not on what they could not control—the public evaluation of that responsibility.

Once that public evaluation occurs, however, public relations must answer whether the organization's policies and conduct are in the public interest. Harlow (1942), citing Arthur Page, wrote that when businesses were small, they had a much easier time staying in touch with their neighbors. In the age of large, multinational corporations, however, it was much more difficult to serve the public interest. Page thought big business could still operate in the public interest by explaining "the problems surrounding the business so that the public sees that the enterprise is in their interest" (Harlow, 1942, p. 27). Public relations was not just publicity or management, it was "what everybody in the business, from top to bottom, says and does in contact with the public" (p. 27). The job of public relations was to sensitize those inside the organization to the needs of the public and inform the public as to how the organization could satisfy those needs. Harlow described a public-minded practitioner as one who facilitated activities that encouraged public inquiry and action.

Harlow (1942) invoked the metaphor of a mirror to describe public relations as a facilitator, expressing the spirit and purpose of an organization and interpreting its role in society. Through that mirror, public relations reflected the organization's present and past good works and helped it get credit for those actions. As America emerged from the Depression, the New Deal gave the impression that the government would protect the public's interests. During World War II, corporate activism replaced the government activism. By the late 1940s, corporations touted a form of "welfare capitalism" (Ewen, 1996, p. 361). Big business employed public relations to convince the public to reject the New Deal's government-sponsored social policy and embrace the idea of corporate social action (Ewen, 1996). Public relations practitioners jumped on the welfare capitalism bandwagon and took ownership of the idea of public relations as the social conscience of an organization.

At trade conventions and conferences across the country, business touted the merits of better public relations (Fitzgerald, 1946). Meeting in 1939, corporate chief executive officers advocated aligning their private interests with the public interest. Representing major corporations, including B. F. Goodrich and Philadelphia Electric Co., these business leaders contended that good public relations served their self-interests and the public interest. It was not a service for getting out of trouble but a sincere expression of a business's personality (Public relations as good business, 1939). Longtime public relations counselor H. M. Miles (1944) echoed these sentiments, arguing that one of the primary jobs of public relations was to help industry conform to the public interest. Publicity played an important part in accomplishing this task, but it was only one of several tools used by public relations counselors.

The war helped win back public confidence in business and industry, and organizations espoused an obligation to adjust and adapt to the public. Modern management should do the right thing and then communicate that to the public. "Modern public relations is a matter of establishing a business with the public by sound policy, procedures and products put over by personnel principles, publicity, advertising, sales promotion and personal contacts" (p. 62). The key for business was to hire "a man of imagination tempered by social consciousness" (p. 67). The public relations "man" also must have the courage to tell the boss when the boss was wrong even if it cost him his job. In organizations, public relations practitioners represented the public interest. Public relations was the "acknowledgement to the public of the social responsibilities of business" (Baus, 1945, p. 62).

Public relations comprised "every phase of endeavor that touches the public interest" (Wagner, 1945, p. 179). Public relations mediated between business and society by creating good will and restoring the public's trust. Through public relations, industry showed the public that it operated in the public interest (Parkes, 1945). "The principle flaw in industrial public relations in the past is that industry managed to get itself pictured as self-seeking; as protecting vested interests. It has somehow failed to establish in the public's mind that its motives are good" (Parkes, 1945, p. 1053). If the public believed that industry wanted to do the right thing, it would lend its support.

This emphasis on public relations as the heroic defender of the public interest helped deflect growing criticism coming from the press and the public sector. The booming postwar economy, along with the expansion of the media to include newspapers, radio and television, increased the demand for public relations expertise. Harlow (1944[1945]) estimated that 75,000 service men and women gained some experience working in public relations for the military. Many of these former military public information officers entered the private sector (Cutlip, 1994). Hardly a week passed without the announcement of some new public relations firm being established (Baus, 1945).

Popularity and success, however, created the false belief that public relations was like Aladdin's lamp and, "All you have to do is to rub it and wealth flows into your coffers" (Harlow, 1944[1945], p. 553). The press jumped on the opportunity to report distortions in public relations practice, labeling it as a parasite on the press and calling upon editors to protect the public from these paid special interests. The field's defenders argued that public relations helped businesses put their best foot forward as they vied for the public's favor. However, unless the field acted to find "an antidote to the poison within it, public relations may never recover and become the force for good that it should be" (Harlow, 1944[1945]).

Harlow and other educators identified publicity as the poison. Though publicity remained central to public relations practice, educators and leading practitioners rejected the idea that publicity alone could serve the public interest. Instead, they embraced professionalism and professional standards. Professionals served the public interest. They wanted to help management balance its responsibility to the organization with its social responsibility to the public (Cutlip & Center, 1964). To do this, public relations needed a place at the management table. Stephen E. Fitzgerald (1946), who had just joined the venerable advertising agency, N. W. Ayer & Son, wanted the field to do more than communicate policy; he wanted to shape that policy. But the field's wide range of actors and activities confused the public and the popular press as to the true nature of public relations. Publicity alone, he argued, "was a poorer substitute for public relations ... when business was in greater need of some really high caliber public statesmanship" (Fitzgerald, 1946, p. 196). The power of public relations rested in its ability "to influence and sometimes control decisions of major public import" (Fitzgerald, 1946, p. 196). Therefore, the public had a stake in public relations practice. While doctors, lawyers, and accountants require professional training and certification, public relations practitioners did not and yet they still held a position of influence with the public on important issues.

Rather than calling themselves professionals, public relations practitioners should simply act more professionally (Fitzgerald, 1946). Increased professionalism would bring order to the field and "help to mobilize, in the public interest, some of the enormously effective skills and techniques which now exist" (p. 197). Fitzgerald intuitively recognized that more professionalism would improve practice but never explained what practitioners should do to better serve the public interest. He claimed that job one was not selling the public as to an organization's value but helping the organization in "the formation of sound public policy and, at times, in the communication of that policy to the public" (p. 197).

Leading practitioners began to formulate their own policies regarding their professional status. In August 1947, they merged the two leading public relations professional groups into the Public Relations Society of America (Advertising news and notes, 1947). Scott Cutlip (1952) claimed that this combined national professional association, along with growth in public relations education and the publication of scholarly and trade journals, provided evidence of the field's professionalism. In 1952, Cutlip published what for decades was the field's most influential textbook, *Effective Public Relations*. In his text, Cutlip cited *PR News* editor Denny Griswold's oft-quoted definition of public relations as "the management function which evaluates public attitudes, identifies the policies and procedures of an individual or an organization with the public interest, and executes a program of action to earn public understanding" (Cutlip, 1952, p. 6).

Another educator, Bertrand R. Canfield, published the first public relations case studies textbook in 1952. In the fifth edition, Canfield (1970) equated good public relations with policy decisions reflecting "the social philosophy of serving the public interest" (p. 8). Policy decisions were the decisions made by management. They were the most important organizational decisions made in an organization. By having an influence on organizational philosophy, public relations represented the public interest inside the organization. As a profession and now a part of management, public relations was now endowed with the power to identify, serve, and protect the public interest.

Professionalism and the public interest

To protect the field's professional reputation and prestige, leading practitioners sought to distance themselves from the poorly educated and unprincipled publicists and promoters whose excesses gave the field a bad name. Edward Bernays proposed a licensing program akin to other professions. A bit of a paradox himself, Bernays refused to join the Public Relations Society of America, the field's leading professional organization. He claimed that PRSA did not demand high enough "standards of character and professionalism of its prospective members" (Bernays, quoted in Cutlip, 1994, p. 217). Government licensing, on the other hand, would establish "sufficient control to make sure that it will serve the public interest, as we have done in the case of other professions" (Bernays, 1953, p. 28). Bernays later acknowledged that public relations' expanding influence in society might lead to abuse, especially from hacks posing as professionals. "We must consider the advisability of establishing sufficient control to make sure that it will serve the public interest, as we have done in the case of other professions" (Bernays, 1953, p. 28).

The majority of practitioners opposed licensing, believing it undermined the utilitarian function of serving the public interest. Licensing, wrote Joseph W. Hicks (1953), would limit practitioners' ability to inform the public and, thus, conflicted with the basic principles of public relations. Citing Ivy Lee's declaration of principles, Hicks argued that the public interest was best served by providing prompt and accurate information *"of value to the public"* (p. 29). Hicks noted that public relations was more than just publicity; it consisted of any effort to improve an organization's stature and dignity. Hicks failed to note, however, that much of the criticism of public relations stemmed from its efforts to manage reputations, engineer consent, and create positive images. Indeed, Boston University professor Albert Sullivan (1964) noted that the "professional" training given practitioners often contributed to the "dim view of its character" by emphasizing techniques over a "responsibility for the public interest" (p. 9).

The field's apologists and critics agreed that the industry needed to emphasize professional values more than professional skills. Sullivan cited two of those critics. In *Image Merchants,* Irwin Ross contended that public relations experts passed off "shoddy corporate practices by wrapping them in beautiful packages" (Sullivan, 1964, p. 11). Vance Packard, a former journalist, voiced similar concerns in his best-selling book, *The Hidden Persuaders* (Packard, 1957). Published in 1957, Packard's book criticized the advertising industry and public relations. Public relations people in particular, Packard argued a year later, needed to be "more forthright, less designing, more strict in their standards, and more respectful of the public, then—and only then—will the discerning public accept them as real professionals" (Packard, 1958, p. 57). No matter how much public relations practitioners wanted professional recognition, they lacked "rigorous academic preparation, licensing, and adherence to a stern code of ethics" (p. 54).

Though Sullivan disliked Packard's "spectacular" critical approach, he agreed that public relations needed to strengthen its professional standards and give more respect to the public (Sullivan, 1964, p. 11). As practiced in the 1960s, public relations lacked two essential elements of professionalism: "an accepted body of knowledge and dedication to the public interest" (p. 12). Despite hundreds of books discussing the practices and techniques, the body of knowledge did not include a theoretical foundation based on research. Public relations faced a similar problem with the public interest. "Most public relations activity is frankly partisan" (p. 12). Citing a popular trade publication *Public Relations Today,* Sullivan wrote that, by its very nature, public relations distorted information by communicating only favorable information. "Communication that conceals unpleasant facts or distorts by changing emphases can hardly be characterized as communication in the public interest, however much it may be defended on partisan grounds" (p. 13). For public relations to rise above partisan promotion, it must have more responsibility than granted by management. Public relations, Sullivan (1964) argued, must be a "custodian of truth, charged with communicating truth and responsible for safe guarding it" (p. 15).

Ironically, Sullivan tried to solve the tensions created by the paradox of the public interest by focusing on the positive aspect of the paradox. Contradictory forces exist simultaneously, meaning that the logical approach of choosing one contradictory aspect of the paradox over the other does not eliminate the existence of the oppositional element. Sullivan emphasized truth and responsibility over partisan public relations activity, but the truth about responsible or irresponsible public relations was that it was inherently partisan. Sullivan's solution may have eased the paradoxical tension inherent in public relations simultaneously serving private interests and the public interest, but it failed to provide a long-term solution to the paradox. To focus on the positive aspect of a paradox and ignore the opposing negative elements actually magnified the tension created by the paradox (Argyris, 1988; Hofstadter, 1979; Lewis, 2000). To view a paradox as an either-or decision actually exaggerates the effects of the paradox (Lewis, 2000). Rather, the solution lies in accepting that partisan and public interest communication exist simultaneously, and the key to solving the paradox lies more in the negative than positive elements of that tension.

Sullivan's views were reflected in how public relations associated the public interest with *responsible* advocacy and publicity, both forms of one-way communication. Even today, the Public Relations Society of America's Member Statement of Professional Values identifies advocacy as its first value: "We serve the public interest by acting as responsible advocates for those we represent. We provide a voice in the marketplace of ideas, facts, and viewpoints to aid informed public debate" (PRSA, n.d., para. 7). The statement implies that serving the public interest is dependent upon whether practitioners and their organizations aid the public's informed debate and discussion. Essentially, serving the public interest depends on whether the responsible advocate initiated public inquiry, an outcome that occurs independent of the responsible advocate's actions.

Stephenson (1971) echoed these sentiments. However, he failed to resolve the paradox of taking credit for serving the public interest before having any evidence as to whether the public was served. For public relations to operate in the public interest, he wrote in the 1960 second edition of his book, it must be part of the management function in an organization. As advocates, they must make sure that everything they wrote and said or caused others to write or say in the interest of their employers "should be in the public interest" (Stephenson, 1971, p. 11). But how would they know whether their communication served the public interest if service to the public interest existed independent of their actions? Stephenson said practitioners must have the personal integrity necessary to rise above their partisan interests. Though they lacked the customary protections due lawyers and other professionals, they were obliged "to put the public interest first, even if that means to sever [a] business connection"

(p. 11). But how could they put the public first if they did not know whether the public was served until after serving the private interests of their client or organization?

Public relations practitioners have long aligned service to the public interest with participation in the court of public opinion or the marketplace of ideas. It was left to practitioners to determine whether their communication served the well-being of society. Ironically, as Douglas (1980) noted, leaving the determination of the public interest to the individual emerged from aligning democratic ideals with an emphasis on "property rights and private benefits" (p. 108). In other words, the individual practitioner determined majority interests through the democratic process of advocating for private interests. Since interests are most commonly identified with personal preference, private interests and public interests often became one and the same. "The more that benefits are linked to personal preference, the more difficult it becomes to demonstrate the existence of benefits which pertain to all members of society" (Douglas, 1980, p. 110). Thus, the paradoxical tension regarding the public interest caused a number of scholars to question its validity and relevance (Schubert, 1960; Johnston, 2017).

Problems with the public

In the same way public relations practitioners embraced the positive side of the public interest paradox, abolitionists began focusing on its negative attributes. Critics argued that the public interest defied definition and measurement, and some went so far as to claim it did not exist but simply represented a multiplicity of competing group interests (Cochran, 1974). Others contended that proponents were simply promoting their own special interests (Diggs, 1973; Cochran, 1974). The whole idea of aligning commercial interests with the public interest appeared self-serving and insincere. The public interest began to be perceived as more of a point of view and less of an absolute (Prout, 1968).

Public relations scholars responded by de-emphasizing the field's obligation to the public interest. Mechling (1975) noted that practitioners struggled to balance private, commercial, and societal interests. Armed with Systems Theory, public relations scholars focused less on advocacy and more on the role of practitioners in organizational systems. Practitioners functioned more as managers and boundary spanners, managing issues and communication for their organizations (Heath, 1997, 2005). Issues management emerged in the 1970s as a "set of functions used to reduce friction and increase harmony between organizations and their publics in the public policy arena" (Heath, 2005, p. 460). As a manager rather than just a counselor, public relations practitioners joined the ranks of the management team.

Although Harlow (1976) and many practitioners still held to the idea of serving the public interest, they also embraced the management function. In a 1970s survey, public relations educators and industry leaders defined public relations as a management function promoting *management's* responsibility to the public interest (Harlow, 1976). The practitioner acted as a two-way conduit between the organization and the public, interpreting the organization to the public. In other words, public relations managers represented both the interests of the public and the organization. Their role had now expanded beyond facilitating communication between an organization and the public; they were now expected to serve as an enlightened mediator and interpreter of the public mind.

By the 1990s, public relations educators and practitioners had lost interest in the field's obligation to the public interest. It was replaced by corporate responsibility, issues management, public relationships, and two-way symmetrical communication. In 1984, Grunig and Hunt introduced a new model for determining *excellence* in public relations (Grunig & Hunt, 1984). Grunig and Hunt redefined public relations as the practice of social responsibility and introduced four models of practice: Press agency/publicity, public information, two-way asymmetric communication, and two-way symmetric communication. Grunig and Grunig (1992) called two-way symmetrical communication the most ethical of the four. It included the same traditional characteristics as public interest public relations, including telling the truth, listening, interpreting and mediating, and managing and understanding the viewpoints of various stakeholders (Grunig & Grunig, 1992). Unlike one-way communication strategies, such as persuasion, advocacy, and publicity, two-way symmetric communication promoted research, engagement, mutual understanding, and adjustment (Grunig & Grunig, 1992). Stated another way, engaging in two-way symmetric communication served the public interest.

In 1993, Bivins tried to direct the field's attention back to the public interest. He admitted that the practitioner served as a mediator and advocate and promoted the public interest by facilitating public debate. As a mediator, public relations served private and public interests. With echoes of John Dewey, he recommended that the profession could tip the scales toward the public by promoting public inquiry and debate, especially on contemporary issues of public concern. The profession would need "to strengthen its code to clarify the public service function of individuals" (p. 125), and figure out how to foster public debate, even for unpopular causes. But then Bivins slipped back into another paradox when he argued that the field's recognition as a profession still depended on it doing a better job of defining the public interest in a way acceptable to the public. In other words, Bivins called for facilitating public debate while at the same time asking public relations practitioners to manage the results of that inquiry. This approach confused the levels of abstraction, assuming that public relations could identify and promote public inquiry and evaluate it at the same time.

Despite Bivins' (1993) examination of the public interest and more recent attempts by Johnston (2017) to re-emphasize the public interest, contemporary public relations scholarship continues to sidestep the term. Symmetry, dialog, and other public relations models imply that dialogic activities, such as open discussion, reciprocity, and an ongoing process of validating truth, serve private and public interests (Weaver, Motion, & Roper, 2006). These dialogic approaches reject the field's historical roots in advocacy, publicity, and persuasion. Brown

(2006) contended that present day public relations scholars have withdrawn from historical scholarship with the intention of promoting a conception of public relations that better reflects the way they want to be perceived by external publics. Scholars deny or ignore elements of public relations history in hopes of creating a more palatable historical narrative. They also have distorted that narrative to reflect "a historically linear, ethically justified, technologically oriented explanation of public relations" (Brown, 2006, p. 207).

Messina (2007) also chided the field's scholars for avoiding and ignoring the role of persuasion in public relations. For the last 50 years, he contended, the academy failed to include persuasion in the development of contemporary theories, processes, and definitions. The fact that professional practice remained "predominantly about communication with intent" (pp. 29–30) made this this void in scholarship even more appalling. He surmised that scholars wrongly associated persuasion with the more pejorative practice of propaganda. Propaganda, he argued, disengages informed choice and reason while ethical persuasion enables reasoned and informed decision making. Public relations practitioners traditionally appealed to the public interest as their moral standard for evaluating the ethics of persuasion and advocacy. Messina rejected that notion, arguing that the determination of whether one's position served the public interest depended upon the outcome of the political process (see Flathman, 1966). Thus, practitioners had no way of knowing whether their actions served the public interest until after the public had passed judgment on their actions. Sorauf (1957) helped shape Messina pessimistic views of the public interest, but Messina is one of the few to consider the implications of the negative side of the public interest paradox.

Contemporary scholars assume that building and maintaining mutually beneficial relationships solves the public interest paradox. Their motivation, however, differs little from their scholarly predecessors. In an effort to make the field more palatable to the public, Albert Sullivan and Rex Harlow also emphasized public engagement and public service. They, too, de-emphasized persuasion, advocacy, and publicity. In other words, the private interests of past and present academics and professionals were best served by defining public relations as a management function employing two-way communication and building mutually beneficial relationships. More recently, public relations scholars have shown a renewed interest in advocacy, especially in social media, but this trend arises out of a desire to justify the use of public relations to promote causes that align with personal interests and values.

Corporate social responsibility (CSR) initiatives also exhibit this same kind of self-serving motive for organizations to be perceived as being good citizens. Public relations helps organizations receive recognition for their socially responsible actions. In one study, companies benefited from corporate responsibility in a variety of ways but only if stakeholders knew about CSR activities (Shuili, Bhattacharya, & Sankar, 2010). Companies can win public support and improve their image if they are sincere in serving the public (Yoon, Gurhan-Canli, & Schwarz, 2006; Kim & Lee, 2012). These studies not only reinforce the need for informing the public about CSR activities, they expose the potential dangers of this kind of communication being perceived as self-serving self-promotion. Like the public interest paradox, companies want public recognition for their good deed but do not want to be perceived as serving their own interests in seeking that recognition. Frankental (2001) identified this paradox and several others, including the oversized influence of shareholder governance, absence of market rewards for ethical practice, the lack of a clear definition of CSR, and the reluctance of companies to admit to social responsibility failures (Frankental, 2001). Until corporations resolved these paradoxes, Frankental noted, CSR would continue to be branded a public relations invention.

In sum public relations scholars and practitioners sincerely believe in serving the public interest, promoting social responsibility, engaging in dialog, and building mutually beneficial relations. They have failed, however, to acknowledge the self-serving motives behind these social initiatives. Formal logic serves as an interpretive scheme or context that influences how people think, feel, and understand their world. When faced with the tensions produced by contradictory ideas, formal logic tends to promote one idea over the other, typically focusing on more positive aspect of a paradoxical situation. Public relations scholars and practitioners have done just that. They have focused on the prosocial effects of their work, including contributing to the marketplace of ideas, informing the public, creating conditions for public engagement, and enhancing capitalism and commerce. On the other hand, practitioners and scholars, with few exceptions, have ignored the negative pole of the paradox—the personal and professional motives for wanting to be perceived as serving the public interest. By denying public relations history, practice, and philosophy, the field has magnified the paradox and stymied its progress. No matter how many prosocial theories scholars develop, the public still perceives public relations as self-serving.

Resolving the paradoxes

To resolve the paradox of the public interest, the first step is to accept its existence and embrace the negative side of the paradox. Persuasion, influence, advocacy, and promotion have long been the de rigueur of public relations (Lamme & Russell, 2010). Practitioners, scholars, and the profession have long served their private interests by emphasizing the public interest. However, they have failed to acknowledge that serving the public interest is a by-product of serving their own interests. As Schocket (1979) noted in his discussion on the public interest, a person does not discard private interests and values when moving from one role to another. The private interests of one's organization, client, or profession are not suddenly discarded because one enters the marketplace of ideas or the court of public opinion. Whether engaging in two-way symmetric communication or advocating for a cause, the professional identity of public relations is to serve the private interests of their client organizations.

That does not mean that public relations should ignore or discard the public interest as a moral standard. Private interests and public interests are not mutually exclusive, but the evaluation of whether an action serves the public interest occurs at a higher level of abstraction. To move to that higher level requires practitioners to talk *about* the social implications of their actions. This is consistent with Johnston's (2017) call for the field to re-emphasize the public interest. By recognizing the paradox and levels of abstraction in language, public relations can begin to break down the walls of its semantic prison.

Korzybski (1933[2000]) contended that a consciousness of abstracting in language provided persons with the "semantic *freedom* of all levels and so helps with *evaluation* and selection, thus removing the possibility of remaining animalistically fixed or blocked on any one level" (p. 441). An understanding of multiordinal communication is a critical first step to resolving paradox. Elson (2010) explained that there is communication and then communication about that communication. "A communication (what is said) and a meta-communication (the relationship aspect of what is said) differ in ways not definable in terms of time and space. They are at different levels of abstraction" (p. 77). In other words, as public relations manages interactions, it serves private interests but has little or no control over public evaluations of those interactions. Stated another way, practitioners manage communication at the lower level of abstraction (identification) but have less power over the public's inferences and interpretations that occur at higher levels.

When people confuse "orders of abstractions and disregard multiordinality" (Korzybski, 1933[2000], p. 449), they build up paradoxes that stubbornly resist logical solutions. My colleague Megan Stoker and I (2012) first recognized this paradox in an analysis of the relationship between public relations and the public interest. We leaned heavily on the philosophical approach to loyalty proposed by Oldenquist (1982). Interests and loyalties enjoy many similarities. They are at once personal and public. Just because a loyalty is personal or subjective, however, does not mean it is unethical or immoral. On the contrary, Oldenquist argued that our narrower loyalties carry more moral weight because they are more personal and concrete. As our loyalties become more abstract, they become broader and thus more impartial and impersonal. In other words, they move to a higher level of abstraction and thus have less claim on us.

Like loyalties, interests wield more power at the personal and private level. The broader the interest, the more difficult it becomes to determine its moral claim on us. At the identification level, public relations practitioners have an interest in their organizations, fellow employees, family, church, community, and friends. When they begin talking about those interests or determining what those interests have in common with their geographic region, country, or world, those relationships between private and public interests become much more abstract and complicated.

We argued that for practitioners to serve the public interest, they should serve private interests in a morally worthy way (Stoker & Stoker, 2012). This paradoxical approach to serving the public interest did not sit well with journal editors who had accepted the paper for publication. They felt uncomfortable with an ethics paper that emphasized individual, proximate interests over more social, public ones. Trapped in the paradox, they viewed our solution as lacking intellectual rigor and ethical justification. Elson (2010) identified this behavioral pattern in her study of paradoxes. "To individuals who have not transcended the binary framework of the paradox, the two opposing options appear to be the only real alternatives" (p. 143). In other words, when faced with whether to serve private or public interests, one should obviously prioritize the social over the individual. In Elson's study, she discovered three stages or levels of abstraction. At Stage 1, the person does not perceive the paradox. In the case of humor, the Stage 1 person takes the joke literally and fails to appreciate the punchline. The Stage 2 person gets the joke but only sees a binary pair of options in which the person must choose one alternative or the other. The Stage 3 person gets the joke but chooses not to react because he or she has heard the joke or finds no humor in its context. The person at Stage 3 accepts the paradox and accepts that both options may have equal relevance. Elson noted that those at Stage 2 misinterpret those at Stage 3 as not being aware of the paradox because they may carry on as if the paradox does not exist.

Thus, the editors questioned our solution that serving private interests paradoxically served the public interest. If practitioners acted with "intelligent good will" and focused on promoting superior interests, such as freedom and justice (Stoker & Stoker, p. 41), they served the public interest. Intelligent good will reflects the philosophy of Immanuel Kant and his emphasis on the objective and subjective necessity of doing one's moral duty (Kant, 2002). Instead of worrying about whether practitioners serve broader public interests, they should concentrate on making morally worthy decisions in behalf of proximate interests (Kant, 2002; Johnson, 2009). We also applied Kant's imperatives to universalize moral laws and treat people as ends in and of themselves. Similar to Bivins' (1993) call for public relations to encourage public debate, we also proposed applying Dewey's (1927) public philosophy of facilitating public education and learning. By promoting "public inquiry, individual autonomy, and human and community improvement," (Stoker & Stoker, 2012, p. 41) public relations practitioners could serve the public interest.

However, in combining private moral action with Dewey's public philosophy, we, like Bivins, breached the levels of abstraction. At the identification level, practitioners could apply intelligent good will in performing their roles as mediators and advocates for private interests. They also could promote superior interests and facilitate conditions for public inquiry, but the description or evaluation of those actions—whether they served the public interest—stood outside their locus of control. Dewey (1927) contended that publics unaffiliated with the direct action of the individual or the group judged whether that action served the public interest (Bozeman, 2007). Messina (2007) argued that the political process determined whether an action served the public interest. In each of these cases, practitioners have little control over whether the public judges an act as serving their interests.

Resolving the public interest paradox

For practitioners and scholars to break free of the paradox of the public interest, they must accept that their actions serve their individual and professional interests and the private interests of their organizations. They should also accept that private interests may be public interests. Private interests are not always in conflict with the public interest, but we can never be completely sure in advance that they are the same. There also is nothing inherently unethical or immoral about promoting personal, private, and partisan interests. What is potentially immoral and unethical is to claim otherwise. Arguing that the intent of public relations activities, such as advocacy, publicity, or two-way communication, serves the public interest is inauthentic and deceptive. Instead, the field should focus on how to be more transparent about and accountable for its activities on behalf of private interests. Public relations is then reframed as a series of morally worthy activities on behalf of private interests that welcome outside scrutiny and public judgment. This recognition then encourages transparency and accountability, two actions that, at a higher level of abstraction, can contribute to the public interest. Intelligent good will at the identification level rises to a discussion about how these practices promote superior interests at the next higher level. At the third level, the organization examines subsequent feedback from organizational members and the public and determines the public interest value of these activities.

By reframing public relations as morally worthy actions in behalf of private interests, the field will shift its research and scholarship inward toward the character and motives of the organization and the ethics of the practitioner and the profession. Professionalism will become less about promoting the public interest and more about celebrating practices that successfully promote superior interests and public inquiry. The academy will worry less about making the field more palatable and worry more about making the field more transparent and accountable. As practitioners take on more responsibility and communicate with more transparency, they can better relate with the public and develop authentic relationships, ones that do not require management.

Note

1 I'm indebted to my colleague and former co-author Brad Rawlins for this analysis of Hiebert's biography on Ivy Lee.

Works cited

Adams, H. C. (1902). What is publicity? *North American Review 175*, 845–904.
Advertising news and notes. (1947, August 21). *The New York Times*, p. 21.
Argyris, C. (1988). Crafting a theory of practice: The case of organizational paradoxes. In R. E. Quinn & K. S. Cameron (Eds.), *Paradox and transformation: Toward a theory of change in organization and management* (pp. 255–278). Cambridge, MA: Ballinger Publishing.

Baus, H. M. (1945, December). Thou canst not then be false. *Nation's Business*, 62–67.

Bernays, E. (1928a). Manipulating public opinion: The way and the how. *American Journal of Sociology*, *33* (6), 958–971.

Bernays, E. (1928b, September 1). The business of propaganda. *Independent*, *123*, 198–199.

Bernays, E. (1936, September). Freedom of propaganda. *Vital Speeches of the Day*, 744–746.

Bernays, E. (1947). The engineering of consent. *Annals of American Academy of Political and Social Science*, *250*, 113–120.

Bernays, E. (1953, June). License the public relations counsel. *Rotarian*, 28—29, 50–51.

Bernays, E. (1962). *Crystallizing Public Opinion*. New York: Liveright Publishing (Original work published 1923).

Bernays, E. (2005). *Propaganda* (M. C. Miller, Ed.). Brooklyn, N.Y.: IG Publishing. (Original work published 1928).

Bivins, T. (1993). Public relations, professionalism, and the public interest. *Journal of Business Ethics*, *12* (2), 117–126.

Bozeman, B. (2007). *Public values and public interest: Counterbalancing economic individualism*. Washington, DC: Georgetown University Press.

Bridgeman, R. L. (1905). Publicity and reform in business, for protected interests. *New England Magazine*, *33*, 459–467.

Brown, R. E. (2006). Myth of symmetry: Public relations as cultural styles. *Public Relations Review*, *32*, 206–212.

Brownell, A. (1922). Publicity—and its ethics. *North American Review*, *215*, 188–196.

Burke, J. J. (1910). Publicity and social reform. *Catholic World*, *91*, 198–211.

Canfield, B. (1970). *Public relations: Principles, cases, and problems* (5th Ed.). Homewood, IL: Richard D. Irwin.

Cassinelli, C. W. (1962). The public interest in political ethics. In C. J. Friedrich (Ed.), *The Public Interest* (pp. 44–53). New York: Atherton Press.

Cochran, C. E. (1974, May). Political science and "the public interest". *Journal of Politics*, *36* (2), 327–355.

Creel, G. (1920). *How we advertised America: The first telling of the amazing story of the Committee on Public Information that carried the gospel of Americanism to every corner of the globe*. New York: Harper & Brothers.

Cutlip, S. (1952). *Effective public relations*. New York: Prentice Hall.

Cutlip, S. (1994). *The unseen power: Public relations. A history*. Hillsdale, NJ: Lawrence Erlbaum Associates.

Cutlip, S. & Center, A. (1964). *Effective public relations* (3rd Ed.). New York: Prentice-Hall.

Dewey, J. (1927). *The public and its problems*. New York: Holt.

Diggs, B. J. (1973, July). The common good as reason for political action. *Ethics*, *83* (4), 283–293.

Douglas, B. (1980). The common good and the public interest. *Political Theory*, *8*, 103–117.

Elson, L. (2010). *Paradox lost: A cross-contextual definition of levels of abstraction*. Cresskill, NJ: Hampton Press.

Ewen, S. (1996). *PR! A social history of spin*. New York: Basic Books.

Fitzgerald, S. E. (1946). Public relations: A profession in search of professionals. *Public Opinion Quarterly*, *10* (2), 191–200.

Flathman, R. E. (1966). *The public interest: An essay concerning the normative discourse of politics*. New York: John Wiley & Sons.

Frankental, P. (2001). Corporate social responsibility—A PR invention? *Corporate Communications: An International Journal, 6,* 18–23.

Grunig, J. E. & Grunig, L. A. (1992). Models of public relations and communication. In J. E. Grunig (Ed.), *Excellence in public relations and communications management* (pp. 285–325). Hillsdale, N.J.: Lawrence Erlbaum Associates.

Grunig, J. & Hunt, T. (1984). *Managing public relations.* New York: Rinehart & Winston.

Hallahan, K. (2002). Ivy Lee and the Rockefellers' Response to the 1913–1914 Colorado Coal Strike. *Journal of Public Relations Research, 14* (4), 265–315.

Harlow, R. F. (1937). "Selling" the university. *Journal of Higher Education, 8,* 14–17.

Harlow, R. F. (1942). Public relations and social action. *Journal of Higher Education, 13,* 25–29.

Harlow, R. F. (1944/1945). Public relations at the crossroads. *Public Opinion Quarterly, 8* (4), 551–556.

Harlow, R. F. (1976). Building a definition of public relations. *Public Relations Review, 2* (4), 34–42.

Heath, R. L. (1997). *Strategic issues management organizations and public policy challenges.* London: Sage.

Heath, R. L. (2005). Issues management. In R. L. Heath (Ed.), *Encyclopedia of public relations* (pp. 460–463). Thousand Oaks, CA: Sage.

Hicks, J. W. (1953, June). License the public relations counsel. *Rotarian,* 28–29, 50–51.

Hiebert, R. E. (1966). *Courtier to the crowd: The story of Ivy Lee and the development of public relations.* Ames, IA: Iowa State University Press.

Hofstadter, D. R. (1979). *Gode, Escher, Bach: An eternal golden braid.* New York: Vintage Books.

Hofstadter, R. (1955). *The Age of Reform.* New York: Vintage Books.

Johnson, R. (2009). Kant's moral philosophy. *The Stanford Encyclopedia of Philosophy.* Palo Alto. CA: Stanford University Press. Retrieved November 11, 2009 from http://plato.stanford.edu/entries/kant-moral/.

Johnston, J. (2017). The public interest: A new way of thinking for public relations? *Public Relations Inquiry, 6,* 5–22.

Kant, I. (2002). *Groundwork for the metaphysics of morals* (A. W. Wood, Ed. & Trans.). New Haven, CN: Yale University Press.

Kim, S. & Lee, Y. J. (2012). The complex attribution process of CSR motives. *Public Relations Review, 38,* 168–170.

Korzybski, A. (2000). *Science and sanity: An introduction to non-Aristotelian systems and general semantics* (5th Ed.). Brooklyn, NY: Institute of General Semantics. (Original work published 1933).

Lamme, M. & Russell, K. (2010). Removing the spin: Toward a new theory of public relations history. *Journalism Communication Monographs, 11* (4), 281–362.

Lewis, M. (2000). Exploring paradox: Toward a more comprehensive guide. *Academy of Management Review, 25* (4), 760–776.

Lippmann, W. (1955). *Essays in the public philosophy.* Boston: Little, Brown and Company.

Lippmann, W. (1997). *Public Opinion.* New York: Free Press Paperbacks. (Original work published 1922).

Mechling, T. B. (1975). Is public interest public relations practical—and desirable? *Public Relations Quarterly, 20* (2), 10–22.

Messina, A. (2007). Public relations, the public interest and persuasion: an ethical approach. *Journal of Communication Management, 11,* 29–52.

McGerr, M. (2003). *A fierce discontent: The rise and fall of the Progressive Movement in America, 1870–1920.* New York: Oxford University Press.

Miles, H. M. (1944, December 30). Wanted: A definition of public relations. *Railway Age, 117* (27), 998.

Moran, F. (2011). Is public relations in the public interest? Francis Moran & Associates. Retrieved May 5, 2017 from www.francis-moran.com.

Oldenquist, A. (1982). Loyalties. *Journal of Philosophy* [On-line], *79* (4), 173–193. Retrieved October 9, 1999 from www.jstor.org.

Packard, V. (1957). *The hidden persuaders.* New York: David McKay.

Packard, V. (1958, May). Public relations: Good or bad? *Atlantic Monthly, 201,* pp. 53–57.

Parkes, H. (1945, December 29). How industry can make friends for itself: First, industry's aim must be in the public interest. *Railway Age, 119* (26), 1053.

Prout, C. H. (1968). Public opinion and public interest. *Public Relations Quarterly, 13* (2), 5–10.

PRSA (n.d.). Code of ethics. Retrieved May 4, 2017 from www.prsa.org.

Publicity, public opinion, and the wily press agent. (1920, October 2). *Literary Digest,* 58–62.

Public relations as good business. (1939, June 3). *Business Week,* 54–55.

Russell, K. & Bishop, C. (2009). Understanding Ivy Lee's declaration of principles: U.S. newspaper and magazine coverage of publicity and press agentry, 1865–1904. *Public Relations Review, 35* (2), 91–101.

Schocket, G. J. (1979). Social responsibility, profits, and the public interest. *Society,* 20–26.

Schubert, G. A. (1960). *The public interest.* Glencoe, IL: Free Press.

Shaw, A. (1909). The opportunity of the publicist in relation to efforts for social betterment. *Proceedings of the National Conference of Charities and Correction,* 318–332.

Shuili, D., Bhattacharya, C. B., & Sen, S. (2010). Maximizing business returns to corporate social responsibility (CSR): The role of CSR communication. *International Journal of Management Reviews,* 8–19.

Sorauf, F. J. (1957). The public interest reconsidered. *Journal of Politics, 19* (4), 616–639.

Steel, R. (1997). Foreword. In Lippmann W. (Ed.), *Public Opinion* (pp. xi-xvi). New York: Free Press Paperbacks.

Stephenson, H. (1971). *Handbook of public relations* (2nd Ed.). New York: McGraw-Hill.

Stoker, K. (2014). Defining public in public relations: How the 1920s debate over public opinion influence early philosophies of public relations. In St. John, B., Lamme, M. O., & L'Etang, J. (Eds.), *Pathways to public relations: Histories of practice and profession* (pp. 340–351). London: Routledge.

Stoker, K. & Rawlins V. L. (2005). The "light" of publicity in the Progressive Era: From searchlight to flashlight. *Journalism History, 30* (4), 177–188.

Stoker, K. & Stoker, M. (2012). The paradox of public interest: How serving individual superior interests fulfill public relations' obligation to the public interest, *Journal of Mass Media Ethics, 27,* 31–45.

Sullivan, A. (1964). The tenuous image of public relations. In A. Sullivan & O. Lerbinger (Eds.), *Information, influence, and communication: A reader in public relations* (pp. 3–16). New York: Basic Books.

The public is not damned. (1939, March). *Fortune, 19,* 83–88, 109–114.

Vance, A. (1907). The value of publicity in reform. *Annals of American Academy of Political and Social Science, 29,* 87–92.

Watzlawick, P., Bavelas, J. B., & Jackson, D. D. (2011). *Pragmatics of human communication: A study of interactional patterns pathologies and paradoxes.* New York: Norton Paperback.

Wagner, R. B. (1945). Don't neglect your relations: Molding the mass mind. *Vital Speeches of the Day, 12* (6), 179–180.

Weaver, K. C., Motion, J., & Roper, J. (2006). From propaganda to discourse (and back again): Truth, power, the public interest, and public relations. In J. L'Etang & M. Pieczka (Eds.), *Public relations: Critical debates and contemporary practice* (pp. 7–22). Mahwah, N.J.: Lawrence Erlbaum Associates.

Wilcox, D. L., Cameron, G. T., Reber, B. H., & Shin, J. (2011). *Think public relations.* Boston: Allyn & Bacon.

Wilson, W. (1913). *The new freedom.* New York: Doubleday.

Wright, M. (1935). *How to get publicity.* New York: McGraw Hill Book.

Yoon, Y., Gurhan-Canli, Z., & Schwarz, N. (2006). The effect of corporate social responsibility (CSR) activities on companies with bad reputations. *Journal of Consumer Psychology, 16* (4), 377–390.

3   The relationship paradox

In 1984, Mary Ferguson (2018) presented an invited paper in which she urged public relations scholars to make public relationships the central focus of their research and theory development. Inspired by Thomas Kuhn's (1996) conception of scientific paradigms, she explained that relationships touched on all aspects of public relations scholarship—organizations, publics, communication, and management. Public relations could explore the nature, attributes, and dimensions of macro-level public relationships. Ferguson proposed organizing a community of scholars around the paradigm of public relationships. As the "niche or domain" of public relations scholarship, the study of public relationships would bring legitimacy to the field and help define public relations "in terms of the activities of those who practice it" (p. 173).

Ferguson (2018) acknowledged that the study of interorganizational relationships moved public relations scholarship to a higher level of abstraction. The higher level of analysis was necessary to incorporate all aspects of public relations, including organizations, the public, and communication. This macro-level study would lead to new methodologies, a new unit of analysis, new considerations of attributes, and new dimensions of public relationships. Relationships offered scholars a chance to explore such dichotomies as static or dynamic, open or closed, mutually satisfying, mutually controlled, or mutually understood. The study of public relationships would "integrate organization-level variables, public or group-level variables, and communication variables" (p. 171).

This reframing of public relations research, coupled with the concept of two-way symmetric communication (Grunig & Hunt, 1984), has emerged as one of the most popular areas of public relations research. A community of scholars has developed around the paradigm of public relationships or, as it is referred to today, organization-public relationships (OPR). They have sought to define public relationships, identify their attributes, measure them, control them, and manage them (Ledingham & Bruning, 1998; Hon & Grunig, 1999; Broom, Casey, & Ritchey, 2000). What they have not done, however, is grapple with semantic problems and implications of public relationships and relationship management. They have failed to recognize that relationships describe a phenomenon that exists at a higher level of abstraction than the interactions that create them. The evaluation and inferences associated with those relationships—the way they are interpreted and valued by the parties in the relationships—also occurs at an even higher level of abstraction. Thus, public relations scholars assume they can define, control, or manage a complex phenomenon over which they have but limited control. To manage relationships, practitioners must hope for the others' willing cooperation or resort to ethically questionable strategies that could include manipulation and control. It is not like one can "manage" a relationship in the same way one manages schedules or a social media account. As Hinde (1997) stated, "Relationships are complicated" (p. 11).

Relationships also are paradoxical, and in this chapter, I will explore these paradoxes and suggest alternative ways of framing relationships that do not breach the levels of abstraction. In other words, I will suggest employing a more precise conceptual language for studying the nature, causal attributes, and social implications of interpersonal and public relationships. First, I will explore the paradoxical issues associated with interpersonal relationships. Next, I examine public relations research on organization-public relationships and managing relationships. Finally, I propose solutions to these paradoxes and recommend an approach that practitioners can manage—the act of relating (Stoker, 2014b).

Levels of abstraction

For language to be effective, it must be structured similar to the thing that it represents (Korzybski, 2000). This is based on mathematician Bertrand Russell's Theory of Logical Types in which the name of a thing, class, or collection is not a member of the thing, class, or collection. In other words, the name exists at a higher level of abstraction than the thing it names. Public relations serves as the name for a class of activities, such as issues management, publicity, and advocacy, and thus exists at a higher level of abstraction than those activities. "Any attempt to deal with the one [level] in terms of the other [level] is doomed to lead to nonsense and confusion" (Watzlawick, Weakland, & Fisch, 2011, p. 8). Bateson (2000) often noted that you do not eat the word steak on the menu, but you can eat the sizzling piece of meat on your plate. The person who does not get the joke is one who takes things literally and fails to move to the higher level of language where the punch line resides. Korzybski (2000) used the example of a map as a representation of a territory. One doesn't walk on the map but treks across a territory. In the process of scientific discovery, Watzlawick et al. (2011) noted that procedures, method, and methodology represented different levels of abstraction. Methodology exists at a higher logical type because it represents the philosophical study of methods.

To grasp ordinality, I imagine the levels of a high-rise retail department store. The merchandise on each floor reflects a different logical type. On the bottom floor, the store offers women's and men's fashions and then on the second floor are appliances. The third floor may include home decor or home furnishings. We describe the spatial relationship by saying the third floor is above the second floor, and the second floor is above the first floor. If we substitute the word about for above, as we might do in language, we can say the bottom level is about what the individual wears, the second floor is about what the individual needs and the third floor is about how the individual lives. This rough analogy reflects the idea that the identity of a thing and our description of the thing, and the inferences we make based on our descriptions coexist at different levels of abstraction.

Korzybski (2000) used the example of anthropologists, who, in the 1930s, measured culture in primitive societies by the way native peoples incorporated orders of abstraction in their languages. Primitives often had names for specific trees, such as poplars or pines, but lacked terms for more abstract classifications, such as woods or forest. Thus, the saying that one cannot see the forest for the trees is the product of levels confusion. It is not that one cannot see the forest but one's frame of reference remains stuck at a lower level of abstraction. We use the saying to describe a failure to move beyond one level, the trees, to abstract frame, the forest. Higher levels of abstraction serve as "expedient devices" because they help to facilitate "mutual understanding in being able to be brief in a statement and yet cover wider subjects" (Korzybski, 1994, p. 377).

Breaches in these levels of abstraction produce paradoxes in language and lead to human pathologies. Bateson (2000) argued that schizophrenia was caused by "formal patterns of breaching [that] occur in communication between a mother and child" (Bateson, 2000, pp. 202–203). Human afflictions, according to Korzybski (1994), stemmed from the use and under use of symbols. Confusion over levels of abstraction can change the way we perceive, interpret, and define the world around us. In other words, semantic breaches distort our sense of reality. Bateson (2000) and Korzybski (1994) warned about the dangers of treating two levels as one. Terrible consequences could result when self-interested persons promoting personal advantage at the identification level exploited common goods at the collective level (Hardin, 1968; Elson, 2010). The short-term gains are offset by long-term problems at a higher level. Like an addict, the person seeks immediate gains without considering the consequences of that behavior. This logic of addiction, as Bateson called it, may promote the survival of the individual at the expense of the rest of the population and society. Elson described it as akin to doing everything in our power to win battles without perceiving the potential implications those efforts might have on winning the war. To avoid having action at one level create havoc at another level requires the discipline to recognize that what's good for the individual at one level may harm or help the individual and the collective at another level.

Advertising uses the abstracting process to create illusions (Elson, 2010). Advertisers seduce consumers by appealing to desires for adventure, conquest, and prestige while all the time selling a vehicle that transports them from point A to point B. The old adage of buyer beware implies that one must recognize the illusion is not the reality. For consumers, this means recognizing that advertising's appeal exists at a higher level of abstraction, and that they need to move to a lower level of abstraction to realize that the promised benefit is an inference and not identified with the product's actual use. We may be seduced into thinking that an expensive car will make us happy but, at a more concrete level, the higher monthly payments will make us miserable. By being aware of abstraction, we now are in position to distinguish between the illusion and reality.

In her study of five paradoxes, Elson (2010) confirmed the value of moving up *and down* the levels of abstraction to resolve common paradoxes. She found that different levels could produce different valences, with something negative at one level turning positive at a higher level. For example, in the Prisoner's Dilemma, the two prisoners were faced with zero, three, or ten years in prison, depending upon whether one or both confessed. At the lowest level of abstraction, individual self-interested action, accepting the prosecutors' deal and confessing, could result in serving no time (if the other prisoner, who would then serve ten years, remained silent) or three years (if both confessed), as opposed to serving ten years if the other prisoner alone confessed. At a higher level, however, if they cooperated with each other and neither talked, they both were set free. The negative consequences of rational self-serving behavior at one level became the positive consequence of moral cooperation at another level. "At one level, choice and strategy and rationality and logic produce a decision to defect; at the next they advise cooperation" (p. 64). It is important to note that though moving to a higher level has its advantages, it also limits the amount of control each prisoner has over the outcome. This is why communication plays a critical role in resolving the paradox. If parties or organizations communicate and determine a willingness to cooperate, they serve their individual interests as well as collective interests.

By proposing public relationships as the central focus of public relations research, Ferguson (2018) ostensibly reframed public relations cooperative relationships. However, the terms public and relationships represent different levels of abstraction, especially in the way subsequent public relations researchers have interpreted and defined the terms. In trying to measure, maintain, and manage relationships, they have confused and breached the levels of abstraction. In other words, public relations scholars have failed to see the trees for the forest. They have assumed that they can bypass the process of communication and negotiation and move right into cooperation. Part of the problem arises from the foundational theories they use to define public relationships. They draw from a variety of disciplines but their descriptions and metaphors predominantly rely on research in interpersonal, one-on-one relationships.

Interpersonal relationships

Relationships serve as the connecting tissue between two or more participants or even groups of people. They are shaped by a variety of internal and external factors, including the mindsets, cultures, and motivations of the participants (Hinde, 1997). A variety of academic disciplines have studied interpersonal relationships, including psychology, philosophy, communication, and sociology. However, the study of relationships has long defied clear definition because the parties engage in such a complex pattern of actions that are accompanied by different emotions and cognitions (Hinde, 1997). Interaction serves as the term generally used to describe these actions and activities that lead to a relationship. These interactions exist at a lower level of abstraction and include past, present, and expected interactions. In other words, they are shaped by a myriad of interactions and relationships outside the influence or control of the other party in the relationship. The secret to cultivating healthy relationships is continued interaction, which sustains the relationship and leads to more interactions (Hinde, 1997).

Researchers must account for interactions over time as well as the type, number, and frequency of interactions. Interactions also occur in a particular society, culture, and physical environment, adding another layer of intrapersonal influences on an interpersonal phenomenon. In addition, existing and developing relationships affect interpersonal interactions, making it difficult for one party to control or manage relational outcomes. Bateson (2000) noted that many aspects of relationships are based on habits and routines that are not conscious but unconscious activities. Critical to relating is the need for both parties to share unconscious material, whether based on personal, cultural, or contextual values and interpretations. We already share some common values and ideals that we may not be able to consciously identify, but that are very much there. The strength of a conscious relationship often depends on shared thoughts, ideas, and values that are part of the unconscious.

This combination of these conscious and unconscious attributes helps to overcome the distance between parties in a relationship. Josselson (1992) identified eight ways in which people reduce the distance and relate with each other. These dimensions, as she named them, emerged from the developmental history of an individual. Thus, the first is holding, the second attachment, the third passionate experience, and the fourth eye-to-eye validation. The other four come into play as individuals move into the social world. They include idealization and identification, mutuality, embeddedness, and tending and care. Although the first four dimensions revolve around the most basic of relationships—filial and romantic—the final four apply to group and organizational relationships.

These relationships dimensions are difficult to measure. Indeed, most relationships research relies on self-reports, which skew evaluations in favor of the one reporting. Each party interprets interactions based on their own backgrounds and experience. These interpretations can change over time, causing one party to evaluate an interaction as positive at one instant and then apply a more negative evaluation at a later time. Personal and social interactions are complex, as are the requisite metaphors used to explain those interactions. Thus, meanings and language influence the relating experience and the relationships resulting from those interactions. "Language serves to structure meanings about the human relationships that we seek to understand and perform" (Duck, 1998, p. 5; citing Duck, 1994).

In describing relationships, people use language to create narratives about the interactions and events. Social contexts, norms, and culture exert a powerful influence over the language employed, often dictating the type of behavior deemed reasonable in developing a relationship. The parties involved make initial judgments about acceptable language and behavior while also considering the judgments and perceptions made by their social communities. This means that the more people or groups involved in a relationship, the more complicated the evaluations and social judgments regarding that relationship. Expanded conceptual contexts, including social and cultural meanings, also influence the interpretations and performances of relationship behaviors. The participants consider their own socially and culturally shared meanings as well as external judgments coming from society and their social network of relationships (Duck, 1993, 1994, 1998).

Communication also plays an integral and essential role in relationships. As Duck (1998) noted, "we talk to relate, whether well or badly" (p. 7). Talking helps to develop, maintain, improve, and change relationships. At a higher level of abstraction, however, other elements of the communication, including content and context, directly affect relationships. Duck (1998) referred to these as levels of abstraction in language (Watzlawick et al., 2011), when noting that verbal messages consist of two parts: "the *content* and *a message about the relationship* between the speaker and the listener" (p. 7). This means that the intended meaning of what is said also includes another evaluative layer about how the person feels about the relationship itself. Thus, every message consists of multiple layers—the verbal, paralinguistic, and nonverbal. In other words, what is said, how it is said, and what is not said combine together to influence a relationship. All are part of relating.

Communication involves persuasion (Duck, 1998). People intentionally engage in relational activities and behaviors. Each party brings various cultural and social baggage to social interactions. Our communications reflect our views, our identity, our interpretations, and our feelings about ourselves and others. In essence, we invite others to accept or at least sympathize with our views. Thus, a deep structural connection exists between persuasion and relationships. "The processes of persuasion are intricately tied up with the processes of relationships so that daily relational activity involves persuasion more widely and deeply than may appear at first" (p. 128). Although some general rules of engagement apply to human relationships, each relationship evolves to establish its own rules. The nature of the relationship determines what type of persuasion is considered appropriate and acceptable.

Duck (1998) described how car salesmen mimic relational activity to better persuade a customer to buy a car. Some acquaintances show an unusual amount of concern about our affairs and welfare before requesting some kind of favor. In a close relationship between family and friends, the parties share personal stories about challenges and triumphs in hopes of gaining acceptance or soliciting sympathy. Organizations often share similar stories in hopes that their customers or community might also accept and relate with them. This attempt at intimacy is paradoxical. Like the car salesman, the organization's efforts to mimic relational behaviors may have the opposite effect and come across as insincere and inauthentic. Maintaining and sustaining a relationship depends on how we relate and the perception that one's relating is sincere and authentic.

Maintenance serves as an effective metaphor to describe the process of sustaining a relationship (Canary & Stafford, 1994). To maintain a relationship, the parties engage in strategic and routine behaviors, both interactive and noninteractive. Maintenance focuses on the critical elements necessary for a relationship to endure and "the dynamic processes involved in relating" (p. 3). This statement exposes the paradox associated with maintaining a socially constructed phenomenon. Canary and Stafford talk about maintaining a relationship, but, in reality, they are more concerned with sustaining the ongoing interactions necessary for a relationship to exist. In other words, maintenance does not focus on relationships but on the dynamic interactions that lead to an ongoing relationship. Canary and Stafford define relational maintenance behaviors as those "actions and activities used to sustain desired relational definitions" (p. 5), but they erroneously assumed that relational definitions represent the way the parties define the relationship. They failed to recognize that relational definitions exist at a higher level of abstraction than relational maintenance. The actions to maintain a relationship are a different logical type than the definitions or descriptions of those actions.

The relational properties that Canary and Stafford (1994) assumed existed in all relationships confirm this breach in ordinality. They contended that the strength of a relationship depended upon the relational properties of control mutuality, trust, liking, and commitment. All four of these concepts are statements *about* the relationship and exist at a level of abstraction above the relationships they describe. Control mutuality means the degree to which the parties in a relationship agree as to when control is mutual or delegated. Trust depends on the perception that one can rely on the honesty and dependability of the other parties in a relationship. If the participants like each other, they share affection and mutual respect. Commitment reflects relational stability and indicates a desire to sustain the relationship. By measuring these relational properties, researchers assume that they can measure the strength of a relationship. Indeed, Hon and Grunig (1999) embraced Canary and Stafford's relational properties and incorporated them into their study of public relationships. The relational properties are similar to Wood's (1995) four dimensions of interpersonal relationships that influenced the public relationship research of Ledingham and Bruning (1998). Wood's dimensions included investment, commitment, trust, and comfort with relational dialectics. A good balance of these dimensions enables interpersonal relationships to flourish, but, once again, they are expressions about the relationship.

Public relations scholars have relied on the relationship maintenance research to study organization–public relationships. However, much of that research focused on married couples or families, not on business and professional relationships. Furthermore, some of the original scales are now considered flawed. Stafford (2010) identified concerns with the wording of questions, the use of certain terms, and overall clarity. She also found problems with "the

correspondence between conceptual and operational definitions of both maintenance and maintenance factors" (p. 281). In particular, she noted that relationship maintenance is defined as behavior, but some concepts, such as liking,
measure a disposition rather than an action. Her proposed new approach to
measuring relationship maintenance focused on behaviors and attitudes that
contributed to the maintenance of relationships. The scales measured activities
more closely associated to relating—openness/self-disclosure/relational talk,
positivity and understanding, networks, assurances, and tasks.

Some of the changes in measuring relationship maintenance reflect criticisms
leveled by Baxter (1994). She argued that healthy relationships are not relatively
stable and static, but constantly adapting and changing (Baxter, 1994). Personal
relationships represent "indeterminate processes of ongoing flux" (p. 233).
Applying a dialogic perspective, Baxter argued that the relational process is
beset by contradictions that promote constant change, making relationships difficult to maintain or repair. Citing the work of social theorist Mikhail Bakhtin,
Baxter contended that the social processes were characterized by a tension
between melding together and differentiation. Relationships reflect the give
and take between interdependence and independence. The parties in a relationship fuse together while at the same time maintaining their own individuality.
Baktin (1981) identified these opposing forces as centripetal and centrifugal—
one pulling the parties together while the other pushing them apart (Baxter,
1994). These opposing tendencies struggle for dominance, producing ongoing
change and realignment.

Viewed through the lens of paradox, Baktin's tension between independence and interdependence may be more paradoxical than contradictory. To
be contradictory, independence and interdependence would have to exist at
the same structural level of language. However, independence represents the
state of being independent and free from external controls while its opposite
is dependence or the state of being dependent or reliant on someone else.
Interdependence, on the other hand, represents the mutuality of two or more
independent people depending upon each other. Interdependence and independence are not so much opposites as they are contradictory elements that
exist at the same time but at different levels of abstraction. Our eyes receive
different inputs but somehow our sight moves to a higher level of abstraction
to produce an interdependent view of the world.

Sociologist Anthony Giddens' (1984) Structuration Theory reflects this
structural paradox. Giddens contended that an individual's interaction with
structure leads to an ongoing process that produces a nearly identical new structure. It may look the same as the original structure but an ever so slight change
occurs because, in the time between interactions, the human actor has changed.
Structuration is a dynamic process in which the medium of interacting with
our structures and the outcome of that interaction are the same. The dynamic
process of structuration allows for individuals to constantly create and recreate
their structures. The structural functionalist approach assumes that structure
dictates human behavior while interpretivists or social action theorists believe

that individuals define their structures. Giddens embraced both assumptions and argued that human agency is both constrained and enabled by structure. Structuration Theory accepts the notion that relationships appear stable and in motion at the same time. Although some scholars have criticized Giddens for giving too much credit to human agency, his theory recognizes the paradoxical nature of human interaction and embraces the idea that relationships are a product of an ongoing interaction between humans and their structures.

The introduction of Information Communication Technology (ICT), such as smart phones, tablets, and personal computers, has dramatically changed the nature of human and organization–public interactions (Stafford & Hillyer, 2012). ICTs have magnified the contradictions associated with relationships. They facilitate connections and disconnections and social interaction and social isolation. They increase control over information and decrease control over information. They enhance autonomy and infringe on autonomy. Organizational leaders and members can now cultivate and maintain relationships through a variety of social media.

In sum, relationships exist at a higher level of abstraction than the human interactions that produce them. They are a complex phenomenon arising from past, present, and expected future interactions and multiple other internal and external factors, including culture, context, language, communication, and intentionality. Researchers invoke "maintenance" as a metaphor to represent the process of sustaining relationships, but the actions and activities they maintain exist at a lower level of abstraction than the relationship itself. Thus, the maintenance metaphor breaks down because it does not represent relationships as much as it represents the foundational interactions that create and sustain them. The dialectical approach recognizes the paradoxical nature of relationships and suggests that a stable relationship is the product of ongoing interactions in which individuals constantly construct and reconstruct their relationship structures. With this recognition of the levels confusion associated with interpersonal relationships, I will now show how public relations scholars have stumbled into the semantic breaches associated with their research in understanding and managing public relationships.

Public relationships

Since the 1920s, when professional publicists reframed publicity as public relations, all types of organizations have sought to cultivate good relations with the public. In particular, the Great Depression required business and industry to adopt "a broader social responsibility" and subsequent economic struggles "increased our awareness of that responsibility" (Fitzgerald, 1946, p. 192). Businesses turned to public relations practitioners to help them rebuild public trust and respond to demands for more accountability and responsible business practices. In particular, the Depression increased the realization by business *"that mutually beneficial public relationships could be built only by coupling responsible performance with persuasive publicity"* (p. 117 [italics in original]). At the time, however, public relations scholars and practitioners did not invoke the concept of mutually beneficial relationships, but instead promoted the need for organizational members to do a better job of relating with other human beings (Harlow, 1942). Interpersonal relations, Harlow added, were analogous to interactions between organizations and publics.

In the 1960s and 1970s, public relations scholars began emphasizing public relationships and mutually beneficial relationships. In the third edition of the popular textbook *Effective Public Relations*, Cutlip and Center (1964) argued that sound public relations depended upon responsible performance that recognized institutional responsibilities to the public. Those responsibilities for "public relationships" rested on the shoulders of the "organization's directing executives" (p. 6) and not public relations specialists. To assume that role, the authors claimed, practitioners needed to be managers or a part of management. Public relations scholars embraced the idea of managing and building mutually beneficial relationships, but practitioners continued to prioritize measuring and influencing public opinion (Broom, 1977).

In the fifth edition of *Effective Public Relations*, Cutlip and Center (1978) tried to reconcile the disconnect between theory and practice by suggesting that practitioners manage relationships rather than manage the professional activities that created those relationships. They defined public relations as "*relationships* with those who constitute an organization's publics or constituents, the ways and means used to achieve favorable relationships, and the quality or status of the relationships" (p. 4). Six years later, in the sixth edition, Cutlip, Center, and Broom (1985) tied two concepts together, defining public relations as "the management function that identifies, establishes, and maintains mutually beneficial relationships between an organization and the various publics on whom its success and failure depends" (p. 4).

As managers, practitioners could shape organizational policy, not just communicate it (Fitzgerald, 1946). They no longer just managed publicity, communication, or even key publics, they planned, managed, and built relationships (Wilcox & Cameron, 2009). By "managing relationships with key publics" (Dozier & Broom, 1995, p. 85; Ledingham & Bruning, 2000, p. xiii), public relations embraced a strategic management function that could justify a seat at the management table and contribute to "strategic planning and other managerial processes" (Ledingham, 2003, p. 182). Never mind that professional practice continued to be dominated by media relations, communication, and influencing public opinion; public relations now claimed a more important role—building and managing mutually beneficial relationships with key publics. Practitioners were now tasked with managing a phenomenon over which they exerted only partial control. In addition, their responsibilities were now limited to only those publics upon which the organization depended. Every other public, including those that might not mutually benefit from the organizational relationship, appeared to be left out.

The shift from managing communication to managing relationships opened the door for publishing research that measured successful public relationships

(Broom, 1977). Among the first was a 1998 study by Ledingham and Bruning testing the willingness of phone company customers to seek an alternative provider. They tested Wood's (1995) four dimensions of relationships—investment, trust, commitment, and comfort with relational dialectics—and found that the higher customers ranked on those dimensions the less likely they were to entertain switching to a newer alternative. Based on the study, Ledingham and Bruning (1998) surmised that public relationships represented actions directly affecting both parties in the relationship. They defined organization-public relationships as "the state which exists between an organization and its key publics in which the actions of either entity impact the economic, social, political and/or cultural well-being of the other entity" (p. 62). Ironically, they only measured the public's perceptions of the state of the relationship and provided little or no insight into what organizational interactions led to increased investment, trust, commitment, or comfort with relations dialectics. Plus, they also limited "public" relationships to include only those publics affected by an organization.

The next year Hon and Grunig (1999) also published an instrument for measuring public relationships. Like Ledingham and Bruning, they turned to interpersonal communication research to identify their variables. Their relational properties were the same as those used by Canary and Stafford: control mutuality, trust, satisfaction, and commitment. Control mutuality was defined as the degree to which each party in a relationship has power to influence the other. Integrity, dependability, and competence contributed to trust. Satisfaction measured favorability toward each other, and commitment represented the level of energy each was willing to devote to the relationship. They also introduced two types of relationships: exchange and communal. Exchange relationships were reciprocal, quid-pro-quo interactions while communal relationships featured mutual concerns and benefits—though not always with the expectation of reciprocity. Although some degree of power imbalance is natural in relationships, Hon and Grunig warned that "unilateral attempts to achieve control by one party are associated with decreases in perceptions of communicator competence and satisfaction with the relationship" (p. 19).

Communal relationships were considered the ideal because they emphasized mutuality and community membership. However, Hon and Grunig (1999) did not explain how communal relationships could be mutual without always being reciprocal. They encountered the paradox of organization-public relationships. On one hand, they wanted to avoid the idea that all public relationships were simply reciprocal, quid-pro-quo self-interested exchanges. On the other hand, they had bought into the idea that public relations was a management function for building mutually beneficial relationships. To accept that all public relationships were exchange relationships meant that all parties were simply motivated by expectations of getting something in return of equal value to what they had contributed. It was a paradox, and their solution was to focus on the positive aspect of the paradox—being a part of community meant more than just what is in this relationship for me. Gallicano (2013) recognized the paradox and argued that to claim communal relationships might not always require reciprocity was unrealistic, particularly if applied to employees working for a paycheck. To solve the logical problems with communal relationships, she suggested the inclusion of more abstract returns, such as quality of life. In other words, Gallicano tried resolving the paradox by moving the relationship to a higher level of abstraction, one that, ironically, does not necessarily include mutuality.

Ledingham and Bruning (1998) avoided the paradox by creating another. They did not distinguish between relationship types, but instead incorporated Grunig's two-way symmetric communication model into the process of managing relationships. Two-way symmetric communication, they contended, envisioned "public relations as a process of continual and reciprocal exchange between the organization and its key publics" (p. 56). The incorporation of two-way symmetric communication means that practitioners are required to engage in dialog with abstract publics and then make sure those abstract groups are as equally pleased as the organization with the interaction and subsequent relationship. By cultivating these long-term relationships, public relations accrued value and proved the financial value of organization-public relationships (Ehling, 1992; Grunig, 1993; Ledingham & Bruning, 1998).

In 2000, Ledingham and Bruning promoted their conception of relationship management in an edited book by the same name. Relationship management served as a metaphor for public relations role as a management function that produced value for client organizations. Rooted in Systems Theory, the management role serves as indicator of power and influence in organizations (Lauzen, 1990; Lauzen & Dozier, 1992; Dozier & Broom, 1995). Systems Theory views human behavior as the product of interacting systems and not as the outcome of human interaction. In a social system, the individual plays a role (Boulding, 1956), such as manager, technician, or boundary spanner. Dozier and Broom (1995) linked organizational roles with other models of public relations practice, including issues management and two-way symmetric communication (Grunig & Grunig, 1989).

Dozier and Broom (1995) based their application of Systems Theory on the research of Katz and Kahn (1978), who described organizational roles as abstractions created to "help scholars make sense of organizational behavior, its antecedence, and its consequences" (p. 5). Later, Broom, Casey, and Ritchey (2000) drew from Systems Theory to define relationships as "patterns of interaction, transaction, exchange, and linkage between an organization and its publics" (p. 18). They applied Systems Theory because it had served the field well since first proposed by Cutlip (1952) in the popular textbook, *Effective Public Relations*. They claimed that interpersonal communication principles did not work in the organizational-public context (Bruning, Castle, & Shrepper, 2004). Thus, relationship management relied on an ecological systems approach in which public relations played a role in helping organizations adjust and adapt to their environment (Broom, 2009). Relationship management became the strategic role of moving the "current state of the relationship" to the "desired state of the relationship" (Dimmick et al., 2000, p. 132). The interjection of Systems Theory has given the impression that organizations can manage their public relationships in the same way they manage their relationships with other systems and the environment.

These systems or "set of interacting units" (Miller, 1978; quoted in Broom et al., 2000, p. 13) serve as abstract representations of anything from single cells to multi-national corporations. The relationships in and among these systems exist at an even higher level of abstraction than systems themselves. There are now multiple interactions involving individuals, units, organizations, and societies. By managing this web of intangible assets, as one scholar described relationships, relationship management creates wealth and promotes organizational success (Phillips, 2006). This emphasis on organization-public relationships also has a darker side; it can dehumanize relationships and categorize them as a part of a system that feels nothing but a desire to survive and thrive. However, studying relationships at a systems level does have merit because it acknowledges that "personal relationships do not operate independently of one another, but instead are influenced by social communication patterns and interactions taking place between relationship participants and important others in their lives" (Sarason, Sarason, & Pierce, 1995, p. 616). Relationship researchers tend to focus too much on individual perceptions of relationships rather than on the dyadic level of analysis, which explore the congruence of perceptions among the parties in a relationship.

Although public relations researchers seem most concerned with system-level relationships, they tend to focus on individual perceptions. Public relations theory would appear to dictate a more dyadic approach to relationship research because successful public relations outcomes depend on developing mutually beneficial, interdependent relationships. Thus, relationship management sets a high bar for practitioners, expecting them to create, develop, and maintain these relationships and guarantee that they are perceived by all parties as "mutually beneficial organization-public relationships" (Ledingham & Bruning, 1998; Bruning et al., 2004, p. 436). To be effective, practitioners must understand "strategic planning and other managerial processes" (Ledingham, 2003, p. 182). They also must make sure the other interacting individuals, units, or systems want to continue the relationship and consider it as valuable to them as it is to the organization. In other words, practitioners are expected to manage the perceptions and evaluations of their organization as well as the perceptions and evaluations of the other parties in these public relationships.

Relationship management researchers soon recognized the near impossibility of measuring these complex relationships in and among systems. They again turned to interpersonal communication research to find metaphors to describe organization-public interactions. Bruning et al. (2004) urged practitioners to develop strategies that personalized the organization, noting that organizations often "fail to attend to the relational aspects of organization-public relationships" (p. 443). Bruning et al. (2004) urged organizations and publics to "determine common interests and goals" (p. 443) and engage in dialog. In other words, public relations manages relationships in and among systems, but interprets and measures those relationships based on the perceptions of human actors.

Subsequent OPR and relationship management research continued to reflect this confusing mixture of systems and interpersonal communication theory. Huang and Zhang (2013) reviewed ten years of OPR research and found that researchers relied on two approaches. Some invoked interpersonal concepts to measure public relationships (Hon & Grunig, 1999; Huang, 2001) while others surveyed the public's attitudes toward the organization (Ledingham & Bruning, 1998; Ledingham & Bruning, 1999). In the former, relationships served as the dependent variable while in the latter research, it was the independent variable. Huang and Zhang (2013) noted that most of the research looked at OPR from the perspective of the public, not the organization. Later research, they added, focused on power imbalances, symmetrical research agendas, and organizational types (Waters & Bortree, 2012). Huang and Zhang (2013) claimed to consolidate the lessons learned from OPR research, but the only lesson apparent from the studies was that they had "situated the concept at a higher operational level" (p. 86). They did not explain why moving to a higher level of abstraction improved OPR research. Indeed, it reaffirms the fact that the study of public relationships has provided little direction on how to cultivate and improve public relationships. In other words, the studies had moved to a higher level of abstraction, meaning they were measuring perceptions about relationships and not the relationships themselves.

Broad abstract assumptions based on self-reports continue to plague OPR research. In a review of 156 OPR studies from 1998 to 2016, Cheng (2018) did not differentiate between OPR and relationship management research. She identified several flaws in the research, including "idealized propositions of mutual benefits" (p. 124), neglect of multi-party relationships, conflicting findings on trust, and too much reliance on self-reports. While research assumed mutual benefits, other research showed that organizations and publics focus on their own benefits. To resolve the problems in OPR research, she recommended combining Relationship Management Theory with Contingency Theory of Accommodation (Cancel, Mitrook, & Cameron, 1999; Pang, Jin, & Cameron, 2010). Cheng (2018) tried to resolve the relationship management paradox by defining relationships as "information flow between an organization and one or more publics who are in the status ranging from mutually beneficial to highly conflictual" (p. 127). She also called for both parties to manage their own relationships and, when possible, those of their key publics. Based on her definition of relationships, she essentially called for each party to manage communication. Thus, after nearly 30 years of OPR research, the solution to the paradox is to redefine relationships as communication and then manage that communication.

In general, OPR research has provided a lot of data *about* the public's perception of organizations but little guidance *about* the actions and activities that actually shape those perceptions. The second-order change promised by Ferguson (2018) has essentially led to a first-order restructuring of public opinion surveys to measure public perceptions of relational properties and dimensions. Public relations scholars now know a lot about how people feel about organizations but little about the communicative interactions that shape those perceptions. Moon and Rhee (2013) reaffirmed the importance of those communicative interactions when they discovered a correlation between positive and negative relationships and positive and negative communication. They provided no guidance, however, on the relational antecedents that proceeded these positive and negative evaluations. Instead, they measured the oppositional tendencies of dissatisfaction, distrust, control dominance, and dissolution and found that they relate to communication behavior. They claimed their study of negative OPR "laid a stepping stone for further development of relationship management theory" (p. 707). In reality, the study supported the contention that the secret to managing relationships lies in the process of relating, interacting, and engaging publics. The very act of trying to manage a phenomenon over which practitioners only have partial control reaffirms perceptions of dissatisfaction, distrust, and control dominance. In sum, public relationship research has sent the field down rabbit holes filled with imprecise language and logical fallacies.

Hung (2008) recognized the paradox and called for an increased emphasis on the strategic cultivation of relationships. Citing Baxter and Montgomery's (1996) dialectical approach of relationships as a preferred process of ongoing communication, she argued that perceptions *about* relationships are *not* the same thing as the class of activities that create and sustain relationships. Organizations have relationships regardless of whether they are planned or unplanned (Blewitt, 1993). Indeed, relationships are not so much intentionally created as something people and organizations *experience* as a part of interactive social units. These interactions will produce relational outcomes with or without the intervention of public relations. To expect practitioners to maintain or manage relational outcomes assumes that they can control and influence the attitudes and perceptions of organizational members and key publics. Relationship management wants all parties to want a relationship with an organization and to like and appreciate it as much as the organization does. No matter how much an organization desires its publics to want a relationship, it cannot—absent force and coercion—manage people's desire for a relationship. People and organizations want the freedom to create, develop, and maintain their own relationships.

Resolving the relationship paradox

Public relations scholars assume that they can manage and control public relationships in the same way they might manage their contacts or social media accounts. They also expect these relationships to be mutually beneficial, especially for those publics critical to the organization's success. This focus on mutual benefit, symmetry, dialog, and relationships is well intentioned but ethically problematic. Like the car salesman, public relations practitioners mimic relational activities that lull publics into thinking that they only have their best interests in mind and want nothing more than to develop a long-term, mutually beneficial relationship. Thus, they imply that the relationship is closer than it actually is, so as to win trust and acceptance. Such is the paradox of centering public relations scholarship around public relationships.

Like interpersonal relationships, public relationships are complex and paradoxical, but recent public relations research is determined to discover how to manage and control them. The goal of this and related scholarship in symmetrical communication and issue management is to imbue public relations with a higher purpose and earn a seat at the management table. Scholars claim public relations builds and manages mutually beneficial relationships, but their OPR and relationship management theories are based on flawed assumptions. No matter how much practitioners desire mutually beneficial relationships, they cannot control the other party's desires or evaluations without resorting to coercion and manipulation. Indeed, OPR and relationship management research are morally problematic. With few exceptions, they focus on public perceptions of relational dimensions, such as commitment, trust, and mutuality, and presume that they can and should manage and control those perceptions.

Public relations scholars' obsession with relationships breaches the levels of abstraction in language by promising to manage a phenomenon that carries so many meanings that it lacks connotative force (Josselson, 1992). Instead, public relations should place more emphasis on helping organizations better understand themselves in relation to their publics. Relatedness plays a central role in "the growth and development of the self" (p. 3.). As Levine (2011) noted, people struggle to relate to others, and that problem is magnified in an organized technological society. "These people, or those they are involved with, have difficulty sustaining good, cooperative, mutually gratifying relationships" (p. 622). They lack the tools necessary to relate to others and then seek counseling and group therapy to resolve those problems. Group therapy does not focus on the abstract relationships but on how to help people gain a great sense of self and improve their ability to effectively relate and connect with others. The organizational equivalent to group therapy would then be for organizations to engage public relations to help them refine their identities and more effectively relate and connect with others. Instead of invoking the legal metaphor to describe public relations counselors, it might be more effective to see practitioners as communicative health care professionals.

By understanding the different levels of abstraction, public relations can begin to match its professional capabilities with its relational activities of the same logical type. Past, present, and future interactions create, sustain, and even destroy relationships. At this lower level of abstraction, the participants' self-interests, unique personal history, culture, and physical environment influence the quality of the relationship. As noted, language, communication, and persuasion play critical roles in how people relate and interact. At this level, public relations can use its communication expertise to influence relational outcomes. Public relations can manage and control how an organization relates and interacts with people, groups, and other organizations (Stoker, 2014a). This is a level of identification that OPR and relationship management research has ignored. Instead, scholars have focused on outcomes outside their control, such as whether the other parties perceive the relationships as mutually beneficial. Although public perceptions are still important to evaluating the effectiveness of personal and organizational communication, they are less effective in telling us how to improve our daily interactions. At the concrete, identification level of interacting, practitioners have the most power over persuasion, communication, and language. It is at that level that public relations research can provide practitioners with practical and theoretical guidance on how to communicate better with other human beings and develop healthy relationships. As Kelleher (2007) noted, practitioners must relate with other human beings and what do organizations relate with if not human beings.

Relating is intentional and sometimes it is simply a natural outcome of living and working in the same space. One does not have to approach them with a willingness to change or change others to still produce positive relational outcomes. Organizations and individuals often move back and forth between states of self-interested action and cooperation. As they do so, they develop a greater sense of self and other-focused relationships (Levine, 2011). This aspect of self-discovery plays an important role in helping individuals and organizations more effectively identify their beliefs and values and relate to others, especially those with the same values and ideals. By focusing on public relationships, public relations has ignored this critical aspect of our personal and organizational character. Ironically, public relations provides the tools necessary to help organizations and organizational members refine their organizational identity and so enable more substantive relationships. Relating requires an understanding of publics as individual human beings who interact with other individuals and organizations for various reasons, including self-interest, socialization, and cooperation. By recognizing those mutual motivations, public relations can facilitate the relational activities that serve the interests of the individual as well as the organization. The purpose of public relations changes from cultivating and managing public relationships to cultivating and managing the organization's critical interactions.

More than ten years of OPR research has offered little evidence of progress in understanding the basic components of relating. Instead it has simply situated the research at a higher level of abstraction (Huang & Zhang, 2013) and failed to provide specific direction on improving organizational relationships. At this higher level of abstraction, relationships serve as a metaphor for the interpretations and evaluations of the interacting parties. By focusing research at this level of abstraction, researchers have relied too heavily on self-reports, typically gathered from an organization's key publics. Based on the public's evaluations of relational properties or dimensions, researchers determined the quality of the relationship. If publics report a lack of commitment or trust, researchers have recommended that the organization focus on increasing commitment and trust. However, they provide little or no guidance on what specific actions or behaviors the organization needs to take to improve in these areas. Because self-reports provide only a descriptive snapshot, they fail to uncover the root properties of relating and interacting. Self-reports also ignore the influence of organizational actors on public relationships. Finally, researchers assume that the relational dimensions of interpersonal relationships are the same as the relational properties of organization-public relationships. There is yet to be a study to confirm this assumption.

The focus on mutually beneficial relationships further complicates research and scholarship in public relations. Past, present, and future interactions exist at the identification level of abstraction. They are a different logical type than parties' description of the interactions as a relationship. Inferences about the relationship exist at the next higher level of abstraction. The determination that a relationship is mutually beneficial is an inference made by all participants. To agree that the relationship is mutually beneficial is a statement about the relationship. At this third level of abstraction, the expectation of mutuality essentially demands that all parties in the relationship evaluate the distribution of goods as equitable. Since participants engage in organization-public relationships to serve their own self-interests, the determination of mutuality depends on whether their individual needs are met and not whether the relationship serves the self-interests of the other parties involved. Ironically, the very demand that public relations build mutually beneficial relationships serves the self-interests of the profession. Mutual benefit implies that public relations serves more than the private interests of clients or organizations—when in reality even the expectation of mutual benefit serves the interests of the organization to sustain the relationship. The paradox becomes more acute when considering the fact that public relations has little or no power to manage or control whether the other party considers the relationship mutual or the other party's desire to continue the relationship.

As a theoretical basis for public relations, public relationships are merely a metaphor for the complex web of interactions occurring between an organization and its publics. Metaphors enable understanding and comprehension, but they also "change the way we think of a concept on an unconscious level" (Burkley, 2017, para. 11). The OPR and relationship management metaphors have emphasized broad abstractions at the expense of the essential components of interacting and relating. Morgan (2006) claimed that metaphors have profoundly affected research in a variety of fields, including organizations, science, and language. Metaphors influence the way we think and express ourselves. Indeed, Morgan contended that "all theory is metaphor" (p. 5). Although metaphors and theory provide new ways of seeing, they also distort what we see. By their very nature, metaphors emphasize similarities and ignore differences. They produce one-sided insight that highlights certain interpretations while forcing others into the background. Metaphors also are paradoxical. They "create powerful insights that also become distortions, as the way of seeing created through a metaphor becomes a way of *not* seeing" (p. 5). As higher-level abstractions, they overemphasize the road map and discourage the exploration of the terrain. For public relations research to move forward, it needs to rediscover the basics of relating and interacting, including language, communication, and persuasion.

By emphasizing relating, interacting, and engaging with individuals, public relations reframes target publics as human beings. They are no longer just abstract classifications of employees, stakeholders, publics, or target audiences. Those groupings may be important to strategic management and communication, but, as higher-level abstractions, they can cause practitioners to overlook the concrete interpersonal activities central to the formation and continuation of meaningful relationships. A paradox of digital and social media is that organizations gather a tremendous amount of data regarding key publics and then crunch that data to learn about individual preferences, interests, and needs. Organizations can now connect with individuals on social media sites, such as Facebook, LinkedIn, Instagram, and Twitter, and develop individual and organizational relationships. The success of companies in the digital age may depend on how well they relate virtually on an interpersonal level and not as an abstract organization or public.

Conclusion

McDonald's Corp. Chief Information Officer Daniel Henry wants to transform the way the hamburger chain relates to its individual customers. "It's getting away from dealing with the masses to how do we deal with you as an individual" (Henry, quoted in Maidenberg, 2019, p. R3). The paradox of OPR and relationship management is that their success depends on relating with their publics on an interpersonal level and allowing them to manage their own relationships with organizations.

By reframing public relations as enhancing and managing relating, public relations scholars can begin to explore the complex signals that communicate interest in creating a relationship (Bateson, 2000). To relate is to accept and promote the humanity and autonomy of the other (Stoker, 2014a). By focusing more on communicating values, including how much the organization values its publics as individuals, we accept the freedom of others to engage and interact on their terms. One manages what one controls, so to manage relationships is to dictate to the other parties the rules of engagement. To manage relating, however, calls for practitioners to manage activities at the level of abstraction over which they are morally responsible.

The reason one can manage relating rather than relationships is that relating starts near the beginning of the relationship and continues throughout the life of the relationship. As noted, the relating process is as much about self-discovery as it is about developing a relationship with others. Early in the relationship process, the parties can identify problems that disrupt our ability to relate with others. This can lead to mutual adjustment and change, not because of symmetry or reciprocity, but because our interactions expose flaws in our persuasion, language, and communication. We have the power to manage and change ourselves. Whether the other parties respond in kind remains with them. They choose to continue to relate in the same way or to make the changes necessary to better relate with us. We cannot control how the other party evaluates or describes the relationship, but we can control how we relate to the other party. Since relating is ongoing and occurs throughout the relationship process, it is the most important part of cultivating and sustaining quality relationships.

Interpersonal and public relationships remain important to public relations but, as higher-level abstractions, they act as a GPS system for achieving strategic goals. However, the actual work of public relations demands that we get behind the wheel and drive. Relating serves as the vehicle by which public relations moves forward by refocusing scholarship on the concrete activities that power meaningful relationships. Relating includes the basic elements of language, communication, and persuasion. It also encompasses personal history, culture, values, the physical environment, and other relationships. How we relate and interact reflects who we are as an organization and profession. For public relations scholarship to progress, it should take into account levels of abstraction and the paradoxes created by breaching those levels in theory and practice. It is time for public relations to return to the fundamentals of good communicative interaction to help organizations better relate with their publics, other organizations, the public sector, and society.

Works cited

Baktin, M. M. (1981). *The dialogic imagination: Four essays* (M. Holquist, Ed., & C. Emerson & M. Holquist, Trans.). Austin: University of Texas Press.

Bateson, G. (2000). *Steps to an ecology of mind.* Chicago: University of Chicago Press.

Baxter, L. A. (1994). A dialogic approach to relationship maintenance. In D. J. Canary & L. Stafford, *Communication and relational maintenance* (pp. 233–254). San Diego: Academic Press.

Baxter, L. A. & Montgomery, B. M. (1996). *Relating: Dialogues and dialectics.* New York: Guilford Press.

Blewett, S. (1993, August). "Who do people say that we are?" *Communication World,* pp. 13–16.

Boulding, K. (1956). General systems theory—the skeleton of science. *Management Science, 2* (3), 197–208.

Broom, G. M. (1977). Coorientational measurement of public issues. *Public Relations Review, 3,* 110–119.

Broom, G. M. (2009). *Cutlip & Center's Effective public relations* (10th Ed.). Upper Saddle River, NJ: Prentice Hall.

Broom, G. M., Casey, S., & Ritchey, J. (2000). Concept and theory of organization-public relationships. In J. A. Ledingham & S. D. Bruning (Eds.), *Public relations as relationship management: A relational approach to the study and practice of public relations* (pp. 3–22). Mahwah, NJ: Lawrence Erlbaum Associates.

Bruning, S. D., Castle, J. D., & Shrepper, E. (2004). Building relationships between organizations and publics: Examining the linkage between organization-public relationships, evaluations of satisfaction, and behavioral intent. *Communication Studies, 55* (3), 435–446, doi:10.1080/10510970409388630.

Burkley, M. (2017, Nov. 28). Why metaphors are important. *Psychology Today.* Retrieved 5/14/2019 from www.pyschologytoday.com.

Canary, D. J. & Stafford, L. (1994). Maintaining relationships through strategic and routine interaction. In D. J. Canary & L. Stafford, *Communication and relational maintenance* (pp. 3–22). San Diego: Academic Press.

Cancel, A. E., Mitrook, M. A., & Cameron, G. T. (1999). Testing the contingency theory of accommodation in public relations. *Public Relations Review, 25* (2), 171–197.

Cheng, Y. (2018). Looking back, moving forward: A review and reflection of the organization-public relationship (OPR) research. *Public Relations Review, 44,* 120–130.

Cutlip, S. (1952). *Effective public relations.* New York: Prentice Hall.

Cutlip, S. M. & Center, A. H. (1964). *Effective public relations* (3rd Ed.). Englewood Cliffs, NJ: Prentice-Hall.

Cutlip, S. M. & Center, A. H. (1978). *Effective public relations* (5th Ed.). Englewood Cliffs, NJ: Prentice-Hall.

Cutlip, S. M., Center, A. H., & Broom, G. M. (1985). *Effective public relations* (6th Ed.). Englewood Cliffs, NJ: Prentice-Hall.

Dimmick, S. L., Bell, T. E., Burgiss, S. G., & Ragsdale, C. (2000). Relationship management: A new professional model. In J. A. Ledingham & S. D. Bruning (Eds.), *Public relations as relationship management* (pp. 117–136). Mahwah, NJ: Lawrence Erlbaum.

Dozier, D. M. & Broom, G. M. (1995). Evolution of the manager role in public relations practice. *Journal of Public Relations Research, 7,* 3–26.

Duck, S. (1993). *Individuals in relationships.* Newbury Park, CA: Sage.

Duck, S. (1994). *Sage series on close relationships. Meaningful relationships: Talking, sense, and relating.* Newbury Park, CA: Sage Publications.

Duck, S. (1998). *Human relationships* (3rd Ed.). London: Sage Publications.

Ehling, W. P. (1992). Estimating the value of public relations and communication to an organization. In J. E. Grunig (Ed.), *Excellence in public relations and communication management* (pp. 617–638). Hillsdale, NJ: Lawrence Erlbaum Associates.

Elson, L. G. (2010). *Paradox lost.* Cresskill, N.J.: Hampton Press.

Ferguson, M. (2018). Building theory in public relations: Interorganizational relationships as a public relations paradigm. *Journal of Public Relations Research, 30,* (4), 164–1789.

Fitzgerald, S. E. (1946). Public relations: A profession in search of professionals. *Public Opinion Quarterly, 10* (2), 191–200.

Gallicano, T. D. (2013). Relationship management with the Millennial generation of public relations agency employees. *Public Relations Review, 39,* 222–225.

Giddens, A. (1984). *The constitution of society.* Berkley, CA: University of California Press.

Grunig, J. E. (1993). Public relations and international affairs: Effects, ethics, and responsibility. *Journal of International Affairs, 47,* 137–162.

Grunig, J. E. & Grunig, L. A. (1989). Toward a theory of public relations behavior in organizations: Review of a program of research. In J. E. Grunig & L. A. Grunig (Eds.) *Public relations research annual* (Vol. 1, pp. 27–66). Hillsdale, NJ: Lawrence Erlbaum Associates.

Grunig, J. E. & Hunt, T. (1984). *Managing public relations.* New York: Holt, Rinehardt & Winston.

Hardin, G. (1968). The tragedy of the commons. *Science, 162,* 1243–1248.

Harlow, R. F. (1942). Public relations and social action. *The Journal of Higher Education, 13,* 25–29.

Hinde, R. A. (1997). *Relationships: A dialectical perspective.* East Sussex, UK: Psychology Press Publishers.

Hon, L. C. & Grunig, J. E. (1999). *Guidelines for measuring relationships in public relations.* Gainesville, FL: Institute for Public Relations.

Huang, Y. & Zhang, Y. (2013). Revisiting organization-public relations research over the past decade: Theoretical concepts, measures, methodologies and challenges. *Public Relations Review, 39*, 85–87.

Huang, Y. (2001). OPRA. A cross-cultural, multiple-item scale for measuring organization-public relationships. *Journal of Public Relations Research, 13*, 61–90.

Hung, C. F. (2008). Toward the theory of relationship management in public relations: *How to cultivate quality relationships?* In E. L. Toth (Ed.), *The future of excellence in public relations and communications management* (pp. 443–476). New York: Routledge.

Josselson, R. (1992). *The space between us: Exploring the dimensions of human relationships.* San Francisco: Jossey Bass.

Katz, D. & Kahn, R. L. (1978). *The social psychology of organizations* (2nd Ed.). New York: Wiley.

Kelleher, T. (2007). *Public relations online: Lasting concepts for changing media.* Thousand Oaks, CA: Sage.

Korzybski, A. (1994). *Science and sanity: An introduction to non-Aristotelian systems of general semantics* (5th Ed.). New York: Institute of General Semantics.

Korzybski, A. (2000). *Science and sanity: An introduction to non-Aristotelian systems of general semantics.* Brooklyn, NY: International Non-Aristotelian Library Publishing Company.

Kuhn, T. S. (1996). *The structure of scientific revolutions* (3rd Ed.). Chicago: University of Chicago Press.

Lauzen, M. M. (1990, August). When marketing imperialism matters: An examination of marketing imperialism at the managerial level. Paper presented at the meeting of the Public Relations Division, Association of Education in Journalism and Mass Communication, Boston, MA.

Lauzen, M. M. & Dozier, D. M. (1992). The missing link: The public relations manager role as mediator of organizational environments and power consequences for the function. *Journal of Public Relations Research, 4*, 205–220.

Ledingham, J. A. (2003). Explicating relationship management as a general theory of public relations. *Journal of Public Relations Research, 15* (2), 181–198.

Ledingham, J. A. & Bruning, S. D. (1998). Relationship management in public relations: Dimensions of an organization-public relationship. *Public Relations Review, 24*, 55–65.

Ledingham, J. A. & Bruning, S. D. (1999). Managing media relations: extending the relational perspective of public relations. In J. Biberman & A. Alkhafaji (Eds.), *Business Research Yearbook* (pp. 644–648). Saline, MI: McNaughton & Gunn, Inc.

Ledingham, J. A. & Bruning, S. D. (2000). Introduction. In J. A. Ledingham & S. D. Bruning (Eds.), *Public relations as relationship management: A relational approach to the study and practice of public relations* (pp. xi-xvii). Mahwah, NJ: Lawrence Erlbaum Associates, Publishers.

Levine, R. (2011). Progressing while regressing in relationships. *International Journal of Group Psychotherapy, 61* (4), 621–643.

Maidenberg, M. (2019, May 14). McDonald's strategy to transform ordering. *The Wall Street Journal*, p. R3.

Miller, J. G. (1978). *Living systems.* New York: McGraw-Hill.

Moon, B. B. & Rhee, Y. (2013). Exploring negative dimensions of organization public relationships (NOPR) in public relations. *Journalism and Mass Communication Quarterly, 90*, (4), 691–714.

Morgan, G. (2006). *Images of organization.* Thousand Oaks, CA: Sage Publications.

Pang, A., Jin, Y., & Cameron, G. T. (2010). Contingency theory and conflict management: Directions for the practice of crisis communication from a decade of theory development, discovery, and dialogue. In W. T. Coombs & S. J. Holiday (Eds.), *Handbook of crisis communication* (pp. 527–549). Malden, MA: Blackwell Publishing.

Phillips, D. (2006). Towards relationship management: Public relations at the core of organisational development. *Journal of Communication Management, 10* (2), 211–226.

Sarason, I. G., Sarason, B. R., & Pierce, G. R. (1995). Social and personal relationships: Current issues, future directions. *Journal of Social and Personal Relationships, 12* (4), 613–619. http://doi.org/10.1177/0265407595124019.

Stafford, L. (2010). Measuring relationship maintenance behaviors: Critique and development of the revised relationship maintenance behavior scale. *Journal of Social and Personal Relationships, 28* (2), 278–303.

Stafford, L. & Hillyer, J. D. (2012). Information and communication technologies in personal relationships. *Review of Communication, 12* (4), 290–312.

Stoker, K. (2014a). Paradox in public relations: Why managing relating makes more sense than managing relationships. *Journal of Public Relations Research, 26* (4), 344–358.

Stoker, K. (2014b). Defining public in public relations: How the 1920s debate over public opinion influence early philosophies of public relations. In St. John, B., Lamme, M. O., & L'Etang, J. (Eds.), *Pathways to public relations: Histories of practice and profession* (pp. 340–351). London: Routledge.

Waters, R. D. & Bortree, D. S. (2012). Advancing relationship management theory: Mapping the continuum of relationship types. *Public Relations Review, 38,* 123–127.

Watzlawick, P., Weakland, J., & Fisch, R. (2011). *Change: Principles of problem formation and problem resolution.* New York: W.W. Norton.

Wilcox, D. L. & Cameron, G. T. (2009). *Public relations: Strategies and tactics* (9th Ed.). Boston: Pearson.

Wood, J. T. (1995). *Relational communication.* Belmont, CA: Wadsworth.

4   The symmetrical/dialog paradox

The more public relations has stressed the importance of public relationships and the management of relationships, the more the field has embraced the ideal of dialog as the most ethical form of communication. In 2006, I claimed that public relations scholars were infatuated with dialog, but now that infatuation has grown into an obsession, particularly among public relations scholars trained in rhetoric and communication studies. They have promoted dialog as the ethical ideal for public relations practice (Pearson, 1989a; Kent & Taylor, 2002; Anderson, Swenson, & Gilkerson, 2016), and dialog research has become "a touchstone for the public relations literature" (Sommerfeldt & Yang, 2018, p. 59). With a few exceptions, public relations practice, however, continues to rely on persuasion and asymmetric communication. Practitioners (and some scholars) tend to view dialog as two-way communication and employ it to achieve organizational (and publication) goals (Theunissen & Wan Noordin, 2012; Lane & Bartlett, 2016; Lane, 2018). Acknowledging this disconnect, public relations scholars lament that the field has made little progress since the 1970s (Podnar & Golob, 2009; Theunissen & Wan Noordin, 2012). But as the cartoon strip character Pogo said, "We have met the enemy and he is us" (Kelly, 1987).

Ironically, public relations scholars shoulder some of the blame for this lack of progress. They have promoted dialog and its predecessor, two-way symmetrical communication, and then wondered why professionals have not embraced their dialogic worldview. One-way statements advocating dialog or two-way symmetrical communication constitute semantical antinomies, meaning the statement is only true if it is untrue. In essence, they demand a form of behavior that leaves no room to engage in that very behavior demanded (Watzlawick, Bavelas, & Jackson, 1967). As a higher-level abstraction and form of metacommunication (Kent & Taylor, 2002), dialog theory describes object-level behavior as well as an evaluation about the ethics of dialog and the actual behavior. The result of this paradoxical injunction is a double bind.

To escape this dialogical double bind, public relations scholars need to step outside popular theoretical frameworks and simply recognize the paradoxes associated with dialog theory and two-way symmetrical communication. By acknowledging the concepts' oppositional and contradictory communicative expectations, scholars can begin to identify the discontinuities in levels of abstraction and the resulting logical fallacies. This type of metacommunication could spark a new wave of creativity and theory building and provide new insight into public relations communication. In our original critique of these concepts, Katie Tusinski and I questioned dialog's basic assumptions of reciprocity, balance, and mutuality. We contended that other types of communication might actually be more just and ethical than dialog. Indeed, by calling attention to these paradoxes, the hope was that we might discover new normative approaches to public relations theory and practice.

Public relations is not just about achieving understanding or finding agreement with people who share or desire to share an organization's values and interests; it is about recognition—recognizing our common humanity and individuality and reconciling our different backgrounds, experiences, and desires. This chapter expands on these ideas, by employing paradox theories to critique the field's emphasis on dialog. In particular, I focus on the pragmatic (language) paradoxes related to dialog and symmetry—those that translate into paradoxical injunctions. I argue that for public relations scholarship and practice to innovate and change, the field needs to grapple with its practical and logical paradoxes and escape from its overly narrow and abstract conception of ethical communication in public relations.

To accomplish this goal, I will first define pragmatic paradoxes and show how two of public relations' most influential communication models—Grunig and Hunt's (1984) two-way symmetric communication and Kent & Taylor's (2002) dialog theory—have placed practitioners in a double bind. I will then introduce several logical paradoxes identified in John Durham Peters' (1999) critique of dialog and discuss their implications for public relations scholarship and practice. Finally, I will reframe dialog in public relations as an act of mutual discovery and interpretation that accepts and recognizes differences, diversity, and individual self-interests while still making room for understanding, agreement, and mutuality.

Pragmatic paradoxes and double binds

All communication presents public relations with several pragmatic and logical paradoxes, but the paradoxical injunctions embedded in two-way symmetrical communication and dialog theories may be the most debilitating. Both models expect practitioners to control or not control their communicative relationships in such a way that they achieve prior agreement on communicative rules and procedures and achieve outcomes satisfying to all parties. They cannot simply resort to two-way communication but must be willing to change and engage those who also have forsaken control and have a willingness to change. The initial goal of dialog is to achieve mutual understanding but the ultimate objective is to achieve a metacommunication that consists of mutuality, propinquity, empathy, risk, and commitment. Two-way symmetry places more emphasis on the process of each party adjusting and adapting to reach mutual understanding and agreement. To comply with these lofty expectations, public relations practitioners must disobey the injunction to control the dialogic features of the communicative relationship to obey dialog's injunction to give up control and be willing to change—even their approach to dialog. It is not surprising that the expectations of dialog and symmetry place practitioners in a double bind.

Double bind theory emerged from the study of the pathological implications of dysfunctional communication within important relationships, such as that of parent/child, commanding officer/soldier, manager/employee, and professor/student. A paradoxical injunction occurs when a parent or superior demands obedience and disobedience at the same time. In other words, the subordinate in the relationship must disobey to obey. In significant relationships, it is difficult for the receiver to step outside the relationship to comment on the statement because that "would amount to insubordination" (Watzlawick et al., 1967). Kutz (2017) applied the concept of double bind to organizational relationships and argued that double bind communication patterns contribute to employee absenteeism, burnout, and depression. In organizations, the paradoxical injunctions may deliver positive information but be delivered in a negative tone or with hostile body language. Responding to the injunction is tricky because fulfilling one aspect of the instruction would make it impossible to fulfill the other part of the instruction. The context of the situation also limits comment or question. "Hinting the discrepancy between the messages or even just asking which one of the messages (e.g., the verbal or the non-verbal or which part of the paradox instruction) might be the valid one is strictly forbidden" (para. 20).

Double binds occur when a significant other punishes or criticizes a person for having accurately interpreted the incoming data from external and internal sources. In the spring 2019, Special Counsel Robert Mueller's report revealed that aides to President Donald Trump refused to execute his orders based on legal grounds or personal concerns (Graham, 2019). The aides could not step out of the frame and respond appropriately by fulfilling the command and likely endured criticism for interpreting the situation as untenable. In other words, to obey, they had to disobey. The same challenge faced a public relations executive of a major corporation in the Southeast. His CEO ordered him to mislead the press about an important issue affecting the company. The executive also knew that the CEO expected him to enhance and protect the reputation of the company. To obey the command to mislead would undermine his personal credibility and that of the corporation. Rather than comment on the incongruency of the CEO's request, he used creativity to explain that a smart reporter would see through the communication and create a crisis worse than the existing problem. By focusing on the damaging effects of the order, the executive skirted the double bind and obeyed by disobeying the CEO's request (Stoker, 2005).

Another type of double bind takes place when the significant other expects the person to express feelings contrary to those actually experienced. Elson (2010) gave the example of a mother who wanted her child to want to clean his room. The child complied with the task and still got into trouble because the mother interpreted the child's actions as compliance to her injunction rather than a sincere desire to clean the room. Teachers often fall into this same trap when requiring students to do an assignment and then criticizing them for not completing the assignment in the same way that the teacher would have done it if given the opportunity.

A final type of double bind occurs when the significant other demands and prohibits actions in the same injunction (Watzlawick, 1990; Elson, 2010). Public relations professionals are expected to have autonomy and act in the public interest. However, at the same time, they are dependent upon the professional standards and codes of ethics, not to mention their fiduciary obligations to a client. Furthermore, practitioners encounter a double bind when expected to manage media relations even though their code of professional ethics prohibits them from manipulating (corrupting) the channels of communication. In crisis communication, organizations want public relations to help ameliorate the crisis but at the same time avoiding legal retribution and liability.

To escape a double bind requires metacommunication (Elson, 2010). One must recognize the breach in the discontinuity between the levels of abstraction and then step out of the frame and recognize a different logical type (Abeles, 1975; Elson, 2010). This often can be accomplished through humor, irony, or even absurdity (Berger, 1978; Elson, 2010). Geico changed insurance advertising from a serious, necessary burden to something likable and fun. In an effort to match Geico's success and connect with younger consumers, other insurance companies also introduced humorous characters, such as Mayhem and Flo. The absurdity of the ads reflects metacommunication and exists at a higher level of abstraction than the basic message of the ads—sell insurance. "That's rule one," said David Fowler, the executive creative director at Ogilvy and Mather. "In Geico's case, most of the ad is crazy but at the end there's the message—15 minutes saves 15 percent" (quoted in Kaufman, 2017, para. 16). The humor serves as a quick exit from the paradoxical injunction. Geico wants consumers to want to inquire about its insurance, and employs metacommunication to change the frame from selling something dull to joining in the fun.

Although we experience double binds in all aspects of our lives, they are often not so repetitive and long-lasting as to become habitual experiences. The effects of double binds also differ, with some leading to pathologies and mental paralysis and others sparking creativity and learning. In public relations, the dialogic double bind has limited scholarly and practical study of other forms of communication and at the same time provided a framework for analyzing digital and social media interactions. Meanwhile, practical success in public relations continues to largely depend upon other forms of communication, including publicity, persuasion, brand journalism, and marketing. The topics covered in recent issues of *PRSA Strategies & Tactics* reflect the dominant themes in professional practice. The themes include social media advocacy, crafting crisis messages, storytelling, media relations, and improving customer relations, all of which have little relation to dialog, except possibly customer relations.

The field's scholarly obsession with dialog raises questions as to whether this communication mandate qualifies as a double bind or just a simple paradoxical injunction. Does a significant or intense relationship exist between public relations scholarship and the practice of public relations? Do practitioners and students feel some kind of subordinate obligation when instructed that two-way symmetrical communication and dialog are morally superior to other forms of communication? I contend that a significant relationship does exist between the academy, students, and practitioners. This relationship is reinforced through textbooks, scholarly literature, graduate curriculum, academic conferences, and professional workshops. Scholars serve as mentors to graduate students, and whichever research paradigm they advocate is mopped up in graduate research. These professors and graduate students then instruct undergraduate students as to the most acceptable methods of public relations practice and then expect them to repeat those ideas back through exams, research papers, and presentations.

The next question is whether the scholarly mandate for symmetry and dialog qualify as a paradoxical injunction. Watzlawick et al. (1967) identified two criteria: First, the structured message "asserts something…, asserts something about its own assertion and… those two assertions are mutually exclusive;" second, the message's recipient "is prevented from stepping outside the frame set by this message, either by metacommunication (commenting) about it or by withdrawing" (Watzlawick et al., 1967, p. 212). To determine whether two-way symmetrical communication and dialog meet these criteria, the next section will review the relevant literature on both concepts and their assertions regarding public relations research and practice.

Two-way symmetrical communication

Since first introduced as the most ethical and desirable of four models of public relations (Grunig & Hunt, 1984), two-way symmetrical communication has achieved wide acceptance among scholars and, to a lesser extent, practitioners across the world. In contrast to the first two models—press agentry/publicity and public information—symmetry promotes communication exchanges that lead to mutual understanding and ultimately collective change. The third model, asymmetric communication, applies social science theory and research to develop communication strategies aimed at persuading the public to align with organizational goals and interests. The four communication models describe both the range and evolution of public relations communication. Thus, the models reflect a developmental approach to history in which one-way dissemination, education, and strategic communication evolved into symmetry and dialog. Although the first three models were not inherently unethical, they did require that practitioners follow certain rules and procedures and make sure their actions did not harm people (Grunig & White, 1992; Grunig, 2001).

The symmetrical model, on the other hand, was inherently ethical because it included reciprocity, mutuality, and adaptation (Grunig & White, 1992; Grunig,

2001). It represented the most advanced form of practical and ethical public relations. It also provided a defense against public relations critics who classified all public relations as asymmetrical and unethical (Grunig & Grunig, 1992). Pearson (1989a) was credited for developing symmetry's ethical rationale and creating rules for its ethical application. By focusing on processes and not the outcome of communicative action, symmetry avoided the pitfalls of ethical relativism. It brought people together and served as a forum for dialog, discussion, and discourse (Grunig & Grunig, 1992). It also associated ethical public relations with dialog and viewed publics as partners in and not targets of communication (Pearson, 1989b). Grunig and White (1992) claimed that "excellent public relations is based on the worldview that public relations is symmetrical, idealistic in its social role and managerial" (p. 56). If all parties participated in making decisions and accepting consequences, "the outcome then must be ethical" (p. 57).

Huang (2004) equated symmetrical communication with ethical communication because it directed organizations to try to understand publics and reach mutually satisfactory results. If persuasion was used in symmetrical communication, the organization had to be as willing to be persuaded as it was to persuade (Phillips, 2019). In the ideal situation, both change and both benefit from the interaction (Laskin, 2009; Phillips, 2019). Shaw (2004) went a step further and claimed symmetry benefited publics at the expense of the organization while asymmetry allowed organizations to achieve their goals at the expense of the public (Shaw, 2004). There was little evidence, however, that public relations professionals fully embraced symmetry as normative or practical. They talked about symmetrical communication but struggled when faced with public expectations that conflicted with the organization's core values and culture.

The Excellence project tested the four models and found that one-way communication models dominated the profession. Little support was found for two-way symmetrical communication, but Grunig and Grunig (1992) continued to advocate it as "a major component of excellence in public relations and communication management" (p. 320; quoted in Laskin, 2009, p. 40). In 2002, Grunig accepted the impracticality of applying the injunctions of symmetrical communication in every situation. He accepted Murphy's (1991) recommendation of a mixed-motives model that recognized that both parties in a relationship can legitimately try to satisfy their own interests as well as mutual interests. Murphy's approach meant that "organizations do not completely relinquish their own interests" (Shaw, 2004, p. 392). As representatives of their organizations, practitioners were still expected to understand and benefit their publics and approach communication with a willingness to change from the inside as well as the outside.

However, subsequent researchers have criticized two-way symmetry as too utopian (Pieczka, 1997), unrealistic (Van der Meiden, 1993), and narrowly focused (Leitchy & Springston, 1993). Contingency theorists pointed to instances when organizations had strong philosophical and constitutional disagreements with activist publics and could not accommodate without undermining organizational standards and values (Cancel, Mitrook, & Cameron, 1999). In a study of South African practitioners, Holtzhausen, Petersen, and Tindall (2003) identified strong support for the mixed-motive model but found no evidence that practitioners adhered to principles of symmetry and asymmetry. They also discovered no theoretical support for the four historical models developed by Grunig and Hunt (1984). The study found that experienced practitioners employed an activist model that included the Western dialogic elements and aspects of asymmetry. Brown (2006) criticized symmetry as a-historical and designed to support an evolutionary, progressive approach to history.

Phillips (2019) contended that critics have overlooked Grunig and Hunt's (1984) emphasis on having the symmetrical intent to bring parties together and achieve mutual understandings. Citing Buber (1970), she stated that the true I-Thou or I-You mindset promotes engagement and interaction without any expected outcome. The desire to persuade is not problematic as long as it does not exclude the I-You relationship. In other words, the intent to persuade also must include a willingness to be persuaded. Phillips (2019) argued that Buber focuses on the mind rather than the actions and outcomes. However, this dialogic mindset only works if the other party shares that same mindset (Phillips, 2019). Symmetry asserts that practitioners must approach communication with a willingness to change but the assertion itself implies an unwillingness to accept any behavior except change. Thus, the practitioner is caught in the trap of being willing and unwilling at the same time.

Dialog theorists' criticism of two-way symmetrical communication, however, runs much deeper than questions about will and intent to engage in two-way communication (Kent & Taylor, 1998, 2002; Theunissen & Wan Noordin, 2012). The biggest problem with symmetry, they argue, stems from its roots in systems theory (Kent & Taylor, 1998, 2002; Stoker & Tusinski, 2006; Theunissen & Wan Noordin, 2012). As a product of systems theory, symmetry reflects adjusting and adapting to the environment so as to maintain the organization's steady state and assure its survival. Systems theory emphasizes roles, structures, and patterns of interaction, and interdependence. The system relies on the flow of information between the interrelated and interdependent parts of the system to maintain a steady state. Interactions with other systems and the environment depend upon their value to the system, and thus system practitioners engage only those individuals and groups based on their value to the success of the system (Stoker & Tusinski, 2006). This means that symmetrical communication would not be universally applied. The growth and survival of the system depends upon how well the critical parts of the system interact among themselves and with the environment. "Communication acts as a systems binder" (Almaney, 1974, p. 36). Thus, public relations practitioners serve as boundary spanners, mediating between internal and external audiences. Symmetry's foundation in systems theory limits the expectations of engagement, adaptation, and adjustment only to the degree that meets the needs of the system. Thus, another inherent aspect of symmetry is that change is strategic and conditional.

Taylor and Kent (2014) argued that rhetorical and dialog-based models were ethically and morally superior to the two-way symmetrical approaches of the 1980s and 1990s. Two-way symmetrical communication dealt with interactions between subsystems and systems and not between human actors. "Regrettably, the systems model as it has been applied in public relations thinking encourages a linear and mechanistic view of such a multifarious and dynamic communication process" (Theunissen & Wan Noordin, 2012, p. 12). By equating dialog with two-way communication, symmetry has done a disservice to a complex organizational communication (Theunissen & Wan Noordin, 2012). The incongruity of symmetry's demands eventually left scholars looking for an alternative. After dominating public relations research for 20 years, symmetry gave way to relationship building and dialog theory (Gower, 2006).

When we questioned the ethics of symmetry and dialog, we did not distinguish between the two forms of communication (Stoker & Tusinski, 2006). We viewed them as conceptually and theoretically similar. Pearson (1989b) also did not differentiate between the two concepts. Advocates of symmetry and dialog both claim Pearson (198) as the first to propose dialog as a standard for public relations ethics. Pearson (1989b) described dialog as a process and product of communication and explained that it "occurs when participants are able to move freely from one level of abstraction to another" (Habermas, 1984; Pearson, 1989b p. 125). At higher levels of abstraction, practitioners could raise questions about their communicative interactions and challenge validity claims against generally accepted norms. To some extent, Kent and Taylor (1998) did exactly that when they rejected symmetry as the normative paradigm for public relations and proposed dialog as something that occurs in relationships and is a product of relationships (Wirtz & Zimbres, 2018).

Dialog

Kent and Taylor (1998) based their theory of dialog on the work of Pearson (1989b) and Johannesen (1983) and philosopher Jurgen Habermas (1984). Pearson (1989b) defined ethical public relations as dialog and added that a commitment to dialog would result in publics being treated as partners and not targets of persuasion. Johannesen (1983) associated dialog with authenticity, mutual equality, and inclusion while Habermas (1984) identified dialog as the most ethical method for achieving mutual understanding (Wirtz & Zimbres, 2018). Kent and Taylor (1998) incorporated these ideas into their conception of dialog and proclaimed it as foundational to ethical relationships. Unlike other communication approaches, dialog was an end in and of itself and reflected agreement among parties for coordinating actions plans. Neither party dominates the relationship but come together as equals. Kent and Taylor defined dialog as "any negotiated exchange of ideas and opinions" as well as "communicative give and take" (p. 325).

The basic ground rules governing dialogic communication are "a willingness to try to reach mutually satisfying positions" (Kent & Taylor, 1998, p. 325) and an intersubjective philosophy of knowing and understanding the world. Intersubjectivity means "the interchange of thoughts and feelings, both conscious and unconscious, between to two persons or 'subjects,' as facilitated by empathy" (Cooper-White, 2014, para.1). Thus, the concern for others creates shared meanings that are not owned by one party or the other (Wirtz & Zimbres, 2018). This approach to dialog resonated with public relations scholars looking for an alternative to the two-way symmetrical communication. Dialog neatly tied into the field's growing interest and fascination in public relationships and interpersonal communication. In the 20 years since first published in 1998, Kent and Taylor's essay ranks "among the most cited and influential articles in public relations history" (Somerfeldt & Yang, 2018, p. 59).

Kent and Taylor (1998) argued that dialog served as a theoretical framework for understanding and studying communication on the World Wide Web. They provided criteria for evaluating an organization's Internet interactions and then, in 2002, they explained how public relations practitioners could incorporate dialog in building relationships. Those relationships included interpersonal and mediated relationships. They also enjoined practitioners to set up procedures for dialogic exchanges. Although reiterating that dialog was a product and not a process of communication, Kent and Taylor proposed several process-oriented strategies for developing interpersonal or mediated relationships. Interpersonal relationships, they wrote, emphasize listening, empathy, contextualizing issues, finding common ground, thinking long term, seeking out groups with opposing viewpoints, and soliciting internal and external positions on policy issues. These skills reflected concrete interactions as well as descriptions and evaluations of those interactions. In other words, they confused the levels of abstraction. Mediated dialogic relationships arose from technologies that promoted interactivity, including the telephone and the Internet, but there was little guidance on how these technologies could be used for something more than two-way communication. The procedural approach emphasizes creating mechanisms for facilitating dialog so as to promote trust, satisfaction, and sympathy. But establishing procedures and the evaluation of those procedures exist at different levels of abstraction. The act of creating rules for dialogic engagement could imply a lack of trust in either party's sincerity, satisfaction, and sympathy. In addition, the obligation for practitioners to create conditions and mechanisms for dialog would likely require persuasion, organizational support, and appeals to self-interests. In other words, the assertion to engage in openness and a willingness to change include an opposing assertion to not change any of the pre-ordained rules or engage in the processes required to achieve a dialogic outcome.

Further confusion of the levels of abstraction occurred when Kent and Taylor (2002) acknowledged that dialog could be immoral if one party resorted to self-interested action, such as "manipulation, disconfirmation, or exclusion" (p. 24). They warned that one party might exploit the trust and vulnerability of the relationship. However, if dialog requires an openness and willingness to change (at least everything except the agreed-to procedures), then one party approaching a relationship with a different mindset would, by definition, not be engaging in dialog. The offending party also would violate the principles and features of dialog, namely mutuality, propinquity, empathy, risk, and commitment. To impose principles to protect against manipulation while at the same time admitting that those principles could be used for manipulation constitutes a pragmatic and logical paradox. Manipulation occurs at a higher level of ordinality than ethical dialog. As such, at the higher level it is something other than dialog.

Kent and Taylor's (1998, 2002) narrow view of dialog has created confusion, even among public relations scholars trying to apply their theory to public relations (Wirtz & Zimbres, 2018). Theunissien and Wan Noordin (2012) identified studies on dialog and social media that equated it with two-way symmetrical communication or two-way communication (Bortree & Seltzer, 2009). They admitted that dialog is abstract in nature and difficult to operationalize in practice and thus more difficult for organizations to control and influence. Indeed, practitioners are caught in the paradox of being expected to engage in dialog as an ethical standard and goal and then violating that expectation if doing it for the purpose of advancing organizational interests and objectives. Intentional, goal-based practices enacted under the guise of dialog are not dialog (Paquette, Sommerfeldt, & Kent, 2015). This ignores the fact that the expectation for practitioners to engage in dialog is an intentional, goal-based communicative act. Furthermore, based on the need to agree on procedures for dialog, the features of dialog—mutuality, propinquity, empathy, risk, and commitment—are subject to negotiation and change.

Dialog's advocates recognize that the abstract nature of dialog makes it difficult to implement in professional practice (Paquette et al., 2015; Kent & Taylor, 2002). They even admit that dialog may be impractical because it expects practitioners and their organizations to relinquish control of communicative outcomes and relationships (Theunissen & Wan Noordin, 2012; Paquette et al., 2015). Indeed, normative dialog rarely exists in practice and all that can be hoped for is the potential for dialog (Paquette et al., 2015). In a case study, Paquette et al. (2015) found that participants engaged farmers as a means to persuade and resorted to dialog only when other strategies failed. They noted the inherent contradiction of using dialog to achieve predetermined goals. The farmers offer an example of disobeying the dialogic double bind in order to obey its paradoxical injunction.

Despite its admittedly abstract nature, dialog theory places impractical restrictions on what the parties can bring to the relationship. Kent and Taylor (1998, 2002) and their supporters rule out any possibility that dialogic communication can be strategic or self-interested. Ironically, Martin Buber, a contributor to their theory of dialog, advocated dialog while at the same time engaging in strategic communication (Toledano, 2018). Dialog and strategic communication can be abused, but they also can be ethical, transparent, and honest. Buber's real-life examples shows that the form of communication is not as important as how it is used. "Ethical practices are not about the communication approach but about the treatment of stakeholders and publics" (Toledano, 2018, p. 140).

Even public relations scholars struggle to accurately interpret the paradoxical injunctions of dialog. In a content analysis of public relations studies on dialog, Wirtz and Zimbres (2018) found that their colleagues studying dialog relied on content analyses of organizational websites, blogs, and social media. The majority of the studies recommended improvements in practice but offered no critique or support for dialog theory. They also conflated dialog with other features of web-based communication and failed to provide concrete examples of actual dialog. Most of those that included theoretical implications did not even link their findings to dialog theory. In addition, few researchers even broached the subjects of ethical communication and relationships. Wirtz and Zimbres concluded that dialogic theory needs to "provide a more comprehensive and convincing account of the ways that power and access to resources influence organization-public relationships than has been articulated thus far" (p. 28). In concluding their insightful critique of dialog theory, Wirtz and Zimbres astonishingly overlooked dialog's flaws and expressed a belief that the theory could be salvaged. They urged scholars to fully embrace dialog as a starting point and make web-based organizational communication the focus and motivating force behind research.

No better evidence of dialog's paradoxical injunction exists than the conclusion by Wirtz and Zimbres (2018) that despite dialog's logical fallacies, public relations practitioners should fully embrace it. They are part of a group of dialog apologists who claim the problem is in how dialog is studied, interpreted, or applied (Sommerfeldt, Kent, & Taylor, 2012; Sommerfeldt & Yang, 2018). Other studies raise questions about components of dialogic theory but continue to advocate its application (Dhanesh, 2017). Others critique dialog as impractical and improbable (Pieczka, 2011; Ihlen & Levenshus, 2017). Two qualitative studies of public relations practitioners found that those interviewed generally viewed dialog as two-way communication (Lane & Bartlett, 2016; Lane, 2018). Although elements of dialog appeared in the practitioners' communication, most of them did not understand what dialog was (Lane & Bartlett, 2016). They participated in dialog because it benefited their organizations (Lane, 2018). Instead of engaging with a willingness to change, some organizations had pre-established non-negotiables. Propinquity had little relevance. Practitioners also showed little empathy, seeing stakeholders as obstacles to overcome rather than as collaborators or partners. Practitioners feared hostile interactions, disclosure of sensitive information, and excessive demands. Rather than being genuine and authentic, practitioners adopted "an organizational persona" (Lane, 2018, p. 663). Lane concluded that dialog "in its purest form is a highly demanding and rarefied form of communication—and one that might not lead to achievement of predetermined agendas" (p. 664). Indeed, in her study of government-mandated dialog, Lane found that pre-existing and sometimes hostile and negative relationships among participants turned two-way communication into a battle for control, with no hope for dialog.

In general, public relations scholars have used their significant relationship with colleagues, students, and practitioners to assert that ethical public relations creates and maintains relationships based on mutuality, reciprocity, and a willingness of both parties to engage and change. These theories also assert that each party approaches this assertion without preconceived intentions or expectations despite implicit and explicit commitments to advance the interests of their respective organizations, including management, employees, stockholders, donors, and community members. Proponents of dialogic communication may argue that dialog advances the interests of an organization, but then this idea conflicts with the idea that practitioners enter into dialog without concern for self-interests and organizational advantage. To commit fully to dialog requires practitioners to be open to modifying and changing organizational interests in response to the interests of key publics. Their moral obligation to represent their organization can collide with their moral obligation to dialog and mutually beneficial relationships. Thus, the mandate for dialog places practitioners in a double bind, expecting them to override their internal and external personal and organizational commitments. They may approach others as human beings with openness and a willingness to change, but they are paid representatives of organizations and have a responsibility to promote organizational interests. All their communicative activities are intentional. To meet Kent and Taylor's (2002) expectation that they be public centered also conflicts with these personal and professional obligations to represent their client.

By acknowledging the oppositional aspects of the double bind, I have stepped outside the frame and engaged in metacommunication. The next step is to further identify the dialogic paradoxes and propose strategies for liberating scholars and practitioners from these additional binds. The secret to resolving paradoxes starts with acknowledging their existence and then looking for answers in the most illogical or negative alternative. In the case of dialog, that would mean exploring the merits of its opposite—dissemination. In his critique of dialog as a normative standard for communication, communication scholar and historian John Durham Peters (1999) argued that dissemination respects the receiver's right to engage or disengage.

Communication as a bridge and abyss

Peters (1999) identified a dualism of communication arising from new technologies and "a long tradition of speculating about immaterial mental contact" (p. 5). The technologies described by Peters were the telegraph and radio, but they also apply to the Internet and social media. When communication travels at great speeds from distant voices, it gives the impression that it flows from angelic or telepathic messengers who bypass our senses and speak directly to our minds and souls. Thus, parents' concerns that video games are destroying their children's brains reflect this kind of thinking. In short, Peters identified several definitions of communication, including connections or linkages, transmission, mutual exchange, and symbolic interaction. He defined communication as simply "the project of reconciling self and other. The mistake is to think that communication will solve the problems of communication, that better wiring will eliminate ghosts" (p. 9). Social media may help a person keep up with friends and even exchange messages, but it is just as much a forum for miscommunication as it is for connection.

The problem with public relations communication models, such as dialog and symmetry, is that they imply that communication can only occur if there is some kind of melding of the minds, mutual understanding, agreement, or at least favorable conditions to meet these goals. Indeed, a popular public relations textbook clearly teaches the idea that any form of communication other than dialogic is not communication.

> The myth of communication suggests that sending a message is the same as communicating a message. In essence, dissemination is confused with communication. This confusion is apparent in public relations when practitioners offer media placements (clippings, "mentions," cable placements, broadcast logs, etc.) as evidence that communication has occurred.
>
> (Broom, 2009, p. 188)

This narrow definition of communication confuses levels of abstraction. To transmit a message occurs at a lower level than a social interaction in which the parties talk *about* their communication. Broom (2009) relied on Wilbur Schram's model that defined communication as "a reciprocal process exchanging signals to inform, persuade, or instruct, based on shared meanings and conditioned by communicator's relationship and the social context" (p. 189). Based on that interpretation of communication, it is easy to understand the field's embrace of dialog and symmetry as the most ethical forms of communication. The paradox of placing such high expectations on communication, or, as Peters ([1999]) described it, the dream of communication, arises from the fact that "it inhibits the hard work of connection" (p. 30). In other words, by expecting every interaction to produce a connection or relationship, the act of connecting and relating with another human being becomes even more difficult. For Peters, "the most wonderful thing about our contact with each other is its free dissemination, not its anguished communion. The ultimate futility of our attempts to 'communicate' is not lamentable; it is a handsome condition" (p. 31).

Peters (1999) noted that dialog had achieved a "holy status" because it encompasses liberalism and participatory democracy (p. 33). In particular, Peters noted, dialog's focus on reciprocity makes it superior to media and other one-way communication methods. In public relations, scholars cite Pearson's (1989a) claim that a person's moral development corresponds with his or her application of dialogic concepts of reciprocity and symmetry (Grunig & White, 1992). However, as spelled out in Stoker and Tusinski (2006), public relations scholars have overlooked or ignored the paradoxical aspects of these concepts, as well as other features of dialog. Based on Peters (1999), the following six logical paradoxes call into question dialog's moral supremacy (Stoker & Tusinski, 2006):

1. Face-to-face human interaction is superior to technology (for example, writing in Socrates' day) because dialog allows for the melding of minds and desires and promotes a mutual love and friendship. Socrates restricted this love, however, to those deserving individuals willing to reciprocate through dialog. Thus, the openness of dialogic communication is selective and limited to those most likely to reciprocate and provide value to the relationship. Today's public relations scholars echo Socrates' concerns about writing and technology when they critique the use of media and other one-way communication strategies as the promiscuous production of uncontrolled messages that elicit multiple, unintended (and unmeasured) meanings and interpretations.

2. Reciprocity promotes mutual discovery, understanding, and agreement, but it also demands a response, and even more important, an equivalent response. The expectation of balance and reciprocity burdens relationships with the expectation of mutual and equal exchanges. While these mutual and equal exchanges play a critical role in healthy relationships, they also can turn the relationship into a cycle of quid pro quo transactions.

3. The success of dialog or symmetry depends upon creating conditions in which both parties exhibit openness and a willingness to change (Theunissen & Wan Noordin, 2012). Thus, the less likely those conditions can be met, the more likely the interactions and ultimately the relationship will fail. Dialog theory and symmetry also mandate predetermined agreements on the procedures and conditions for dialog. This raises the possibility that organizations engage only with parties presenting the greatest potential for reciprocity and mutual change. The beautiful other, the willing pupil, gains priority over the more diverse and independent student. Instead of encouraging inclusion and diversity, dialog could promote exclusion and selectivity. The potential for failure actually increases with expectations of mutuality, propinquity, empathy, risk, and commitment. Instead of promoting public relationships, dialog can encourage "closed communication circuits" (Peters, 1999, p. 46; quoted in Stoker & Tusinski, 2006, p. 161).

4. Dissemination and other one-way techniques can be more just than dialog because they recognize the rights of the receiver to accept, interpret, and react to messages according to their own will and pleasure. One-way and asymmetric communication make no distinctions between receivers; anyone can receive or reject the message. It treats all receivers the same and promotes universal access to information. In some cases, dissemination displays more respect and trust for receivers because it acknowledges their ability to receive and interpret messages as they see fit. Chasms between sender and receiver reveal opportunities for building bridges. The gaps or differences "are sometimes vistas to be appreciated or distances to be respected" (Peters, 1999, p. 59; Quoted in Stoker & Tusinski, 2006, p. 162).

5. Advocates of dialog consider dialog theory superior to two-way symmetrical communication because dialog focuses on the products of interactions between people and not objects. With roots in systems theory, symmetry is simply another function of the system and its interrelationships with other systems. Those relationships between systems take precedence over the human actors and their relationship with other humans. Intersubjectivity, however, is not without its problems. It also minimizes the role of the individual and what each individual brings to the interaction. Instead, it prioritizes the social, the common, and the shared. Thus, the unique, distinct, and diverse, especially those developed through social interactions outside the mainstream, threaten the goals of understanding and agreement. By definition, organizational brands refer to a set of unique characteristics and history. Thus, dialog's advocacy of a stronger version of intersubjectivity minimizes individual subjectivity and the possibility of a "presocial core or dimension" (Cooke, 2003, p. 284).

6. Dissemination may promote clearer, more accurate communication because it does not make feedback and response mandatory. Members of the public actually have more freedom to decide whether, how, or when they respond. To be effective, disseminated communication has to engage individuals on their terms, and therefore has to be more relevant to potential receivers. Twitter interactions may be dialog in name only, but they also represent dissemination aimed at eliciting response and discussion. Indeed, organizations may use one-way communication on social media, but their use of the social media creates opportunities for two-way communication. The responsibility for responding, however, rests with the receiver, enabling them to choose for themselves the nature of their communicative engagement.

By identifying these oppositional elements, the goal is not to dismiss dialog but to help public relations scholars and practitioners gain more insight on how to resolve them. We can begin to transcend the "bind by becoming aware of it" (Elson, 2010, p. 87). Awareness of dialog's oppositional tendencies provides insight and can stimulate creativity, leading to second-order change and innovation. Dialog's appeal to public relations reflects the field's self-interested desires for public acceptance and recognition. It also reflects scholars' academic training in rhetoric and interpersonal communication. In a profession plagued by criticism for positivity, persuasion, and propaganda, dialog offers a cure. Mutuality, understanding, and agreement represent universal goals and aspirations. As public relations scholars claim, dialog exhibits deontological values, such as treating people as ends (although its intersubjectivity questions the existence of Kantian absolutes). A closer examination of the concept, however, exposes its paradoxical nature. Peters' (1999) historical analysis showed that dialog is not always the balanced and fair approach that its advocates claim it to be. As Peters (1999) concluded, "dialogue can be tyrannical and dissemination can be just..." (p. 34).

In Stoker and Tusinski (2006), we proposed stepping out of the paradoxes by recognizing and reconciling differences. Recognition is a uniquely human trait that allows us to acknowledge others and how they differ from us and yet are similar to us. Recognition also enables us to appreciate the literal and the abstract. Incorporating the philosophy of Hegel, Peters (1999) defined communication as more than the sharing of information but as recognition and the process of collective discovery.

> One gains knowledge of the world as one comes to understand how particulars make up the whole. In other words, the building of communities and relationships is a product of reconciling the mutual recognition of others' differences, not only in what they say but how they say it.... Recognition involves interpretation. Communication becomes the process of interpreting one's world and then reconciling the subjective recognitions with objective meanings [vice] versa. Thus, meanings are both private and public phenomena.
>
> (Stoker & Tusinski, 2006, p. 169)

The recognition of the unique other promotes an appreciation of disparate interests and goals. Communication breakdowns and misunderstandings become opportunities for learning and revising. Instead of facing the paradox of suppressing differences for agreement, public relations practitioners acknowledge differences and then work to reconcile them.

> Thus, the goal of public relations [communication] changes from finding agreement to discovering differences. As differences become transparent, even those differences between who we think we are and who others perceive us to be, they can be reconciled in a way that places a high value on our common humanity. Using this framework, we engage people or publics in communication, not in an effort to change them or even to change us, but because as human beings, we value our relationships with other human beings. The outcome of this type of relationship is a different kind of change, one not of adaptation or adjustment in response to outside pressures, but constitutional change in who we are and how we perceive ourselves—which then leads to changes in the way we interact and communicate. Our external publics are empowered to change themselves based on internal values and loyalties rather than outside coercion or obligatory reciprocity.
>
> (Stoker & Tusinski, 2006, p. 171)

Reconciliation also allows practitioners to step out of the narrow frame of dialog theory and begin to mend breaches in the levels of abstraction. It also means moving our thoughts, ideas, and intentions closer together through identifying, acknowledging, and validating differences in ourselves and others. As noted, dialog exists at a high level of abstraction. It is communication about communication in relationships. It is considered more ethical than other forms of communication because it focuses on mutuality, propinquity, trust, risk, and commitment. However, when applied to public relations, it moves up and down between levels to include classes of actions that establish procedures and build interpersonal and mediated dialogic relationships. Furthermore, it dismisses motivations for establishing relationships, including self-interests, persuasion, and communicative action (the need to understand). Dialog theory also ignores the personal, organizational, and professional pressures and expectations associated with representing private and partisan interests. Most important, dialog theory demonizes the concept of control. Dialog is about giving up control and not knowing the outcome of communicative activities (Theunissen & Wan Noordin, 2012). However, the mandate for dialog is in and of itself a demand for control, controlling the type of communication acceptable for ethical public relations practice.

If there is no control, there is no personal or professional responsibility. Indeed, practitioners surrender their personal, professional, and social obligations to the will of the dyad. They may gain trust with their partners in dialog while losing the trust of the people whose interests they have hired to advance and represent. Control is not at the opposite end of a continuum from collaboration (Sloan, 2009). On the contrary, control enables organizations to collaborate and relate with publics. Uncontrolled communication empowers practitioners to be more transparent and engage others with more sincerity and authenticity. Instead of establishing ground rules and procedures for dialog, practitioners negotiate ground rules through the give and take of various forms of communication. They reconcile differences rather than trying to eliminate them. They value others for their uniqueness, not for their ability to reciprocate.

To recognize the others for their distinctiveness and individuality is to appreciate them for their common humanity and not just for their beauty and compatibility. Reconciliation is often associated with bringing together warring parties to enable closure and understanding, but it also applies to all parties who differ in their thinking. Reconciliation is ongoing in all relationships; it's not just a concept that applies to parties coming from two extremes. The closer we come to appreciating and valuing difference, the more likely we can actually enter into dialog. Dialog remains an abstract ideal, but reconciliation offers a more pragmatic frame because it carries no mandates to discard self or group interests. Public relations professionals can take responsibility over how they communicate and their intentions behind that communication. They accept that dialog is a valued ideal but not always practical or even ethical. Instead, they take responsibility to find ways to draw closer to others without demanding that others reciprocate. This approach places more responsibility on practitioners and their organizations to hold themselves accountable for miscommunication and misunderstandings. In these instances, the melding of the minds is not as important as the mindset of the communicators and their commitment to be accountable for their decisions and actions.

Works cited

Abeles, G. (1975). The double bind: Paradox in relationships. Unpublished doctoral dissertation, Boston University: Boston.

Almaney, A. (1974). Communication and the systems theory of organization. *Journal of Business Communication*. Retrieved from http://journals.sagepub.com/doi/pdf/10.1177/002194367401200106.

Anderson, B. D., Swenson, R., & Gilkerson, N. D. (2016). Understanding dialogue and engagement through communication experts' use of interactive writing to build relationships. *International Journal of Communication*, *10*, 4095–4118.

Berger, M. M. (1978). *Beyond the double bind*. New York: Brunner/Mazel.

Bortree, D. S. & Seltzer, T. (2009). Dialogic strategies and outcomes: An analysis of environmental advocacy groups' Facebook profiles. *Public Relations Review*, *35*, 317–319.

Broom, G. M. (2009). *Cutlip & Center's Effective public relations* (10th Ed.). Upper Saddle River, NJ: Prentice Hall.

Brown, R. E. (2006). Myth of symmetry: Public relations as cultural styles. *Public Relations Review*, *32*, 206–212.

Buber, M. (1970). *I and thou*. (W. Kaufman, Trans.). New York: Charles Scribner's Sons.

Cancel, A. E., Mitrook, M. A., & Cameron, G. T. (1999). Testing the contingency theory of accommodation in public relations. *Public Relations Review*, *25*, 171–197.

Cook, M. (2003). The weaknesses of strong intersubjectivism: Habermas's conception of justice. *European Journal of Political Theory*, *2* (3), 281–305. Retrieved August 1, 2019 from www.journals.sagepub.com.

Cooper-White, P. (2014). Intersubjectivity. *Encyclopedia of Psychology and Religion*. New York: Springer Reference.

Dhanesh, G. S. (2017). Putting engagement in its Proper place: State of the field, definition and model of engagement in public relations. *Public Relations Review*, *43*, 925–933.

Elson, L. G. (2010). *Paradox lost*. Cresskill, NJ: Hampton Press

Gower, K. K. (2006). Public relations research at the crossroads. *Journal of Public Relations Research*, *18* (2), 177–190.

Graham, D. A. (2019, April 19). No one listens to the President. *The Atlantic*. Retrieved July 19, 2019 from www.theatlantic.com.

Grunig, J. E. (2001). Two-way symmetrical public relations. In R. L. Heath (Ed.), *Handbook of public relations* (pp. 11–30). Thousands Oaks, CA: Sage

Grunig, J. E. & Grunig, L. (1992). Models of public relations and communication. In J. E. Grunig (Ed.), *Excellence in public relations and communication management* (pp. 285–325). Hillsdale, NJ: Lawrence Erlbaum.

Grunig, J. E. & Hunt, T. (1984). *Managing public relations*. New York: Holt, Rinehart and Winston.

Grunig, J. E. & White, J. (1992). The effect of worldviews on public relations theory and practice. In J. E. Grunig (Ed.), *Excellence in public relations and communication management* (pp. 31–64). Hillsdale, NJ: Lawrence Erlbaum.

Habermas, J. (1984). *The theory of communicative action Vol. 1: Reason and the rationalization of society*. Boston: Beacon Press.

Holtzhausen, D. R., Petersen, B. K., & Tindall, N. T. J. (2003). Exploding the myth of the symmetrical/asymmetrical dichotomy: Public relations models in the new South Africa. *Journal of Public Relations Research*, *15* (4), 305–341.

Huang, Y. H. (2004). Is symmetrical communication ethical and effective? *Journal of Business Ethics, 53* (4), 333–352.

Ihlen, O. & Levenshus, A. (2017). Panacea, placebo, or prudence: Perspectives and constraints for corporate dialogue. *Public Relations Inquiry, 6,* 219–232. doi:10.1177/2046147X17708815.

Johannesen, R. L. (1983). *Ethics in human communication* (2nd Ed.). Prospect Heights, IL: Waveland Press.

Kaufman, J. (2017, September 17). It began with a Geico. Mayhem (and Flo and Peyton) ensued. *The New York Times.* Retrieved July 21, 2019 from www.nytimes.com.

Kelly, W. (1987). *Pogo: We have met the enemy and his is us.* New York: Simon & Schuster.

Kent, M. & Taylor, M. (1998). Building dialogic relationships through the World Wide Web. *Public Relations Review, 24* (3), 321–334.

Kent, M. L. & Taylor, M. (2002). Toward a dialogic theory of public relations. *Public Relations Review, 28,* 21–37.

Kutz, A. (2017). How to avoid destroying your employees and organisations due to burnouts, braindrain and fading performance? Stop double-bind communication in your organization! *Journal of Organization Design, 6* (5). Retrieved July 19, 2019 from www.jorgdesign.springeropen.com.

Lane, A. B. (2018). If it's so good, why not make them do it? Why true dialogue cannot be mandated. *Public Relations Review, 44,* 656–666.

Lane, A. B. & Bartlett, J. (2016). Why dialogic principles don't make it in practices—and what we can do about it. *International Journal of Communication, 10,* 4074–4094.

Laskin, A. (2009). The evolution of models of public relations: An outsider's perspective. *Journal of Communication Management, 13,* 37–54.

Leitchy, G. & Springston, J. (1993). Reconsidering public relations models. *Public Relations Review, 19,* 327–339.

Murphy, P. (1991). The limits of symmetry: A game theory approach to symmetric and asymmetric public relations. In L. A. Grunig & J. E. Grunig (Eds.), *Public relations research annual* (Vol. 3, pp. 115–132). Hillsdale, NJ. Lawrence Erlbaum Associates.

Paquette, M., Sommerfeldt, E. J., & Kent, M. L. (2015). Do the ends justify the means? Dialogue, development communication and deontological ethics. *Public Relations Review, 41,* 30–39.

Pearson, R. A. (1989a) A theory of public relations ethics (Doctoral dissertation). Available from ProQuest Dissertations and Theses database. (UMI No. 9011334).

Pearson, R. A. (1989b). Business ethics as communication ethics: Public relations practice and the idea of dialogue. In C. Botan and V. Hazelton (Eds.), *Public relations theory* (pp. 111–134). Hillsdale, NJ: Lawrence Erlbaum.

Peters, J. D. (1999). *Speaking into the air: A history of the idea of communication.* Chicago: University of Chicago Press.

Phillips, A. (2019). Reframing symmetry: Returning to its roots for a new paradigm. Unpublished paper.

Pieczka, M. (1997). Understanding in public relations. *Australian Journal of Communication, 24* (2), 65–79.

Pieczka, M. (2011). Public relations as dialogic expertise? *Journal of Communication Management, 15* (2), 108–124.

Podnar, K. & Golob, U. (2009). Reconstruction of public relations history through publications in Public Opinion Quarterly. *Journal of Communication Management, 13,* 55–76.

Shaw, B. L. (2004). Noether's Theorem: The science of symmetry and the law of conservation. *Journal of Public Relations Research, 16* (4), 391–416.

Sloan, P. (2009). Redefining stakeholder engagement: From control to collaboration. *Journal of Corporate Citizenship, 36,* 25–40.

Sommerfeldt, E. J. & Yang, A. (2018). Notes on a dialogue: Twenty years of digital dialogic communication research in public relations. *Journal of Public Relations Research, 30* (3), 59–64.

Stoker, K. (2005). Loyalty in public relations: When does it cross the line between virtue and vice? *Journal of Mass Media Ethics, 20* (4), 269–287.

Stoker, K. L. & Tusinski, K. A. (2006). Reconsidering public relations' infatuation with dialogue: Why engagement and reconciliation can be more ethical than symmetry and reciprocity. *Journal of Mass Media Ethics, 21* (2&3), 156–176.

Taylor, M. & Kent, M. L. (2014). Dialogic engagement: Clarifying foundational concepts. *Journal of Public Relations Research, 26,* 384–398. http://doi.org/10.1080/1062726X.2014.956106.

Theunissen, P. & Wan Noordin, W. N. (2012). Revisiting the concept "dialogue" in public relations. *Public Relations Review, 38,* 5–13.

Toledano, M. (2018). Dialogue, strategic communication, and ethical public relations: Lessons from Martin Buber's political activism. *Public Relations Review, 44,* 131–141.

Van der Meiden, A. (1993). Public relations and "other" modalities of professional communication: Asymmetric presuppositions for a new theoretical discussion. *International Public Relations Review, 16* (3), 8–11.

Watzlawick, P. (1990). *Munchhausen's pigtail.* New York: Norton & Company.

Watzlawick, P., Bavelas, J. B., & Jackson, D. D. (1967). *Pragmatics of human communication: A study of interactional patterns, pathologies, and paradoxes.* New York: W. W. Norton.

Wirtz, J. G. & Zimbres, T. M. (2018). A systematic analysis of research applying "principles of dialogic communication" to organizational websites, blogs, and social media: Implications for theory and practice. *Journal of Public Relations Research, 30,* 5–34.

5 The accountability paradox

Social media has rewritten the rules of communication, and the opportunities for dialog with affiliated and unaffiliated groups and individuals have dramatically increased. The resulting interactions are not always efforts to develop relationships but to express concerns and demand accountability. Indeed, Flinders (2014) claimed that "accountability appears to be emerging as the uber-concept of the twenty-first century" (para.1). The paradox of these increasing demands for corporate accountability arises from the fact that companies can receive a black eye even when they meet external expectations for accountability.

> With swarms of skeptical reporters and editors, social media backlash and a general public quick to label everything a PR stunt, it is hard to change the perception of companies or entire industries by throwing an issue in the PR spin cycle.
>
> (Terenzio, 2018, para. 1)

The "quick" answer for Terenzio was for public relations to be more accountable and stop promising to be better and simply be better. Public relations has responded by helping organizations establish high standards for corporate social responsibility (CSR). Having CSR standards in place, however, does not guarantee that organizational actors will take more responsibility or even be more accountable. Indeed, formalizing accountability can contribute to decreases in personal and organizational responsibility because organizational actors lose sight of the original purpose of prosocial behavior (De Colle, Henriques, & Sarasvathy, 2014). Formal standards can diminish the importance of internalizing rules and discourage organizational members from taking responsibility (Peterson, 2002; De Colle et al., 2014).

Voluntary acts of accountability present their own problems, especially if the public perceives them to be self-serving and inauthentic. This is especially true when organizations seek out public relations services to help minimize the negative effects of a crisis. Even a good public relations crisis team can struggle to restore public confidence in an organization that has not already established itself as a good citizen. The effectiveness of a public apology often depends on the pre-existing level of trust between an organization and the public (Ulmer,

2012; MacLachlan, 2015). A paradox for public relations arises when its efforts to ameliorate the crisis comes across as insincere and self-serving. To resolve this and other paradoxes associated with accountability, public relations is particularly well positioned to help organizations develop an authentic form of accountability, one not dependent upon external pressure or CSR standards.

This chapter proposes dealing with the paradox of accountability by reframing public relations from an externally focused model of answerability to an internally focused standard of virtue and responsibility. To explain this inversion of public relations priorities, I will first introduce the concept of reframing and the fluid center of Kirk Schneider's Paradox Principle. Second, I detail the current frames for understanding accountability and identify potential opportunities for reframing. Third, I will briefly examine the role of public relations in organizational accountability and show how different forms of accountability are manifested in the personal experiences of veteran practitioners. Finally, I will incorporate a metalanguage that reframes accountability to focus internally on organizational virtue and values rather than externally on third party expectations. This new frame also promotes a new approach to transparency that recognizes the dialectical complexity of modern life.

The art of reframing

Reframing means to change the way one perceives a situation and place it in another frame with new perspective that still fits the situation. The phenomenon or event remains the same, but our conceptualization and emotional response to the experience changes (Watzlawick, Weakland, & Fisch, 2011). Most people might perceive scaling the sheer face of a mountain as absurd and foolhardy, but extreme climbers see it as exciting and exhilarating. One company might deal with an economic downturn by scaling back production and expansion while another interprets the same conditions as an opportunity for growth and expansion. Some organizations react to government compliance by only providing the information required by law while others over comply and cite their compliance as evidence of their civic and social responsibility. These contradictions can produce paralysis and indecision in some individuals and organizations while inspiring creativity and innovation in others.

To reframe is to change the meaning of a situation but not the facts associated with the situation. It calls for viewing the situation from a higher, meta-level of abstraction and accepting the ordinality of language (Watzlawick et al., 2011). In public relations, for example, reframing might change our perception of our place in the community. Group memberships are not the absolute or ultimate truth; they change as we move to higher and lower levels of abstraction. At a meta-level, for example, the public, particularly the general public, is a meaningless abstraction, inferring a solidarity and uniformity inconsistent with a diverse society. To talk about specific groups, such as customers, local community members, and local political leaders, is more concrete but still excludes the organization from group membership. Somewhere in between these two levels, we can reframe individuals, stakeholders, and organizational members as part of a community, which, though an abstraction, is more concrete than the broad description of the public. The organization and its employees are now a part of the same logical type, which enables relationships within the group. The way we relate with others greatly depends upon how we perceive our group relationships. If we refer to our friends or colleagues as part of our family, we change the nature of our interactions and open the door to stronger, more meaningful relationships.

Reframing qualifies as second-order change because it changes the class membership of an object to another, equally valid class membership (Watzlawick et al., 2011). The meaning attributed to a given situation changes but not the facts. What has changed is our opinion about the thing. To express an opinion *about* something is to engage in metacommunication, which represents the next higher logical type (Watzlawick et al., 2011). In the vernacular of the theory of logical types, the act of reframing simply means reassigning membership in the group or simply changing the rules that define group membership. Instead of organizations viewing publics as entities external to them, they reframe themselves as members of the community. The organization can now have relationships with individual members because, like the other community groups, it is a part of the same logical type. Granted the individual members relate to the organization and its employees as a subgroup of the community, but they still claim membership in the larger community and can relate and interact with them at that same level of abstraction. It is akin to seeing ourselves as Americans, rather than Texans or New Yorkers.

As we enlarge our frame, we still have to set boundaries. Our level of transparency with family, friends, colleagues, and neighbors varies depending upon what information should be public and what should remain private. We respect sports fans who support their teams but reject those who become obnoxious and critical of our affiliations. To navigate social interactions, we need to know when to expand and when to contract. As Schneider (1990) noted, individuals need to simultaneously engage and withdraw depending upon the situation. This process of dealing with life's oppositional forces is known as integration. Schneider (1990) referred to this dialectic of constriction and expansion as the Paradox Principle. "The human psyche is a constrictive/expansive continuum only degrees of which are conscious" (Schneider, 2014, para. 10). To deny or avoid the polarities leads to dysfunction and pathological problems, but to embrace and integrate them promotes a healthy, dynamic flexibility and adaptability. "In short, optimal people have well-developed centers—they are more able to choose their retractions and expansions, whereas dysfunctional and conventional people are greatly diminished in this capacity" (p. 141). As Kenny Rogers sang, "you got to know when to hold 'em, know when to fold 'em" (The gambler lyrics, 2017).

The Paradox Principle also applies to groups and organizations. Healthy organizations confront opposites and oppositional forces by reconciling the extremes. This direct approach to contradictions promotes authenticity and creativity. Healthy organizations integrate the need to control and innovate at the same time.

> They tend to "draw back" (inspect details, define tasks, restrict funds) and "burst forth" (explore, innovate, persist) as needed. They use space and time liberally when change, participation and sensitivity are called for, and conservatively when stability, direction, and logic are relevant.
>
> (Schneider, 1990, p. 160)

More recently, Schneider argued that the development of a "fluid center" cultivates "inclusiveness, pliability, constraint, and humility and boldness as the context and circumstance demand" (Schneider, 2014, para. 10). The paradoxical nature of accountability, especially as it applies to public relations communication, requires an ability to integrate opposites.

Accountability

Accountability in its most basic form means answerability (Roberts, 2002; Newton, Hodges, & Keith, 2004). An individual or institutional authority imposes expectations on one or more persons with a demand for answers and the power to reward or punish based on those answers. "Accountability assumes that the agent of whom such answerability is demanded is both self-aware and in possession of the necessary means to cause an event or act to occur" (Harmon, 1995, p. 25.) Although the media and public demands for accountability have increased since the rise of social media, its roots trace back to bookkeeping and accounting (Bovens, Shillemans, & Goodin, 2014). Accountability meant keeping track of costs, supplies, and income. To be accountable meant to essentially tell a story "based on some obligation and with some consequence in view" (para. 5). As the complexity of bookkeeping increased so did the complexity of the stories. This definition places public relations practitioners at the center of accountability reporting. In telling the organization's story, they account for an organization's actions and provide an explanation as to what happened.

This conforms to Haines' (1955) definition of accountability as first, explicability, and second, liability. "In ordinary speech," Haines noted, "an act is accountable not only when it is 'liable' but also when it is 'explicable'" (p. 142). Explication differs from liability and responsibility in that it focuses on the act rather than the actor. In any given action, he wrote, there are two ways of explaining what happened: Causes of and reasons for. Haines gives the example of a driver who turns the wheel and crashes into another car. The "causes of" explanation might consist of the driver saying he or she turned to avoid a child running out in the street. This would be a non-rational explanation. The "reasons for," on the other hand, would be a rational explanation: Say, the driver had planned to kill the person in the other car.

In 2013, global carrier Matson, Inc. leaked 233,000 gallons of molasses into Honolulu Harbor. The molasses eventually settled on the ocean bottom and killed an estimated 26,000 fish and marine life. The company followed the traditional crisis communication game plan and accepted responsibility, but the press wanted more. In facing reporters demanding answers, senior vice president of the Pacific Division Vic Angoco said it was too early to explain what happened, but the company was sorry and concerned about the spill's damage to the environment. "We take pride in what we do. We take pride in being good stewards of the land, of the ocean. *In this case we didn't live up to our standards"* (italics added; quoted in Gutierrez, 2013, para. 2). Four days later, Matson's President and CEO Matt Cox reiterated that the company took responsibility for the spill and promised to pay for the cleanup and cooperate with state authorities (Matson takes responsibility, 2013, para. 3). Matson's response hit the right notes in regards to crisis communication, but it missed an opportunity to communicate its standards and explain how it would hold itself accountable for failing to be a good steward. The company paid a heavy price for the spill, not only in damage to its reputation but in the millions spent to clean up the molasses and pay civil penalties, settle lawsuits, and provide restitution (Inefuku, 2017).

Matson's public apology represented a performative model of accountability—an effort to restore public trust following wrongdoing (Koehn, 2013; MacLachlan, 2015). The company took responsibility for the spill and created a "sense of accountability, and, at the same time, a sense of belonging and identification" (MacLachlan, 2015, p. 451). However, Matson focused too much on direct accountability to the state and legal system and failed to reassert its standards and values, especially those consistent with community norms. Subsequent media coverage reported on how the state and the courts held Matson accountable, but the company never communicated its internal efforts to right itself and hold itself accountable.

Explicability obligated Matson to explain the causes of crisis and give reasons why the company acted as it did and how it corrected the underlying problem that caused the spill. The public does not expect companies to be perfect, but it does expect companies to provide an explanation, give the reasons why it happened, and then tell how the company plans to change to make sure it does not happen again. Explanation serves as the first important difference between accountability and responsibility: Explanation "is primarily concerned with acts and events; but responsibility is interested first of all in persons" (Haines, 1955, pp. 142–143).

Haines' (1955) second meaning of accountability is liability, a word more synonymous to responsibility. The actors, those accountable for their actions, are responsible for the act and considered liable. The degree of their liability depends upon the causes of and reasons for the act. Explanation determines the separation between the act and the actor. Although it seems that the closer the actor is to the act, the greater the responsibility, that is not always the case. In the case of British Petroleum's investigation of the explosion on its Deep-Water Horizon oil platform and subsequent oil spill, the company provided rational reasons and non-rational causes for the disaster, leading commentators to say the company was defining the extent of its liability. Though far removed from the act, the company's CEO was reassigned and was held accountable for company decisions that led to the disaster. Removing the decision-maker reflects the social nature of liability. In large-scale public disasters, society has come to expect the CEO should be held accountable for the system's failure. Though often not objectively responsible and not guilty of violating any of the agent-accountant expectations, the leaders are often held accountable for the subjective decisions that led to the disaster.

When Toyota answered to the U.S. Congress for accelerator problems in its cars, the company relied on CEO Akio Toyoda, grandson of the company's founder, to answer for the company's actions. "I have personally placed the highest priority on improving quality over quantity," he said, "and I have shared that direction with our stakeholders" (Maynard, 2010, para. 1). For more than three hours, Toyoda responded to lawmakers' questions regarding "the recall of more than 6 million vehicles in the United States and the carmaker's delay in responding to problems of sudden acceleration" (para. 2). Congress wanted to know when Toyota became aware of the problem. In response, Yoshimi Inaba, the chief executive of Toyota of North America, claimed that Toyota did not hide the problem, but then had to explain why the company made changes to vehicles in Europe weeks before announcing its U.S. recall. Inaba confessed that the information was not properly shared with the North American division of the company (Maynard, 2010).

The hearing represented an effort by Congress to hold Toyota accountable for its actions. Congress demanded that Toyota answer for its action or inaction in regards to informing the public about its accelerator flaws. Congress and the public wanted to know who was responsible. Why did the company wait so long to take action? Why applaud a memo boasting that the company had saved money by just recalling floor mats (Maynard, 2010)? In other words, the public wanted an explanation that included who was liable and reasons why the company took so long to correct the problem. Congress and the public did not want to hear from public relations, they wanted to hear from the company's decision-makers.

When those in particular positions and situations are expected to account for a company's actions, they are addressing determined liabilities (Haines, 1955). This relates to the World Bank definition of social accountability: "An approach to building accountability that relies on civic engagement, that is, in which its ordinary citizens and/or civil society organizations who participate directly or indirectly in exacting accountability" (Social accountability, 2010, para. 1). In scandals or disasters, it is rare to hear that the public relations director was canned. In cases of determined liability, public relations practitioners advise corporate leaders on how to respond, help tailor a response, and deal with the subsequent public and media scrutiny. But most appeals for accountability are not based on laws or reason but on moral values, such as freedom, responsibility, self-determination, and self-protection (McKeon, 1960). The public may interpret the act of simply providing good "public relations" as hiding and ducking behind corporate communicators to avoid direct accountability. The way in which public relations can truly communicate accountability is to transcend determinations of liability and express a sense of responsibility.

Haines (1955) referred to the person or organization with this sense of responsibility as the *ideal accountant*. Ideal accountants do not need to be scrutinized by external accountants but scrutinize and take responsibility for their own work and actions. Thus, accountability becomes "an expression of self" (p. 150). The ideal accountant transcends determined liabilities "because his principles, his reason, his motives, his character and so on drive him" (p. 150). In some relationships, we do take responsibility or are held accountable for the actions of our organization or group. But for us to take moral responsibility for a specific behavior, it must be done by us directly. We are not directly liable for the actions of another, but we may be responsible for explaining what happened, the root causes, etc. The law tends to impose the severest penalties on those directly involved; others peripherally responsible are punished proportional to their direct actions.

Organizations reflecting this personified sense of responsibility are those with a well-defined character and credo. The company feels a sense of responsibility that goes beyond any legal and public accountability. The ultimate act of public relations accountability is to assume liability even when no one is there to hold practitioners and their organizations accountable. Lewis (1948) argued that a structure or society in general "cannot be the bearer of moral responsibility" because both are "abstractions which we must be careful not to hypostatize" (p. 13). Others may be responsible for failing to act or taking actions that resulted in something bad happening. "But they are responsible for this as individuals, and strictly in proportion to what each might have done, directly or indirectly, to ameliorate her lot" (p. 13).

To have a sense of responsibility means moving beyond questions of compulsion and free will to the point of adopting a personal sense of duty and principle. The negative freedom associated with free will is replaced by the positive freedom associated with self-discipline and personal responsibility. This provides a clearer distinction between accountability and responsibility: Accountability is external, responsibility is internal. Ideal accountants recognize the paradox and accept that external and internal expectations can be complementary and conflicting at the same time. Ideal accountants do not distinguish between the internal and the external but hold themselves responsible to their own character, virtues, and values. In contrast, agent-accountants are liable to external forces. Ideal accountants embrace accountability as a virtue and sense of responsibility (Harmon, 1995; Bovens, 2010). By nature of their communication expertise, public relations practitioners are well positioned to reconcile external and internal obligations through ongoing communication and develop the courage necessary to deal with the anxiety, complexity, doubt, ambiguity, and paradoxes associated with private and public accountability (Harmon, 1995). The ideal accountant views the reconciling of these paradoxes as a personal and professional responsibility.

Some writers contend that accountability and responsibility are two distinct concepts with two separate and distinct meanings. Goetz and Jenkins (2002) described accountability as enforced obligation while responsibility is a voluntary act. Public accountability scholars include accountability as an aspect or type of responsibility, one that includes imposed obligations and moral agency. In his study of the paradoxes of responsibility, Harmon (1995) made accountability one of three subsets of responsibility. The others were agency and obligation. Bovens (1998) included accountability in his definition of passive responsibility. He identified four criteria of responsibility-as-accountability: Some action or inaction that qualifies as transgressing a norm, a causal connection between the act and its consequences, someone who is to blame, and a close relationship with the accountable agent (pp. 28–30). Active responsibility emphasizes virtue and having a sense of responsibility. It values the autonomous actor who, through the power of moral reasoning, recognizes when norms have been violated and the consequences of those violations. Other characteristics include acting consistent with norms and standards and fulfilling duties associated with role obligations (pp. 34–37).

In 2010, Bovens enlarged his conception of accountability to include both passive and active responsibility. He divided accountability in two camps— accountability as a virtue and as a mechanism. The first approach treats accountability in much the same way as active responsibility—a normative standard for evaluating one's performance. This kind of accountability serves a personal and organizational virtue. Accountability as a virtue equates the concept with "clarity, transparency, and responsibility" as well as "involvement, deliberation and participation" (p. 949). The focus of this type of accountability is on the actor's performance, responsiveness, "sense of responsibility, willingness to act in a transparent, fair, and equitable way" (p. 949).

The second conception of accountability treats it as social relations or a mechanism that describes an institutional arrangement in which some kind of forum holds actors to account (Bovens, 2010). The forum has the power to expect explanations and impose consequences for the actions. As a mechanism, accountability consists of the obligation to inform others and the "possibility for the forum to interrogate the actor and question the adequacy of the information" (p. 952). The forum then passes judgment and imposes consequences. Questions arise as to whom one is accountable, who is the accountant, and why is the actor compelled to account to the forum.

Both approaches are related to "transparency, openness, responsiveness, and responsibility" (Bovens, 2010, p. 962). They differ in regards to where those properties reside. For accountability as a virtue, these are virtues of the actor while accountability as a mechanism entrusts them in the mechanism or the outcome produced by the mechanism. In terms of research, accountability as a virtue serves as the dependent variable, measuring the behavior of actors. Accountability as a mechanism, on the other hand, serves as an independent variable that produces virtue as an outcome through the use of various mechanisms, such as clear moral expectations and the threat of punishment for failing to meet those expectations. Bovens (2010) contended that mechanisms without virtue are meaningless as is virtue without mechanisms. The primary difference arises from their influence on the actor. Mechanisms may provide the norms and produce virtuous actions, but they do not necessarily develop virtuous actors. Indeed, Bovens identified this outcome as the accountability paradox: More accountability arrangements or mechanisms do not guarantee more accountable actors. Organizations may meet expectations but still not perform better or more responsibly.

Corporate ethics programs can produce a similar paradox. An organization's efforts to control behavior can produce the opposite effect and undermine employees' desire and capability to make moral decisions, especially when faced with new dilemmas (Stansbury & Barry, 2007). Employees actually reacted negatively to compliance-oriented ethics programs, perceiving them as efforts by top management to avoid blame for bad actions. Instead of increasing reports of misconduct, these programs discouraged misconduct reporting. This same scenario plays out in organizations as well. As they come under more scrutiny and external demands for accountability, they resort to delaying and disrupting tactics. Highly coercive programs undermine employee moral agency and diminish their capability to "manage ethical ambiguity" (p. 253).

Another paradox emerges from the fact that, in complex organizations, responsibility is shared by many people. This phenomenon is known as the paradox of shared responsibility or "the problem of many hands" (Bovens, 1998, p. 45). The more people share responsibility for a certain conduct or behavior, the less responsibility individual members accepts for themselves. The bigger the organization, the more diffuse the responsibility. As with the Matson example, the problem of many hands has practical and normative implications. It is impractical to expect the largest carrier of goods in the Pacific region to monitor every loading procedure that occurs across that vast region. Though Matson espoused a strong commitment to environmental stewardship, it faced no small challenge to have this normative standard adopted by each of the thousands of employees working for the company. Any possible solution to the shared responsibility paradox needs to include accountability as a virtue and as a mechanism. However, like the virtue-mechanism dichotomy, public accountability theories tend to emphasize either moral agency and standards or a structural-functional approach.

Relational aspects of accountability provide somewhat of a middle ground. Based on the relational approach, one party expects certain activities or outcomes and has the power to punish the other actor if those expectations are not met. Based on the concept's relational components, Painter-Morland (2006) interpreted accountability as relational responsiveness and argued that accountability only gains meaning and significance through relationships. These accountability interactions help shape moral knowledge and moral decision-making. In the relational context, accountability shifts from being accountable for something to being accountable towards those for whom we have responsibility. Relational responsiveness would place less emphasis on compliance-driven accountability and more emphasis on our moral obligations and duties to people inside and outside an organization. Relational responsibilities and duties develop together and thus external expectations (duties) and personal responsibility go hand in hand.

The two most cited theories are the principal-agent and social contingency model (Bovens et al., 2014). At its core, the principal-agent theory determines who is accountable to whom. It includes aspects of Bovens' (2010) conceptions of accountability as a virtue and as a mechanism. The principal-agent focuses on dyadic relationships in which a principal party structures the incentives for the agent. In other words, the principal establishes expectations, rewards, and punishment (Gailmard, 2012). Principal-agent theory aligns accountability with the goal-directed behaviors of the agent, along with relationships in which the parties feel a sense of ownership (Bovens et al., 2014). The social contingency model, on the other hand, centers on bridging the gap between individual and external accountants (Bovens et al., 2014). Social contingency is functionalistic and rooted in systems theory and, thus, focuses on how the social environment impacts individual behavior. Human agents adapt their behavior to meet expectations to justify their actions and conform with what is deemed socially acceptable. It posits that having the right accountability mechanisms produces right action.

The agent-accountant relationship is reflected in a background paper for a United Nations Human Development Report (Goetz & Jenkins, 2002). Accountability is simply defined as one party being accountable to another for its actions. Accountability, Goetz and Jenkins contended, is a relationship of power in which the second party can demand justifications from the first party for its behavior and/or has the power to penalize the first party for that behavior if it violates accepted norms. In addition, accountability imposes on the first party an obligation to answer questions posed by the party holding it accountable. This act of voice—asking questions and giving reasons or answers—means that voice is inseparable from accountability. "For there to be answerability—the obligation of the power-holders to justify their decisions and actions—someone has to be asking the questions" (p. 10). Based on this definition of accountability, organizations must respond to outside interest groups and activists.

Unions prefer to promote the social contingency model over voluntary initiatives by transnational corporations because they see corporate citizenship as "more of a public relations slogan than a legal reality" (Henderson, 2002, para. 9). Also referring to transnational corporations, Koenig-Archibugi (2004) argued that the accountability relationship requires "a flow of information to the principals and other stakeholders about the decision-makers' actions, and the capacity of stakeholders to impose sanctions on the agents" (p. 236). Koenig-Archibugi noted that collective financial entities have a duty to the public because governments, acting in the public interest, have granted special legal protections and financial benefits to corporations. For accountability relationships to work, there must be watchdogs or other stakeholders who can punish or hold organizations accountable for their actions. For transnational corporations, Koenig-Archibugi suggested that non-governmental organizations (NGOs) fill this role.

In the public sector, public servants encounter what Harmon called the three paradoxes of accountability. The first is the paradox of obligation. Public officials are obligated to an authority but are still expected to make decisions for themselves. The second is the paradox of agency. Public officials have moral agency but at the same time answer to others. The third is the paradox of accountability. Public officials achieve the ends mandated by authority and have no personal responsibility over those ends, but at the same time, as public servants, they have personal responsibility and are expected to take actions they consider to be in the public interest (Harmon, 1995; Roberts, 2002). Harmon (1995) proposed engaging with citizens, colleagues, and elected officials in the type of ongoing dialog espoused by theologian H. Richard Niebuhr. For Niebuhr, moral life was the dialog of "ongoing interactions between actions upon me, my interpretation of them, my response, and the response to my response" (Marshall, 2018, p. 150). For Niebuhr, dialog was about reconciling external expectations and perceptions with internal thoughts and interpretations. Accountability includes responding to "actions upon me" and others' responses to my reactions (p. 150). Harmon (1995) described Niebuhr's definition of accountability as dialog "involving the mutual interpretation of people's actions in the process of cooperatively discovering what sorts of practices are worth engaging in" (p. 195). This approach embraces the paradox of accountability by taking into consideration external constraints, informing those engaged with relevant knowledge, and facilitating learning, creativity, and innovation. To resolve these paradoxes, Harmon (1995) appealed for actors to have the courage to deal with doubt, ambiguity, imperfection, anxiety, and yes, paradoxes. In other words, actors needed to be more personally responsible.

All of the aforementioned definitions and approaches to accountability directly affect public relations practice, especially for national and transnational corporations. But outside of answerability, they provide little clarity as to the role of public relations in the organizational accountability. In dealing with compliance reporting and other expectations from external accountants, practitioners answer to mandated duties and activities with little opportunity for responsible, autonomous action. In cases in which practitioners have more latitude, such as in crisis communication, they battle the perception that their professional expertise served to deflect or minimize accountability. The crisis communication game plan enacts a check list of steps that may or may not reflect back on the organization's (or the practitioners') purposes, standards, and character. Companies may heed public relations' counsel and give the appearance of doing the right thing but lack sincerity and authenticity. In those cases, public relations serves to reinforce negative perceptions of the field and undermines the intended morality of crisis communication. This paradox also arises in one of the most significant manifestations of public relations accountability—corporate social responsibility.

Accountability in public relations

With immediate communication and heightened scrutiny by media, activist groups, and consumers, companies have touted corporate citizenship but faced the same skepticism expressed by Henderson (2002). In particular, they have embraced the corporate social responsibility movement and employed public relations to manage CSR initiatives. CSR emphasizes "ethical values, compliance with legal requirements, and respect for people, communities and the environment" (Garsten, 2003, p. 362). The rise of CSR can be attributed to pressures exerted by activist groups, particularly those concerned about society and the environment. CSR activities coincided with an increased emphasis on corporate and political transparency. As noted earlier, transparency is often associated with accountability, and laws, such as the Sarbanes-Oxley, have mandated corporate transparency, including the publication of ethics codes. Gelb and Strawser (2001) found a positive relationship between corporate disclosure (transparency) and corporate social responsibility.

Rawlins (2009) defined transparency as making information accessible and providing open and honest communication. The Internet and social media allow companies to provide an enormous amount of information, and public relations has played a major role in managing organizational websites, social media, and information disclosure. Like publicity in the Progressive Era, transparency is associated with building public trust and promoting ethical action (Gower, 2006; Rawlins, 2009). But Wakefield and Walton (2010) contended that transparency only works if organizations have already developed trust through open and prompt communication over a period of time. They proposed "translucency" as a more accurate description of the need to provide more quality information than just a quantity of information. Combs and Holladay (2013) went a step further and called for an emphasis on transparency as a process rather than just a quality of Internet communication. Organizations should engage activists and stakeholders as part of the process of transparency. Otherwise, the burden of demanding accurate and verifiable transparency shifts from the organization to activist groups and other stakeholders.

Public relations has to accept some of the blame for CSR transparency being perceived as strategic and self-serving. This close relationship between public relations and CSR has contributed to a negative perception of CSR communication (Benn, Todd, & Pendleton, 2010). Indeed, corporate leaders have tried to distance CSR from public relations (The role of PR within CSR, 2009). Another problem associated with CSR reporting is that, despite its good intentions, CSR actually discourages actors from taking responsibility (De Colle, Henriques, & Sarasvathy, 2014). For all the positive outcomes associated with CSR programs, there are several "unintended (counterproductive) consequences" that can undermine the positive effect of an organization's CSR standards and its "social performance" (p. 184). These negative outcomes have shifted the focus away from corporate responsibility and voluntary initiatives and moved organizations more toward external partnerships and accountability through law, public policy, and verification (Utting, 2008). But even these voluntary efforts by transnational companies to work with activist groups has led to accusations that corporations have co-opted their accountants.

CSR and voluntary initiatives expose a paradox associated with agent-accountant relationships. Even if organizations meet external expectations, they may earn little credit from a skeptical public. The compulsory nature of agent-accountant relationships can foster adversarial, distrustful interaction from the accountant and the one being held accountable. Communicative interactions become legalistic and compulsory, aimed at meeting legal requirements rather than moral obligations. Research has shown that legislated transparency forces companies to communicate only that information required by law. As one vice president of communications noted, legislated corporate reporting often acts as much as a disincentive as it does an incentive to communicate (personal communication, October 15, 2010). The goal of the communication is not to provide an accountable response but to avoid accountability for anything that might invite prosecution. Thus, the agent-accountant approach to accountability actually can discourage responsibility because the organization is only concerned with its legal obligations and transactions with the government.

Although public relations, especially in the health care industry and investor relations, deals with compliance issues on a regular basis, it can become a stark exchange and lacking in sincerity and authenticity. Public relations serves as a subset of legal counsel, communicating to prevent scrutiny and ultimately a sense of responsibility. In a philosophical essay aimed at delineating between accountability and responsibility, Haines (1955) described the agent-accountant relationship as compulsory accountability. The agent-accountant relationship turns into an act of going through the process of meeting required objective liabilities and nothing more. Typically, the agent-accountant relationship is based on objective standards, those provided by law or contract, and the organization is bound to communicate according to those rules. The Sarbanes-Oxley Act that mandates CEOs reporting to the government is an example of the agent-accountant relationship. Compulsory communication creates "public relations" problems for organizations because it comes across as pejorative "public relations," communication aimed at mechanically addressing a list of imposed requirements rather than expressing sincere accountability.

To overcome the cynicism associated with agent-accountability, public relations must accept the limitations of answerability and begin to take the initiative and move organizational communication towards social accountability. Like accountability as a virtue, social accountability shifts the focus from agent-accountability mechanisms and structures to more voluntary forms of accountability based on shared values and societal norms. Corporate citizenship and corporate social responsibility communicate that an organization is a part of society and therefore seeks to conform its behavior to socially responsible behavior. Social accountability requires more than simply answerability; it demands *active* responsibility (Bovens, 1998).

Public relations can be much more effective if it helps organizations cooperatively establish a set of values and principles that communicate ideal accountability. Practitioners can then tell the accountability story. If the organization makes mistakes or deviates from its own character, then the organization communicates that it holds itself accountable and thus communicates its values to its external accountants. This reframes public relations accountability from responding to external publics, such as the media, to making public the way the organization holds itself accountable. To make public rather than communicate to the public reframes transparency as opening up the organization to allow the public to peer inside while retaining the private space necessary to learn, adapt, and innovate.

PR professionals' perspectives of accountability

Communicating accountability helps organizations create public legitimacy, win public confidence, and narrow the evaluative gap between publics and organizations (Bovens, 2010). Public relations may minimize the effects of the crisis on a company's reputation, but in the end the organization and its leaders are the ones held accountable. An analysis of interviews conducted in 2010 and 2013 with high-level veteran public relations practitioners revealed that they first held themselves accountable by seeking out organizations that reflected their values and placed a high priority on accountability and responsibility. Their responses to questions regarding accountability provides insight into accountability, ranging from agent–accountability to ideal accountability.

Agent-accountability

An agency executive said, "Companies are being held accountable if they get tax payer dollars and especially if they are publicly traded companies and you have stakeholder dollars involved" (Agency executive, personal conversation, Jan. 25, 2010). In her opinion, the Internet and the lack of privacy have contributed to an increasing demand for accountability. "It's much, much harder to keep things under wraps. Companies are having to deal with coming clean and being honest and forthright from the beginning" (Agency executive, personal conversation, January 25, 2010). A corporate public relations account executive added that companies are held accountable by their employees and customers, the "ultimate stakeholders" (Corporate public relations account executive, personal conversation, October 11, 2010). She explained that listening for negative feedback from stakeholders is critical to the long-term health of a company because most people do not report their concerns and simply leave, stop purchasing products, or start telling others about their bad experiences.

A public affairs chair of a health care organization noted that, in the past, public relations sent out emails with internal e-messages and external messages. Now the organization does not distinguish between internal and external talking points. "Organizations have learned to be honest because you learn that all we are doing is under a magnifying glass. They operate differently when everything is being looked at from the outside" (Health care public affair chair, March 3, 2010). The companies that fare best in this transparent environment are those that continue learning, listening, and renewing (Ulmer, Sellnow, & Seeger, 2019).

Based on this type of transparency, a national transportation company pioneered direct relationships with the customer when it bypassed middlemen to show rates for every route and allow the direct purchase of tickets. Transparency in regards to pricing provided "a look at what it was like to be in an online space" (Corporate communication executive, personal conversation, February 11, 2010). The culture of a direct relationship with customers helped the airline to deal with the challenges of having corporate communications "keep up with what is already a transparent brand" (Corporate communication executive, personal conversation, February 11, 2010).

This concept of direct accountability to the consumer has helped the transportation company in its approach to monitoring online traffic and responding immediately to blogs, tweets, or posts about the company. True to transparency, the communications representatives make it clear that they are associated with the company before responding online.

> It took us about a year to figure out where the online spaces and forums were…. We figured out who the influentials were. We know to immediately go to those websites. Our representatives are instructed that when they engage, they engage in a transparent way. There's no other way to do that. When we do weigh in, we weigh in with who we are and where we're from. We don't used paid bloggers.
>
> (Corporate communication executive,
> personal conversation, February 11, 2010)

This kind of responsibility requires autonomy, and, unlike its competitors, the company does not have to have every press release and communication approved by its legal department. Corporate communication has the discretion to bring legal into the conversation when necessary. Legal is sought out when the issue deals with federal agency filings and regulations. If the company is at fault, the culture dictates a contrite response.

Explanation plays a big role in online communication because the online world demands immediate response. There is not just the evening news interview for which to prepare, practitioners must deal with multiple channels all at the same time. Gone are the times in which a well-informed reporter held a company accountable for its actions. Now the person on the story is more likely to be a young, general assignment reporter with little knowledge of the industry. Corporate communication must determine the channels for telling the story and prepare a mitigation plan if the story goes wrong.

An agency executive noted that "Companies have to do a better job of explaining what's going on" (Agency executive, personal conversation, January 25, 2010). If the companies don't decide on their own to explain what's happening, the non-governmental organizations will hold them accountable, either through the press or the courts. For example, extractive companies know that what they do is very complicated, but their close ties to the environment and their potential effect on the environment means they can't go into a place and "shove everything under a rug. They have to be up front and show people what they are going to do and that will save a lot of headaches in the future" (Agency executive, personal conversation, January 25, 2010).

Social accountability

An agency professional experienced this first hand in her work with an oil and gas company. The president went around the country and spoke in 50 different cities and held one-on-one town hall meetings where people could ask questions. People were livid about high gas prices and oil company profits. "Most people don't understand what goes into the price of a gallon of gas, and I think oil companies have not done anything to help the consumer understand this" (Agency executive, personal conversation, January 25, 2010). The petroleum industry, she said, was going to protect the companies and not look out for the consumers. That constrictive approach meant that the industry did a poor job of educating consumers on what factors played into the price of gasoline.

> Once [the CEO] was able to engage people one on one, whether they agreed or disagreed, they at least had some answers…. It was very eye opening to me. The information came from the top. People want to know what's going on and where their money is going.

People want to hear from the CEO. "But they don't want CEOs following a script. They want proof points. The best CEOs not only speak to the press but go out and talk to the people" (Agency executive, personal conversation, January 25, 2010).

This kind of social accountability approaches communication from the standpoint of explanation and liability. In one-on-one conversations, the oil company CEO recognized the industry's social responsibility to explain the causes of the situation—in regards to the high oil and gas prices—and the reasons for the company's actions in response to the high prices. The additional emphasis on the CEO speaking as a person also reflects that, in this case, he was taking personal responsibility, holding himself accountable. As already mentioned, society expects the person in charge to be accountable for organizational actions. By engaging the public as well as the media, the CEO was being socially accountable for company decisions. Another important aspect of this case is the public relations professional's alignment of accountability with personal authenticity. By not speaking from a script, the CEO is more likely to provide authentic answers, those reflecting true feelings and concerns. This moves social accountability closer to an ideal accountability in which the company and its leadership transcends basic agent-accountant answerability and moves toward a sense of accountability that sincerely reflects the core values of the organization.

Another corporate public relations executive faced a similar situation when her company made the decision to lay off hundreds of employees. The company philosophy was to be answerable to stakeholders when making the "hard" decisions. The practitioner persuaded the CEO to go on the road and personally face the laid-off employees, explain the decision, and take questions. She later received several unsolicited emails in which employees expressed respect for company leadership even though they did not like the message.

A branding specialist echoed this transition to ideal accountability when she noted that the health care communicators "have learned the painful lessons as to why it is not a good idea to diminish the importance of things that happen" (Health care brand management director, personal conversation, March 3, 2010). Confidentiality and privacy remain important, but her company learned "the hard way" about their responsibility "to be honest and up front about things that happen here. We've done a better job of that. We've had to struggle to help our leadership understand that it's important" (Health care brand management director, personal conversation, March 3, 2010). Public relations practitioners have helped the company's executives learn from their mistakes. "You can't un-ring the bell. What you say officially is what people hold you to" (Health care brand management director, personal conversation, March 3, 2010). Health care professionals acknowledged a difference between short-term and long-term accountability. "You make decisions in the short term that really affect the long-term reputation of the organization" (Health care brand management director, personal conversation, March 3, 2010).

Ideal accountability

Soon after joining the not-for-profit company, the branding director witnessed the way that her company held itself accountable.

> I remember the moment very clearly. I had been on the job maybe a month. And I don't remember the exact thing, but something happened working with a health care plan at the time. We had lost a contract or something. We were concerned with people not having access to health care. I was called into a meeting very quickly of the board of directors. What struck me so powerful was that the board members were unanimous in saying we were going to do what's right for the patients and make sure they have access to the health care they need. That meeting had a powerful effect on me as to the kind of organization I work for. It is a part of the culture.
>
> (Health care brand management director,
> personal conversation, March 3, 2010)

The mantra of the organization, she explained, was that the patient's needs come first and it permeated everything the organization did. Organizational members were given autonomy to make things better for the patient. "That environment has created a real sense of accountability." The company has a strong internal sense of accountability "that is part of who we are" (Health care brand management director, personal conversation, March 3, 2010). The company was committed to accountability and transparency. "You have to be transparent and accountable in health care. People in health care are not perfect human beings. We try to handle things a candidly as possible" (Health care brand management director, personal conversation, March 3, 2010).

A vice president in corporate communication used different terms to describe the same ideal-accountant relationship. She viewed communications as an act of transparency. "Public relations should be a window to the brand" (Corporate communication executive, personal conversation, February 11, 2010). That definition incorporates enhancing positives and mitigating negatives, but it does not mean being a "spin doctor" or providing misleading and false information. Transparency, giving "our publics a view into the brand," means that the communications professional is accountable for the trust and credibility built into the brand. In other words, as the window to the brand, public relations is individually and collectively liable for upholding and protecting the integrity of the organization (Corporate communication executive, personal conversation, February 11, 2010). She never mentioned reputation. Instead, she focused on the company's identity and character.

This approach helps eliminate conflicts among different accountants. By having a clear sense of what the brand is and what it stands for improves the communication of company actions internally and across multiple media outlets, most of which rely on other published accounts. Consistency and clarity in the message strengthen the company's relationship with internal constituents and customers and builds trust with media, especially those willing to do their homework. That approach communicates accountability even when not actively communicating. The corporate public relations account executive noted that her company did not want to be driven by "squeaky wheel" employees, NGOs, shareholders, and activists but to hold itself accountable to all of its stakeholders. The company tries to give equal consideration to all of its stakeholders, not just to those making the most noise (Corporate public relations account executive, personal conversation, October 11, 2010).

The changing media landscape has reinforced the need for an ideal-accountant relationship. The vice president for strategic communication at a multinational technology company explained that digital and social media has made the present time the age of radical transparency.

> The situation we are facing is that there are no places to hide anymore. For individuals, organizations, for nations and for communities, there are all kinds of issues that not of themselves are anything new but that now have a new level of urgency or consequence. As a result of this shift, largely dealing with privacy and security, we really have crossed the Rubicon on that. There are places, there are organizations, there are limited periods of

time when temporarily, attempts to control may work but they are quixotic and won't last. In that sense everybody is more or less now permanently accountable.

(Vice president of strategic communication,
personal conversation, March 4, 2013)

The vice president noted that research shows that an organization's people and its place in the community drives public perceptions of the organization's authenticity, legitimacy, and worth. Advertising has less effect. The success of an organization depends on it being what it claims to be. The idea that organizations can control their messages, the content of those messages, and the channels of communication are not possible anymore. Public relations has moved beyond simply messaging work. It has to now intervene in corporate culture or, in other words, it has to help organizations hold themselves accountable. "Identity, that is what pops out in a radically transparent world" (Vice president of strategic communication, personal conversation, March 4, 2013).

In the traditional agent–accountant relationship, journalists held industry accountable, but now companies receive calls from journalists offering to publish 5,000 words on the company's CEO for a certain amount of money. "We get a whole lot more pay for play phone calls now" (Corporate communication executive, personal conversation, February 11, 2010). Although the communication executive's company earns enough media attention that it does not need to pay for play, it's now facing a new dilemma: Journalists laid off from newspapers are starting websites and offering to write three positive stories on the company if it pays a $5,000 underwriting fee. "PR people really have to step up if they don't want to face the pitfall of having their information show up and people say, 'Oh, that's a pay for play site'" (Corporate communication executive, personal conversation, February 11, 2010).

Relying on trusted organizational values reflects an ideal-accountant approach. For the public relations professional with a health care not-for-profit organization, the ideal accountant meant that the company did not make a distinction between internal and external audiences. There are few firewalls between internal and external communication, which has caused public relations professionals to be more consistent and thoughtful. The health care branding manager said that, "We know it's going to get public attention. That knowledge has made us more organized and prepared" (Health care brand management director, personal conversation, March 3, 2010). The company lives by the philosophy that everything internal is external, so internal and external talking points are now the same. This kind of internal-external consistency also was exemplified in a recent company decision to limit new patients because the government pay-out did not cover expenses. "We have chosen to be very honest about what we're doing and why we're doing it. We got a lot of negative press. We firmly believe we've done it the right way" (Health care brand management director, personal conversation, March 3, 2010). Other health care providers made the same decision but kept quiet and did not face media scrutiny.

Reframing accountability in public relations

By reframing accountability as ideal accountability, public relations turns its focus inward, facilitating internal discussions and debates to reconcile company values and standards with its actions. The role of public relations is not so much to mediate between the organization and the public but to shine a light on organizational virtues, especially those that resonate with public values and expectations. Public relations serves not so much as public conscience within the organization but as a keeper of the flame, reminding organizational members of its identity and purpose. Since external accountants typically do not hold public relations practitioners accountable for these actions, public relations must serve an early warning system to alert management to inconsistencies. This early warning system is not to be confused with the public relations role associated with issues management and systems theory. These warnings do not originate so much from feedback coming from outside an organization; they come from inside, when loyalists see leaders deviating from the course they themselves claim to espouse.

Ideal accountability communicates through public relations and not because of it. This approach helps to diffuse the perception that organizations use public relations as a strategy for avoiding accountability. Accountability for public relations is about helping executives take personal responsibility rather than delegating responsibility to strategic public relations campaigns. The more the company and its leaders embrace a sense of responsibility, the more likely that they will cultivate the internal and external trust necessary to renew and re-engineer after a crisis. The Paradox Principle then guides organizational accountability, expanding out through socially responsible initiatives consistent with organizational values and contracting to bring about renewal and second-order change (Ulmer, 2012; Schneider, 2014). The centered practitioner and organization views crises, negative feedback, and environmental changes as threats but also opportunities. These challenges can act as a catalyst for innovation and change. At other times, the organization constricts to take stands consistent with its virtues and values, willing to answer for and explain the ideals and standards it considers integral to its culture and identity.

Veteran public relations practitioners have told me that they gravitate to organizations that share their values. The success of ideal accountability depends upon the character and ethics of the organization. If organizational deterioration or change lead to actions contrary to those values, practitioners may find their loyalty tested. When does their loyalty turn from virtue to vice? The next chapter addresses practitioners' conflicting loyalties to their organization and the public.

Dr. Bradley L. Rawlins contributed to some earlier iterations of this chapter and provided thoughtful feedback on the current version.

Works cited

Benn, S., Todd, L. R., & Pendleton, J. (2010). Public relations leadership in corporate social responsibility. *Journal of Business Ethics, 96* (3), 403–423.

Bovens, M. (1998). *The quest for responsibility: Accountability and citizenship in complex organisations.* Cambridge, UK: Cambridge University Press.

Bovens, M. (2010). Two concepts of accountability: Accountability as a virtue and as a mechanism. *West European Politics, 33* (5), 946–967. doi:10.1080/01402382.2010.486119.

Bovens, M., Shillemans, T., & Goodin, R. E. (2014). Public accountability. In M. Bovens, T. Shillemans, & R. E. Goodin (Eds.), *The Oxford Handbook of Public Accountability.* Retrieved August 8, 2019 from www.oxfordhandbooks.com.

Coombs, W. T. & Holladay, S. J. (2013). The pseudo-panpticon: The illusion created by CRS-related transparency and the internet. *Corporate Communication: An International Journal, 18* (2), 212–227.

De Colle, S., Henriques, A., & Sarasvathy, S. (2014). The paradox of corporate social responsibility standards. *Journal of Business Ethics, 125* (2), 177–191.

Flinders, M. (2014). The future and relevance of accountability studies. In M. Bovens, T. Shillemans, & R. E. Goodin (Eds.), *The Oxford Handbook of Public Accountability.* Retrieved August 8, 2019 from www.oxfordhandbooks.com.

Gailmard, S. (2012). Accountability and principal-agent theory. In M. Bovens, T. Shillemans, & R. E. Goodin (Eds.), *The Oxford Handbook of Public Accountability.* Retrieved August 8, 2019 from www.oxfordhandbooks.com.

Garsten, C. (2003). The cosmopolitan organization—an essay on corporate accountability. *Global Networks, 3* (3), 355–370. doi:10.1111/1471-0374.00066.

Gelb, D. S. & Strawser, J. A. (2001). Corporate social responsibility and financial disclosures: An alternative explanation for increased disclosure. *Journal of Business Ethics, 33*, 1–13.

Goetz, A. M. & Jenkins, R. (2002). Voice, accountability and human development: The emergence of a new agenda. Background paper for *Human Development Report 2002* (Report No. HDOCPA-2002–04). New York: United Nations Development Program. Retrieved August 8, 2019 from hdr.undp.org/en/reports/global/hdr2002/papers.

Gower, K. K. (2006). Truth and transparency. In K. Fitzpatrick & C. Bronstein (Eds.), *Ethics in public relations* (pp. 89–106). Thousand Oaks, CA: Sage.

Gutierrez, B. (2013, September 13). Matson apologizes for massive molasses spill in Honolulu Harbor. *HawaiiNewsNow.* Retrieved August 8, 2019 from Hawaiinewsnow.com.

Haines, N. (1955). Responsibility and accountability. *Philosophy, 30* (113), 141–163. Retrieved October 30, 2009 from www.jstor.org/stable/3748424.

Harmon, M. M. (1995). *Responsibility as paradox: A critique of rational discourse on government.* Thousand Oaks, CA: Sage.

Henderson, H. (2002). Tough talk for transnational corporations. *The Worldpaper.* Retrieved November 02, 2009 from www.lexisnexis.com.

Inefuku, T. (2017, January 19). EPA settlement resolves 2013 molasses spill into Honolulu Harbor. *Khon2.* Retrieved August 8, 2019 from www.khon2.com.

Koenig-Archibugi, M. (2004). Transnational corporations and public accountability. *Government & Opposition, 39* (2), 234–259. doi:10.1111/j.1477-7053.2004.00122.x.

Lewis, H. D. (1948). Collective responsibility. *Philosophy*, *23* (84), 3–18. Retrieved October 30, 2009 from www.jstor.org/stable/3747383.

MacLachlan, A. (2015). "Trust me, I'm sorry": The paradox of public apology. *Monist*, *98* (4), 441–456. Retrieved November 2, 2009 from www.jstor.org

Marshall, E. O. (2018). *Introduction to Christian ethics: Conflict, faith, and human life.* Louisville, KY: Westminster John Knox Press.

"Matson takes responsibility for Honolulu Harbor molasses spill." (2013, September 16). *PR Newswire*. Retrieved August 8, 2019 from www.investor.matson.com.

Maynard, M. (2010, February 24). In Congress, Toyota chief takes "full responsibility." *New York Times*. Retrieved February 24, 2010 from www.nytimes.com.

McKeon, R. (1960). The ethics of international influence. *Ethics*, *70* (3), 187–203. Retrieved February 24, 2010 from www.jstor.org.

Newton, L. H., Hodges, L., & Keith, S. (2004). Accountability in the professions: Accountability in journalism. *Journal of Mass Media Ethics*, *19* (3–4), 166–190.

Painter-Morland, M. (2006). Redefining accountability as relational responsiveness. *Journal of Business Ethics*, *66*, 89–98.

Peterson, V. C. (2002). *Beyond rules in society and business.* Cheltenham: Edward Elgar.

Rawlins, B. L. (2009). Give the emperor a new mirror: Toward developing a stakeholder measurement of organizational transparency. *Journal of Public Relations Research*, *21*, 71–99.

Roberts, N. C. (2002). Keeping public officials accountable through dialogue: Resolving the accountability paradox. *Public Administration Review*, *62* (6), 658–669.

Schneider, K. J. (1990). *The paradoxical self: Toward an understanding of our contradictory nature.* New York: Plenum Press. https://doi.org/10.1177/0022167814537889.

Schneider, K. J. (2014). My journal with Kierkegaard: From the paradoxical self to the polarized mind. *Journal of Humanistic Psychology*, *55* (4), 404–411.

Social accountability (2010). World Bank. Retrieved November 2, 2009 from http://go.worldbank.org/Y0UDF953DO0.

Stansbury, J. & Barry, B. (2007). Ethics programs and the paradox of control. *Business Ethics Quarterly*, *17* (2), 239–261.

Terenzio, C. (2018 April 11). Accountability is the best public relations strategy. Forbes Community Voice. Retrieved August 8, 2019 from www.forbes.com.

The gambler. (2017). Lyrics. Retrieved August 16, 2019 from lyrics.com.

The role of PR within CSR. (2009, January 29). *Business & Finance Magazine*. Retrieved November 2, 2009 from www.lexisnexis.com.

Ulmer, R. R., Sellnow, T. L., & Seeger, M. W. (2019). *Effective crisis communication: Moving from crisis to opportunity.* Thousand Oaks: Sage

Ulmer, R. R. (2012). Increasing the impact of thought leadership in crisis communication. *Management Communication Quarterly*, *26* (4), 523–542.

Utting, P. (2008). The struggle for corporate accountability. *Development & Change*, *39* (6), 959–975. doi:10.1111/j.1467-7660.2008.00523.x.

Wakefield, R. I. & Walton, S. B. (2010). The translucency corollary: Why full transparency is not always the most ethical approach. *Public Relations Journal*, *4* (4), 870–888.

Watzlawick, P., Weakland, J. H., & Fisch, R. (2011). *Change: Principles of problem formation and problem resolution.* New York: W. W. Norton.

6   The loyalty paradox

The Public Relations Society of America has enshrined loyalty as one of its six core values. "We are faithful to those we represent, while honoring our obligation to the public interest" (PRSA Member Statement of Professional Values, set out in PRSA Code of Ethics, n.d.). And yet public relations scholarship has virtually ignored loyalty as a professional value. Instead, loyalty is addressed as a by-product of communicative action. In practice, however, loyalty involves a number of virtues valued by public relations professionals, including courage, gratitude, and justice. Loyalty also can promote some well-known vices, such as chauvinism, nationalism, and barbarism (Ewin, 1993). The nature of one's loyalty often depends on a person's judgment. Choosing objects worthy of loyalty leads to positive outcomes while applying poor judgment in choosing loyalties tends to promote the opposite. The reason loyalty plays such a critical role in producing ethical or unethical behavior arises from the fact that loyalists subordinate their interests to their chosen objects of loyalty (Ewin, 1993). For public relations professionals, the implications of loyalty are even more significant because they serve as representatives, mouthpieces, and advocates for their organizations. They publicly defend their organizations' mission, values, products, and people. Ethical loyalists base their loyalty on more than being employed and earning a salary; their loyalty is founded on the legitimacy of organizational interests, purposes, and products and the virtue of its people (Ewin, 1993). These proximate, concrete loyalties exert a greater claim on personal loyalties than more abstract public interests. As Ewin (1993) described this counterintuitive approach, "Sacrificing the interests of the corporation to those of the nation is improper, and cannot be the basis of proper loyalty to the corporation" (p. 392).

Paradoxically, that is exactly what the PRSA statement asks practitioners to do. They represent the concrete interests of their clients but are expected to sacrifice or at least subordinate those interests when they conflict with the public interest. Indeed, their faithfulness to their organizations' purposes, products, and values is conditional on coinciding with higher-level abstractions, such as organization-public relationships and the public interest. The PRSA statement breaches the levels of abstraction by combining obligations to objects that represent two different logical types. The expectation to serve private interests while honoring an obligation to public interests inevitably produces paradox-ical tensions. To resolve the tension, public relations professionals and scholars contend that public obligations supersede private loyalties. And why not? It appears reasonable that the broader interests of the public should take prece-dence over more proximate personal interests, such as loyalty to co-workers or organizational leaders. But is that always the case? Does this shift moral respon-sibility away from the practitioner? How then is the practitioner to determine when an organization, acting in its own interests, undermines or endangers the interests of the public, the community, or society? Should a loyalty determined by the public exert equal or greater moral claims than personal, professional, and partisan loyalties? By looking at public relations loyalty through the lens of paradox, I argue that the loyal practitioner's first obligation is to concrete loyal-ties, those that exert the strongest moral claim on their devotions.

By honoring those obligations, practitioners will enhance personal respon-sibility and become truth seekers. More important, they will strengthen loyalty as a public virtue (Royce, 1908[1971]; Ewin, 1993). This paradoxical approach incorporates the dynamic equilibrium theory of paradox proposed by Smith and Lewis (2011). Dynamic equilibrium acknowledges that contradictory yet interrelated concepts create tension that can lead to virtuous or vicious cycles of behavior. The virtuous cycle occurs when practitioners choose legitimate loy-alties while the vicious cycles take over when practitioners become spectators and have their loyalties chosen for them. To some extent, contemporary public relations models propose that practitioners show loyalty to certain types of communicative practices and outcomes, such as symmetrical communication and dialog or to abstract notions of mutually beneficial relationships and rela-tionship management. This means moral autonomy and personal responsibility take a back seat to social roles and obligations.

In this chapter, I propose a different approach to public relations loyalty that prioritizes both personal and professional responsibilities and provides a pro-cess for choosing and testing the validity of one's loyalties. First, I introduce the theory of dynamic equilibrium and show how it applies to public relations loy-alty. Second, I will examine philosophies of loyalty, particularly the concept of loyalty to loyalty (Royce, 1908[1971]). Third, I will introduce economist Albert Hirschman's (1970) theory of exit, voice, and loyalty as an alternative decision-making model for testing the legitimacy of one's loyalty, particularly in the case of organizational deterioration and moral decline. Fourth, I will review how the public relations literature has dismissed loyalty as a by-product of commu-nicative action. Finally, I show how practitioners can invoke loyalty to loyalty in choosing objects of loyalty and employ exit, voice, and loyalty to test the virtue of those loyalties.

Dynamic equilibrium

Paradoxes exist in all organizations, but organizational actors fail to notice them until faced with organizational change, complexity, or deterioration. As noted in Chapter 1, organizational members expect organizations to know what they are doing, but the reality is that they inevitably encounter disorder (Weick, 1979). The resulting paradoxes are especially acute when the two opposing elements are interrelated, pressuring organizational actors to choose one or the other. Paradoxical tension arises from conflicts between narrower loyalties to one's organization and broader loyalties to the public. These contradictions exist in all individuals, organizations, and society. They are the product of plurality, change, scarcity, and complexity. In terms of loyalty, the paradoxes emerge from personal, family, professional, and occupational commitments. Smith and Lewis (2011) developed the dynamic equilibrium model of organizing to explain how contradictory elements become salient to organizational actors. As noted, these contradictory yet interrelated elements create tensions that lead to virtuous and vicious cycles of behavior. In the virtuous cycles, organizational actors accept paradoxical tensions and adopt proactive responses, such as splitting or integrating the contradictory elements. By embracing paradoxes, organizational actors enable "sustainability by fostering creativity and learning enabling flexibility and resilience, and unleashing human potential" (p. 394). In the vicious cycle, organizational members focus on one of the opposing elements, typically the more positive of the oppositional forces, and ignore or minimize the effects of the other. This kind of rational, logical approach results in magnifying and prolonging paradoxical tensions. In one case a corporate board placed too much emphasis on collaboration over individual initiative and ended up with rigidity and group think (Sundaramurthy & Lewis, 2003; Smith & Lewis, 2011). Another study found that "most management practices create their own nemesis" (Clegg, 2002, p. 491; quoted in Smith & Lewis, 2011, p. 391).

The dynamic equilibrium theory of paradox accepts paradoxical tensions as integral to complex systems and posits that responses to these tensions should be sustainable, repetitive, and simultaneous. In other words, paradoxes happen, so organizational members should take purposeful action to embrace them, deal with them, and learn from them. Paradox theory works best to deal with persistent and synergistic tensions. "At its core a paradox theory presumed that tensions are integral to complex systems and that sustainability depends on attending to contradictory yet interwoven demands simultaneously" (Smith & Lewis, 2011, p. 397).

The PRSA Statement of Professional Values regarding loyalty implies this kind of simultaneous attention to private and public loyalties. Though interrelated, private and public loyalties represent two different classes of activity, one operating at a concrete level of action and the other existing at a higher level of abstraction. Bateson (2000) described the Theory of Logical Types as a communication theory in which a class cannot be one of its members and the members cannot be the class. In other words, loyalty to an organization exists at the different logical level than loyalty to society. No matter how much we might try to address these two loyalties at the same time, they still exist at different logical levels. The key for public relations practitioners is to find a way to move their obligation to serve public interests to the same level of abstraction as their narrower loyalties to their client or organization. This will require an approach to loyalty that provides a way for practitioners to choose private loyalties that reflect public values. Hirschman's (1970) theory of exit, voice, and loyalty provides a formula for practitioners to create the dynamic equilibrium necessary to balance private and public loyalties.

Exit, voice, and loyalty

The rise and fall of organizations is a natural if not inevitable process of the competitive market system (Hirschman, 1970). Factors shaping the development of organizations include age, size, stages in evolution, growth rate of the industry, and economic turbulence (Greiner, 1998). More recently, technology has put extreme pressure on organizations to find ways to transform, re-engineer, and improve (Dervitsiotis, 1998). Hirschman (1970) noted that with the passage of time, the rationale that guided decisions in an organization's early years often fails to deal with contemporary problems and conditions. Less-experienced people replace veterans, increasing the likelihood of mistakes, miscommunication, and mismanagement. Over time these changes can result in inferior products, poor decisions, and ethical shortcuts.

As quality drops, customers stop buying and employees begin leaving, signaling a problem exists and needs to be remedied. This is known as exit. When customers or employees remain with the firm and protest quality declines to management, they invoke the voice option. In theory, exit leads to re-engineering and revival (Hirschman, 1970, pp. 21–29), but it only works if drops in consumer demand or the departures of organizational members are significant enough to attract management's attention. In instances of high demand and low supply (little or no competition), customers and employees may stick with a firm because they have no alternatives. In industries where prices remain constant, such as with gas stations, it may serve some organizations' best interests to maintain competition and keep consumers searching for improved products that do not exist (pp. 27–28). Relationships play a minor role, because the company simply replaces those lost to exit with new customers or employees.

In a more competitive environment, customers and employees can exit at the first signs of decline. Exit without voice is generally motivated by simple self-interest, a calculated quid pro quo. If all the customers exited at the same time, a firm might collapse and never recover. "For competition (exit) to work as a mechanism of recuperation from performance lapses, it is generally best for a firm to have a mixture of alert and inert customers" (Hirschman, 1970, p. 24). Alert members and customers are most sensitive to a quality decline and tend to leave first. The exit of these alert stakeholders means the organization may lose those "who could best help fight its shortcomings and its difficulties" (p. 79). Inert customers generally provide companies with time to make corrections. Sometimes exit alone may attract management's attention and allow for the organization to correct the problems that led to the decline. This is not always the case, however, especially if replacements are readily available or the culture of the organization has undermined individual freedom and autonomy.

Not all alert members and customers exit at the first signs of trouble. Some feel bound to the organization and resort to voice by appealing directly to management or to some group or individual with the power to influence management to make changes. Inherent in the use of voice is a belief in organizational purposes and values and management's capacity to make necessary course corrections. When voice fails, exit serves as a last resort (Hirschman, 1970, pp. 36–37). The degree to which customer-members will trade the certainty of exit for the uncertainties of some future organizational improvement is what Hirschman defined as loyalty. Thus, loyalty arises from a deeper belief in organizational goals and leaders.

Loyalty "activates voice" (Hirschman, 1970, p. 78) and holds exit at bay. The likelihood of voice increases in proportion to the amount of influence members and customers feel they have in the organization. Despite stakeholders' affinity for the organization, they still retain a sense of personal responsibility. As Henry David Thoreau wrote, "It is truly enough said that a corporation has no conscience; but a corporation of conscientious men is a corporation with a conscience" (as cited in Simon & Wylie, 1993, p. xiv). Loyalty is not an act of faith, but a "reasoned calculation" that over a period of time the right decisions of "conscientious men" and women will more than balance out the wrong ones they may make (Hirschman, 1970, pp. 78–79).

Whistle blowers would qualify as loyalists if they still believe in the organization's capacity to change if pressure comes from the outside. In these extreme conditions, the loyalist might believe strongly in the mission of the organization but discovers that no matter what concerns are voiced internally, key leaders will not listen. Loyalty remains a virtue as long as one believes in the virtuous character of the organization despite the actions of those who the loyalist believes have deviated from the organization's mission and values. Whistle blowers generally have lost faith in company leaders or fear retribution if they speak out. In some cases, however, whistle blowers may realize the only way to influence intransient or even good-intentioned leaders is to go public. Loyalists generally use internal channels to voice concerns, but may have to resort to making dissent public when paradoxically proximate and broader loyalties take precedence. In other words, one's personal loyalty to organizational values and the long-term health of the organization coincide with the loyalty of others. These are the same values that the loyalist universalized as being legitimate when accepting the organization as an object of loyalty. In this case, the long-term health of the organization and community are the same. This is especially true in cases in which organizational behavior poses a threat to its character (and ultimately its reputation) and the welfare of members of the organization and their community. The public relations practitioner's personal integrity and broader loyalties to community coincide, causing one to blow the whistle and go public with one's concerns in hopes of alerting management to a needed change of course.

Bok (1989) identified "dissent" as the first of the three elements of whistle blowing. The other two were breach of loyalty and accusation. In an approach that reflects a recognition of public and private loyalties, Bok wrote that whistle blowers "make revelations meant to call attention to negligence, abuses, or dangers that threaten the public interest" (p. 211). Whistle blowing also is considered a "breach of loyalty" because the whistle blower pits an insider's obligations to clients and colleagues against broader public interests (p. 214). However, instead of a breach of loyalty, this could qualify as a more ethical loyalty because those leading the organization have ignored or neglected those virtues that earned one's loyalty in the first place. Bok's final element, "accusation," accuses superiors of an unethical or illegal abuse of public trust. Accusation differs from voice in that the goal is not to influence leaders but to have them removed and replaced. In summary, the loyalist becomes a whistle blower and publicizes voice only as a last resort—when an external public is the only group that can influence a change in course, especially in cases in which organizational decline threatens the public welfare. The whistle blower who called attention to President Trump's actions requesting Ukraine to investigate Joe Biden seems to have felt that only a broader public could influence the President to change course because the President refused to listen to State Department insiders.

Some have argued that the downsizing of the 1980s and early 1990s, and the high-tech economy of the 2000s, undermined the importance of loyalty (We aren't all free agents, 1999, p. 47). Some in the computer industry question whether loyalty is an asset or a liability (Loyalty: Asset or liability?, 1999, p. 52). However, after the 2009 recession, a third of employees in one survey actually said the economic downturn had made them more loyal, and the majority of the others surveyed said it made no difference (Economic recession raising loyalty, 2010). Starting in the late 1990s, a new definition of loyalty emerged in which workers held companies more accountable by demanding employee ownership plans, influence, and recognition of other loyalties, such as family, church, and personal growth (Laabs, 1998; Profits from loyalty, 1998; Hays, 1999). More recently, millennials have begun to define loyalty based on their assigned job. Once that job is mastered, they move to a new organization and a new opportunity. Thus, they are more likely to change jobs than past generations (Murdock, 2017; The 2019 employee engagement report, 2019).

Reichheld (1996) argued that businesses rise and fall depending on the loyalty or defection of customers, employees, and investors. The better an organization listens to its members and customers, the more likely it will recognize organizational decline. Research on Hirschman's (1970) exit, voice, and loyalty model supports Reichheld's conclusion that voice and loyalty increase with the expectation that one's voice can make a difference. Freeman (1980) showed that union contracts reduced exit by providing opportunities for workers to voice dissatisfaction with conditions (see also Freeman & Medoff, 1984). Cahuc and Kramarz (1997) also found reduced employee turnover when power was exchanged for loyalty. When customers and employees feel that management will listen and respond to voice, they will stick with the company, fully expecting declines to be temporary and reversible (Cusack, 2009). One does not need to wield great power and influence in organizational decisions to qualify as a loyalist, but Hirschman (1970) contended that loyalty can hardly exist "without the expectation that someone will act or something will happen to improve matters" (p. 78). To remain with an organization populated by managers unwilling to change or improve is not loyalty; it qualifies as an internal exit from personal responsibility. This internal exit may help reduce the moral discomfort created by the organization's economic or moral deterioration, but it also transforms loyalty into passive submission and subjugation.

For example, what Hobson (1997) called "individual voice" reflects this kind of internal exit and no longer serves as an act of loyalty. "Individual voice expressed by avoiding work and withholding enthusiasm appears to be common across diverse settings" (p. 1208). Avoiding work or withholding enthusiasm is indicative of a lack of faith in the organization's capacity to change. In other words, organizational members have renounced their loyalty and replaced it with disloyalty. They remain with the group but resort to voice that expedites deterioration. They have made an internal exit while physically remaining with the organization (Turnley & Feldman, 1999).

Further support for this explanation comes from Boroff and Lewin (1997), who studied employees reporting unfair treatment by employers. Loyal employees were less likely to exercise voice or leave the firm and more likely to "suffer in silence" (p. 9; see also Barry, 1974; Birch, 1975). In other words, instead of holding exit at bay, as Hirschman (1970) attested, this type of loyalty promotes internal exits that allow members to remain with the organization despite dissatisfaction with its performance. One could argue that an internal exit is not loyalty but a surrender to the status quo. Submissive employees transform loyalty into a vice because they no longer choose their loyalties. They become pawns, having their loyalties chosen for them. According to Harvard philosopher Josiah Royce (1908[1971]), an ethical loyalty must be freely chosen or it will undermine the validity of all loyalty. Royce's approach to loyalty helps to resolve the paradox of public relations loyalty by providing a way for practitioners to determine when our loyalties are no longer worthy of our devotion.

Loyalty to loyalty

> Loyalty, the desire to be and remain with the group, the willingness to bear some cost for that and, at least to an extent, to take the interests of others as one's own, is the raw material for the virtues. It is also the raw material for at least some of the vices.
>
> (Ewin, 1992, p. 419)

Philosophers have generally neglected any discussion about loyalty despite the fact that loyalty "is the most common thing in the world for a person to decide that he should (or should not) do so-and-so on grounds of loyalty to his friend, family, organization, community, country, or species" (Oldenquist, 1982, p. 173). Writing in 1908, Josiah Royce (1908[1971]) proposed that loyalty, if properly defined, was "the fulfillment of the whole moral law" (p. 15). He defined loyalty as "The willing and practical and thoroughgoing devotion of a person to a cause." This devotion must be expressed "in some sustained and practical way, by acting steadily in the service of [the] cause" (p. 17). Royce urged people to freely choose or find a cause and "serve it with all your might and soul and strength; but so choose your cause, and so serve it, that thereby you show forth your loyalty to loyalty" (p. 138; as cited in Fletcher, 1993, p. 152). Poorly chosen causes (or organizations) undermine loyalty's value as a moral law. The opposite also is true. Aligning with a good, noble cause strengthens loyalty as a moral law for ourselves and others. In other words, the very act of choosing a narrow loyalty affects the broader loyalties, not only of the individual but of society as a whole.

Fletcher (1993) defined loyalty to loyalty as meaning, "each person should exercise the maximum amount of loyalty compatible with respect for the loyalty of others" (p. 152). Unlike Royce, however, Fletcher contended that loyalties are inherited and not freely chosen. I argue that there comes a time when even inherited loyalties must be chosen, or the loyalist exercises no moral autonomy. Failure to universalize loyalty or determine whether it strengthens or undermines the loyalties of others denigrates loyalty into blind obedience, submission, and self-deception. Thus, employees avoiding work or sabotaging the operation would exhibit disloyalty because they would undermine the loyalty of others. Suffering in silence also fails Royce's loyalty-to-loyalty test because it releases customers and employees from any moral obligation to try to correct problems. Silent suffering is not loyalty, but submission.

Blind obedience, Ladd (1968) wrote, perverts loyalty because it lacks the moral value of showing loyalty to something worthy of that loyalty. "A loyal Nazi is a contradiction in terms, although a loyal German is not" (p. 98). However, loyalty is not just a reciprocal relationship of binding oneself to a group because it merits loyalty. Ewin (1992) noted that reciprocity "is simply accepting the best tender, and loyalty requires an emotional commitment that goes beyond such commercial-sounding calculation" (p. 406). Loyalists often sacrifice for the group without expecting to receive an equal amount in return. One might remain loyal despite the realization that present circumstances might delay or deny an equitable return on investment. Social relationships governed by reciprocity, warned John Durham Peters (1999), can deteriorate into "a monotonous round of quid pro quo" (p. 56). He argued that other principles, such as hospitality, gift giving, forgiveness, and love, are just as crucial as reciprocity.

In the corporate world, loyalists believe in the company's purpose, products, and people, but more important, they embrace the company's values and standards (Ewin, 1993). One's loyalty is not to a specific person but to what that person represents "as the manager devoted to the corporation's proper ends, and it is only devotion to the firm's proper ends, which include concern with the excellence of the product, that will earn that loyalty" (p. 394). In other words, my loyalty to organizational leaders is dependent on upon their shared commitment to those qualities that promote loyalty to loyalty. However, people and organizations are susceptible to the ups and downs of the economy, new technology, political unrest, and the fickle nature of organizational stakeholders. Worthwhile organizations also are subject to human error, poor management, and shortsighted decision-making. However, even the best-run organizations can be subject to deterioration and decline. As noted, loyalty is not just based on paychecks, personal relationships, and comfortable routines. These are easily discarded when a better alternative comes along. Deeper loyalties, those most morally defensible, reflect a commitment to universal principles, goals, and values.

> Where we are loyal to a group, then, we have come to entertain certain social beliefs and practices. To the group, an abstraction, we are never truly loyal. To the group, the living embodiment of all those things we believe, do, and feel, we cheerfully give our allegiance because in doing so we are simply gazing at ourselves in social breadth. These, then, constitute not the basis of our loyal ties but our deepest loyalties. For the constancy of a relationship to some group persists only as long as the group stands for these underlying activities, whether in actuality or in symbolic reference.
>
> (Bloch, 1966, p. 52)

Bloch's (1966) deeper loyalties move one beyond individual personalities and preferences to values and purposes shared by the group, whether it be the public or one's organization. It focuses loyalty on the collective will of the group, what it has achieved, what it contributes now, and what it can accomplish in the future. This kind of commitment expands one's personal responsibility to abide by universal human values. According to Royce (1908[1971]), loyalty is not a passive state, inevitably determined by history and tradition, but an active process in which the individual seeks after universal truths and loyalties. The seeker of truth is loyal to loyalty because "whatever [the] truth you try to discover is, if true, valid for everybody, and is therefore worthy of everybody's loyal recognition" (p. 376). Ethical loyalty goes beyond fulfilling physical needs; it is a commitment to universal values, such as honesty, fidelity, doing good, non-maleficence, gratitude, freedom, and justice.

A person governed simply by emotions, desires, and cognitive needs is what Danish philosopher Soren Kierkegaard (1843[1983], 1846[1987]) called the aesthetic (also spelled "esthetic") person. In his History of Philosophy, Frederick Copleston (1985) described Kierkegaard's "aesthetic consciousness" as the absence of "fixed universal moral standards and of determinate religious faith" (p. 342). For Kierkegaard (1846[1941]), the aestheticist can be a young man with great potential or a sexual predator, both of whom experiment with everything but without ever becoming anything. Both lead inauthentic lives doomed to despair. To overcome despair, they must choose and commit to, both acts of self-will, universals and higher moral laws (Kierkegaard, 1846[1941], pp. 119–121, 262–264). The authentic or ethical person gains ethical form and consistency through these acts of choice and commitment (see Copleston, 1985, p. 342). Kierkegaard's (1843[1983]) loyalist is like the authentic tragic hero who sacrifices himself and everything that is his for the universal; "his act and every emotion in him belong to the universal; he is open, and in this disclosure he is the beloved son of ethics" (p. 113; see also Copleston, 1985, p. 343).

Loyalists resort to voice, despite its risks, because they believe in the organization, its mission, its people, and its ability to change and improve. To exit at the first hint of problems would indicate that one had not committed in the first place. One would expect organizational members to harbor a greater commitment than customers, but the more closely the loyalty is based on a common cause or mission, the more likely that customers would move beyond the aesthetic to embrace the authentic. By Hirschman's (1970) definition of loyalty, customers and members surrender some certainty of exit for the uncertainty of voice because they believe in the capacity of the organization and its members to recuperate. As Hirschman contended, the most alert members or customers are likely the ones best able to help an organization recover from a crisis or decline. As a truth seeker, the loyalist would qualify as an alert organizational member who would be among the first to notice deterioration in the quality of products, performance, or relationships. Instead of exiting, however, loyalists activate and facilitate voice, two duties inherent in contemporary public relations.

Loyalty and public relations

The Public Relations Society of America institutionalized practitioner loyalty as one of its six core professional values, but then confused the levels of abstraction by bifurcating that loyalty between the private interests of clients and the broader interests of the public. Practitioners are expected to defend and promote their companies' products and actions (White & Dozier, 1992, p. 103), but only as long as those products and actions conform to the public interest. The public expects companies to produce quality products or services and to act in a socially, environmentally, and morally responsible way (Dilenschneider & Salak, 2003; Pruzan, 1998). Crises or cases of organizational deterioration and decline may for a time put private interests in conflict with public interests, but the practitioner may still believe in the organization's mission, values, and people. PRSA and public relations scholars offer little guidance on how practitioners should deal with such situations. Indeed, if practitioners desert an organization in its greatest need, they undermine loyalty's value to themselves and their profession. These are serious considerations for public relations to consider, but the profession and the academy offer little guidance. Public relations research all but ignores practitioner loyalty but instead focuses on loyalty as a by-product of dialog, symmetrical communication, and relationships.

The lack of interest in the loyalty of the individual practitioner arises from the paradoxical tension created from serving self-interests and public interests at the same time. In an effort to make public relations more palatable to the academy and the public, public relations scholars have embraced abstract commitments. The idea of developing relationships with other people has been replaced by cultivating relationships between organizations. With good intentions, public relations scholars have placed emphasis on communication processes and symmetrical group relationships. Organization-public relationships are based on reciprocity, exchange, and interdependence (Broom, Casey, & Ritchey, 2000, p. 17). Interdependence means that the success of the organization rests on its effectiveness in selling products while at the same time winning public approval for its mission and practices. This includes how the organization treats its customers, employees, community, and the environment. Relationships emerge as key publics become aware of shared cultural and social perceptions and expectations (Broom et al., 2000).

A popular public relations textbook has long advocated the field's role in building mutually beneficial relationships (Cutlip, Center, & Broom, 2000). It is assumed that loyalty is shared between the parties involved in the relationship. Interdependence and relationships, however, take loyalty out of the hands of the practitioner and turn it over to the communication process of developing and maintaining relationships that promote mutual respect and change. By focusing on relationships and then communicating that focus to key publics, an organization produces more loyalty (Ledingham & Bruning, 2000, p. 66). Loyalty results from "known organizational activities that demonstrate openness, trust, commitment, and investment" (Wilson, 2000, p. 138). These types of relationships engender loyalty among organizational stakeholders. While business and marketing relationships are based on exchanging one thing of value for another or producing goods to meet customer needs, public relations relationships are based on openness, dialog, and mutuality. Practitioners are expected to subordinate their interests and the interests of their organizations to agenda-free communication outcomes that create and maintain reciprocal, interdependent public relationships. This approach, however, contrasts with loyalty as defined in the PRSA Statement of Professional Values because it mandates that practitioners neither represent the interests of their clients or the public but prioritize mutual interests.

A commitment to mutual interests helps to maintain relationships and build "greater employee loyalty and productivity" (Center & Jackson, 2003, p. 2). Through the ethical use of dialog, practitioners also promote social responsibility (Pearson, 1989; Leeper, 1996). Using technology, they identify key publics and engage in dialogs that produce mutually beneficial relationships (Heath, 1998). Cutlip et al. (2000) argued that a key objective of public relations was to help organizations adjust and adapt to the public interest. These prosocial actions also produce loyalty outcomes that strengthen and build community (Kruckeberg & Starck, 1988; Leeper, 1996). Public relations also serves to inform stakeholders and customers that they have been heard and their voices have made a difference. A leading professional described effective public relations as informing management about what the organization's key constituencies are thinking and then showing "to those constituents how their input has helped inform top management's decisions" (Mieszkowski, 1998, pp. 195–196). Focusing on key constituencies, however, leaves out other publics, particularly those unwilling to engage in dialog or symmetrical communication.

External loyalties are shaped by the loyalty object's capacity to reciprocate and support organizational interests. This kind of loyalty weakens broader loyalties because it is dependent upon quid-pro-quo exchanges. Stated another way, symmetrical communication's reliance on negotiation, reciprocity, and mutuality engenders trust and loyalty. On the other hand, it also promotes a reciprocal relationship in which loyalty depends on the other party's potential for returns of equal value. One need only consider the ramifications of Dilenschneider's (1990) "favor bank" to see the potential dangers in pure symmetry. According to Dilenschneider, those with power and influence leverage stakeholders who are dependent on one's services, pick only favors that do not cost anything to do, avoid those who cannot return favors of equal value, seek credit for one's favors, and advertise the favors performed (pp. 11–17). The favor bank provides a model for serving mutual self-interests, and makes loyalty conditional on the other party's ability to reciprocate. Although a worthy ideal, two-way symmetrical communication and dialog theory place more emphasis on the communicative processes and outcomes than on whether practitioners choose worthy objects of loyalty. Indeed, loyalty paradoxically emerges as a self-interested outcome of the process rather than a catalyst for virtuous action in behalf of a cause or organization.

The process of relating and communication are important, but the other side of the paradox empowers the practitioner to actively choose loyalties and then promote public loyalties within the organization. Public relations practitioners show loyalty to loyalty by persuading management that the organization's interests are intertwined with the interests of the community. This is especially true if the values and mission of the organization coincide with public and community values. Promoting values that cut across organizational and community boundaries strengthens loyalty to the organization as well as enhancing loyalty as a virtue. Public loyalties are manifest through universal private loyalties. Problems arise, however, when practitioners assume that they can represent the public to the organization. Harold Burson, founder of one of the country's largest public relations agencies, may have had this role in mind when he identified being a corporate conscience as basic to the public relations job description (Simon & Wylie, 1993). Ostensibly, as a corporate conscience or public advocate, the practitioner serves as the voice of the public inside the organization. But this role compromises the practitioner's loyalty to the organization. To be loyal and a corporate conscience, practitioners must also represent the organization to itself. That means giving voice to the values and purposes that practitioners first embraced as worthy of their loyalty and the loyalty of others. Based on dynamic equilibrium, both interrelated elements, though contradictory, are true, and practitioners must strike a balance between those loyalties.

Anytime public relations professionals find themselves disagreeing with management decisions, their first loyalty is to the more identifiable purposes and values of the organization. Having subjected their interests to the organization, they have already indicated that the organization's values are in line with their personal values. Thus, they can give voice to personal and internal group concerns that management decisions conflict with the purposes and values that they themselves represent. Second, they can communicate public concerns and express the public implications of organizational behavior that conflicts with broader societal values. The very act of giving voice to their concerns shows that practitioners believe that they can influence management to change plans or stop programs altogether. Organizational leaders may disagree with opinions voiced by public relations practitioners but accept their counsel, not because it reflects a public consciousness, but because they have appealed to the mission and values shared by practitioners and organizational leaders.

For example, a year after joining a worldwide financial organization, a practitioner (K. T., personal communication with promise of anonymity, November 14, 2002) with more than ten years of experience helped change the marketing plan for a new payment card product aimed at the $150 million teenage market. The product team wanted to market the cards directly to teens, but the public relations department took "the high road" on the issue. Public relations argued for policies that would restrict member banks from marketing to teens and also insisted that parents buying the card would agree to a financial skills assessment.

> Now our product team here probably would have not have done that if we would not have brought our influence to bear, insisted on some of these things that we thought it was necessary to protect the brand and take the responsible approach in doing it.
>
> (K. T., personal communication, November 14, 2003)

The public relations department took a lot of criticism but stood its ground.

C. C. (personal communication, March 13, 1998), a practitioner with 30 years of experience in manufacturing, often voiced opposition to "powerful manager-types" who perceived public relations as making up outrageous claims or saying whatever would sell the product. On occasion, a company president would ask C. C. to come up with a way to make a hazardous product, process, or procedure appear safe. C. C. made effective use of voice by identifying worst case scenarios, inconsistencies in the company's position, and potential responses from the media. As a last resort, C. C. would contend that, "What we are saying is an outright lie, and I will resign before I let this company release this information." He said one must be prepared to follow through on that threat.

Hirschman (1970) argued that the use of voice demanded more courage and creativity, and he emphasized that voice is most effective when backed by the threat of exit (pp. 82–83). Practitioners may not wield the influence necessary to improve conditions in an organization unless they are willing to place their job on the line to bring about change. In other words, the ultimate act of loyalty may be to risk the loss of one's job to promote the overall welfare of the organization and society. As the organization's private and social conscience, C. C. (personal communication, March 13, 1998) often found that arguing against the "popular" position did persuade the top brass to rethink their position. However, asking "Can you imagine the headlines this would make?" and then coming up with all sorts of expository and embarrassing headlines actually opened eyes.

C. C.'s experience raises the question as to whether loyalty to principle equates with loyalty to society. Parsons (1993) argued that practitioners owed their highest loyalty to society, with self, organization, and profession coming in second—in no particular order. Self, organization, and profession are essentially subsets of one's loyalty to society, and the professional "should have other significant reasons for choosing an alternative" (p. 56). However, Parsons did not say what those significant reasons might be. She did say that the practitioner's loyalty to society required refusing to follow orders and trying to change the organization's approach before resigning and risking negative effects on society. By associating resigning with negative effects on society, Parsons implied that leaving a bad situation would be in the best interests of the practitioner but not necessarily in the best interests of the organization or society. Parsons gave little guidance in determining when leaving or staying would produce the greatest benefits for society.

A survey of 100 subscribers to *PR Journal* revealed that they were conflicted about whether they owed their greatest loyalty to society or to the client. This conflict is further complicated by a free-market system in which society or the public interest benefits as a whole from the efforts of individuals serving their self-interests. Bivins (1993) noted that professionals can serve the public interest by championing the cause of their clients. Martinson (1995[1996]) argued that loyalty to a client or management did not necessarily conflict with broader loyalties to society as long as "no direct harm is done to others or the public interest" (p. 3). However, this logic seems contradictory. If serving the client serves the public interest, then serving the client would not cause harm to others or the public interest. This presents a circular argument—serving the client serves the public interest; serving the public interest serves the client (Judd, 1989).

Like Parsons (1993), Martinson (1995[1996]) presented another version of this argument when he contended that society benefits from a practitioner's loyalty to a client or organization, as long as this narrower loyalty does not necessarily conflict with broader loyalties to society. However, this provides little guidance to a practitioner facing situations where loyalty to the organization conflicts with society on some issues and not others. Royce (1908[1971]) provided a solution that does not create discontinuity in the levels of abstraction. Loyalty to loyalty would require practitioners to choose a client or organization possessing the qualities worthy of a universal loyalty. Showing loyalty to an organization to which all might not be loyal perverts the value of loyalty. Even when choosing loyalty to loyalty, one's loyalty might conflict with society now and again, but one could justify continued association based on loyalty to the organization's constitutional mission and vision. The question is not whether serving the client serves the public interest or society but whether one shows loyalty to loyalty in choosing and continuing to associate with worthwhile causes.

The practitioner's loyalty to the organization plays a critical role in developing public relationships because the practitioner interacts with more authenticity and passion. Authentic interactions produce more loyalty on both sides of the relationship. Public relations also enables voice to influence management and bring about organizational recuperation. Practitioners' sensitivity to public relationships empowers them to advocate for the public while serving partisan interests. Problems arise, however, from a lack of clarity as to how to handle loyalty conflicts between society and the client organization. Dialogic models mandate that loyalty is equally meted out to all parties with the goal of achieving understanding, agreement, and consensus, but this diffusion of loyalty undermines moral autonomy and personal responsibility. An equitable distribution of loyalty also conflicts with professionalism and its implication that one's greatest loyalty is to the public interest. Equating service to the client with service to society also creates a circular argument and provides little effectual guidance to practitioners facing loyalty conflicts. A better approach is to encourage loyalty to loyalty, standing by organizations worthy of loyalty even when they succumb to the effects of market deterioration (Hirschman, 1970).

Loyalty as virtue and vice

In the competitive marketplace, the natural ups and downs of organizational life make exit, voice, and loyalty factors in every organization. As monitors of the organization's relationships, as communicators of organizational policy and activities, as counselors in organizational decision-making, and as spokespersons for the decision-makers, public relations practitioners are directly affected by deterioration. They are the alert members most sensitive to the ebb and flow of organizational performance. They also are most apt to contribute to the organization's recuperation. Communicating loyalty strengthens relationships and increases the likelihood that organizational stakeholders will delay exit to give voice a chance. By augmenting and facilitating voice, public relations may persuade alert customers and members to remain loyal and eschew the certainty of exit for the uncertainty of recuperation.

Public relations' approach to loyalty has long reflected Kierkegaard's aesthetic consciousness: The field has been governed by a desire to defend its role as a partisan, advocate, and loyalist. With the best of intentions, public relations scholars have espoused obligations to a variety of abstract concepts, such as the public interest, mutually beneficial relationships, two-way symmetrical communication, dialog, and corporate social responsibility. The field continues to experiment with everything without ever becoming sure about anything. Indeed, public relations properly practiced should communicate an organization's deepest loyalties, those arising from its purpose and values. The manner in which practitioners communicate those loyalties is not as important as their decision as to whether those loyalties could be shared by others. Their private loyalties then become public loyalties and have the power to enhance the value of loyalty across personal, professional, and organizational relationships. They also establish a concrete formula for honoring legitimate loyalties even through the ups and downs of the market economy.

Public relations also can help management by giving voice to those who choose early exits. An early exit by the practitioner might deny management the negative feedback necessary to bring about change and improvement. Loyalty to loyalty would not justify an immediate exit for aesthetic reasons. Early exits may serve one's self-interest but, if universalized for all practitioners, might mean leaving organizations at the time of their greatest need for public relations support. Internal exits or suffering in silence also are morally suspect. Mike McCurry ("McCurry on McCurry," 1999), former White House press secretary under President Bill Clinton, avoided seeking the truth about Monica Lewinski. Defending the President in public would have undermined his work, and so he "delegated controversy and scandal to the specialists—the lawyers" ("McCurry on McCurry," 1999, p. 3). McCurry later wondered whether he did the right thing. He applied an aesthetic justification, saying that he stayed out of the information loop because paying for a legal defense would have been a financial burden. By choosing to stay out of the controversy, McCurry robbed the President of counsel from arguably one of history's best press secretaries. The decision haunted him after he left the White House.

As practitioners show loyalty to loyalty or loyalty to universal values, they empower their voices with the threat of exit, signaling that their commitment to the deeper loyalties goes beyond their loyalty to the organization. S. B. (personal communication, April 5, 1999), who logged nearly 20 years with a major electric and power company, said company executives would not ask her to mislead the public because they knew she would refuse to do it. Practitioners unwilling to make such a commitment are candidates for an internal exit, an exit from personal and professional values and ethics.

Loyalty expresses a faith and optimism in the ability of organizations and people to respond to public relations counsel and do the right thing. Refusing to give voice to one's concerns forsakes responsibility. Philosophers and public relations scholars argue that the broader loyalties to the public and society should take precedence over narrower loyalties to friends, family, colleagues, and self. However, loyalty to loyalty is at once loyal to society and loyal to self.

It exists at the same level of abstraction. This approach embraces the paradoxical nature of public relations loyalty and applies a dynamic equilibrium that balances loyalties to one's organization and society. For Royce, there are times when one's loyalty to society reflects personal loyalties to the values and principles governing society. Whether in an organization or a family, one never loses membership in the larger community of humanity. Based on Ewin's (1992) definition, loyalty means remaining with the group, bearing the cost of that decision, and taking the interests of others as one's own. Practitioners rise above the aesthetic when they put the collective welfare of the whole ahead of concerns over their own careers. If they contributed to the organization's past success, they also contributed to its inevitable decline. The loyal public relations practitioner remains with an organization despite deterioration and looks at exit as a last resort, a decision reached only after exhausting voice options.

There is rarely a problem with having too much voice (Hirschman, 1970), but the loyal practitioners, after having voiced personal or group concerns, must consider the effectiveness of voice in bringing about change. This does not mean that one's concerns have to be heeded, but the expectation of having an influence at the moment of expression or at some future time must exist. The organization may reject public relations counsel and still remain worthy of loyalty. To simply jump ship because management refused to consider public relations counsel calls into question the legitimacy of the loyalty and the practitioner's commitment to the object of loyalty. The only exception to this approach may be if management asks the practitioner to act contrary to personal and professional values, such as a demand for dishonesty. Even then, loyalty would require creativity, voice, and the threat of exit.

Superiors who stifle voice and dissent assume infallibility and impose a form of tyranny that persecutes or marginalizes diverse opinions. "To refuse a hearing to an opinion, because they are sure that it is false, is to assume that their certainty is the same thing as absolute certainty" (Mill, 1859[2002], p. 19). To universalize one's loyalty to such a person or persons would undermine the liberty of the loyalist as well as any other person willing to express voice. The same is true for showing loyalty to a person of influence who refuses to pass along the practitioner's concerns to the dominant coalition. As Mill said, "If we were never to act on our opinions, because those opinions may be wrong, we should leave all our interests uncared for, and all our duties unperformed" (p. 20). In this instance, continued loyalty becomes a vice because management has cultivated a "yes man" culture that supersedes otherwise honorable organizational missions, values, or goals. As Ladd (1968) said, loyalty loses its moral value when choosing to show loyalty to persons, objects, causes, or organizations unworthy of that loyalty. Moral loyalty could never justify such statements as, "I was just following orders. It was my job. I didn't have a choice."

One has to determine whether top management has the capacity to change. If practitioners' protests have no influence whatsoever and there is little to no chance that their voices will be heard in the future, then their loyalty to higher values of authenticity, character, and integrity require exit. This reflects one's loyalty to loyalty, a reconciliation of one's narrower loyalties to personal and professional integrity and one's broader loyalties to the organization, community, and humanity. Ethical loyalty separates the decision from the aesthetics—financial uncertainty, social sanctions, and emotional discomfort—and aligns it with the authentic—character, integrity, freedom, and responsibility (Stoker, 1995).

Thus, loyalty to a struggling organization or one embroiled in a crisis is a virtue as long as public relations practitioners perceive that giving voice to their concerns will make a difference. Practitioners do not need to have a direct influence on decision makers but at least have an influence on the influential—those who do have the power to bring about change. As long as hope for change exists, the practitioner serves the narrower interests of fellow employees and the broader interests of the public by helping the organization recover and reassume its role as a productive member of society. The loyal practitioner will use reason, creativity, expertise, experience, wit, and the threat of exit to counteract forces contributing to the organization's decline.

To depart too soon and desert one's organization or cause in its time of distress would promote one's aesthetic self-interests over organizational and community interests and undermine the loyalty of others. If organizational leaders refuse to listen, disregard negative feedback, and pursue a course of action contrary to one's personal and social conscience, the public relations practitioner must exit. Remaining with an organization or cause in which one sees no possibility of change or improvement transforms a virtuous loyalty into a vice.

A moral autonomous loyalty

Public relations professionals are expected to show loyalty to the interests of their clients and organization as well as the public. However, public relations scholarship has provided little guidance on how practitioners can resolve the paradoxical nature of private and public loyalties. Instead, the literature focuses on loyalty as a by-product of public relations processes and outcomes rather than a virtue or moral duty of public relations professionals. Broader public loyalties are to take precedence over narrower loyalties, despite the fact that they are more abstract and have less of a moral claim on the loyalist. To resolve the paradox of public relations loyalty, I argue that the field focus on the narrower, private loyalties and the decision-making process that goes into choosing loyalties and ethically representing those loyalties. Once practitioners choose a *legitimate* object of loyalty, they should remain truth seekers, constantly evaluating and validating the purpose and values of that loyalty. This includes enabling the voice of others and listening to those voices inside and outside an organization. Loyalists also should bear some of the costs of loyalty, voicing concerns to management and assuming responsibility for recuperation and recovery. Practitioners then should put authenticity ahead of aesthetics by backing up voice with creativity, honesty, and, if necessary, the threat of exit. Finally, practitioners show loyalty to loyalty by determining whether those in power are willing to listen, change, or improve the situation. To remain loyal through the ups and downs of modern organizational life can strengthen loyalty in society and enhance its moral value. Exit serves as a last resort but takes precedence over an internal "suffering in silence" exit. To stay with an organization or cause unworthy of loyalty to loyalty perverts loyalty as a virtue and transforms it into the raw material for vice.

Loyalty to loyalty may help resolve the paradox of serving narrower loyalties while at the same time honoring and respecting the loyalty of others and loyalty as a virtue. However, it does not address the broader loyalties that shape our sense of self as well as the culture and character of social organizations. Although those broader loyalties have less of a moral claim on us, they are critical to our development as individuals and social being. If society and the public interest are too abstract to command our loyalty, to what broader loyalty do we anchor our social responsibility. In a book published after his death, Josiah Royce argued that the true source of loyalty was community. Indeed, our deepest loyalties have their expression in the ideals and values of our communities.

Parts of this chapter appeared in Stoker, K. (2005). Loyalty in public relations: When does it cross the line between virtue and vice? *Journal of Mass Media Ethics, 20* (4), 269–287. (Used by permission.)

Works cited

Barry, B. (1974). Review article: Exit, voice, and loyalty. *British Journal of Political Science, 4*, 79–107.

Bateson, G. (2000). *Steps to an ecology of mind.* Chicago: University of Chicago Press.

Birch, A. H. (1975). Economic models in political science: The case of exit, voice, and loyalty. *Industrial and Labor Relations Review, 34* (4), 69–82.

Bivins, T. H. (1993). Public relations, professionalism, and the public interest. *Journal of Business Ethics, 12* (2), 117–126. doi.org/10.1007/BF00871931.

Bloch, H. (1966). *The concept of our changing loyalties.* New York: AMS Press.

Bok, S. (1989). *Secrets: On the ethics of concealment and revelation.* New York: Vintage Books.

Boroff, K. E. & Lewin, D. (1997). Loyalty, voice, and intent to exit a union firm: A conceptual and empirical analysis. *Industrial and Labor Relations Review, 51*, 50–64. Retrieved September 9, 1999 from http://web1.searchbank.com/itw/.

Broom, G. M., Casey, S., & Ritchey, J. (2000). Concept and theory of organization-public relationship research. In J. A. Ledingham and S. D. Bruning (Eds.), *Public relations as relationship management* (pp. 3–22). Mahwah, NJ: Lawrence Earlbaum Associates.

Cahuc, P. & Kramarz, F. (1997). Voice and loyalty as a delegation of authority: A model and a test on matched worker-firm panels. *Journal of Labor Economics, 15* (4), 658–689. Retrieved September 9, 1999 from http://web1.searchbank.com/itw.

Center, A. H. & Jackson, P. (2003). *Public relations practices: Managerial case studies and problems.* Upper Saddle River, NJ: Prentice Hall.

Clegg, S. R. (2002). General introduction. In S. R. Clegg (Ed.), *Management and organization paradoxes* (pp. 1–10). Amsterdam: John Benjamins.

Copleston, F. (1985). *A history of philosophy: Volume VII: Fichte to Nietzsche.* New York: Image Books.

Cusack, G. P. (2009). Willingness: A reflection on commitment, organization citizenship and engagement from the perspective of Albert O. Hirschman's concept of exit, voice and loyalty. *Review of Business*, *29* (2), 19–29. Retrieved September 3, 2019 from ABI/INFORM Collection www.search.proquest.com.

Cutlip, S. M., Center, A. H., & Broom, G. M. (2000). *Effective public relations* (8th Ed.). Englewood Cliffs, NJ: Prentice Hall.

Dervitsiotis, R. L. (1998). The challenge of managing organizational change: Exploring the relationship of re-engineering, developing learning organizations and total quality management. *Total Quality Management*, 9, 109–122.

Dilenschneider, R. L. (1990). *Power and influence: Mastering the art of persuasion.* New York: Prentice Hall Press.

Dilenschneider, R. L. & Salak, J. (2003). Do ethical communicators finish first? Walking the straight and narrow information path. *Communication World*, 32–36.

Economic recession raising loyalty among U.S. employees, Kelly Workforce Survey. (2010, March 8). *GlobalNewswire*. Retrieved September 3, 2019 from www.globalnewswire.com.

Ewin, R. E. (1992). Loyalty and virtues. *Philosophical Quarterly*, *42* (169), 403–419.

Ewin, R. E. (1993). Corporate loyalty: Its objects and its grounds. *Journal of Business Ethics*, *12* (5), 387–396.

Fletcher, G. P. (1993*). Loyalty: An essay on the morality of relationships.* New York: Oxford University Press.

Freeman, R. B. (1980). The exit-voice tradeoff in the labor market: Unionism, job tenure, quits and separations. *Quarterly Journal of Economics*, *94*, 643–673.

Freeman, R. B. & Medoff, J. (1984). *What do unions do?* New York: Basic Books.

Greiner, L. E. (1998). Evolution and revolution as organizations grow. *Harvard Business Review*, *76*, 55–67.

Hays, S. (1999, February). Ownership cultures create unity. *Workforce*, pp. 60–64.

Heath, R. L. (1998). New communication technologies: An issues management point of view. *Public Relations Review*, *24* (3), 273–278.

Hirschman, A. O. (1970). *Exit, voice, and loyalty: Responses to decline in firms, organizations, and states.* Cambridge, MA: Harvard University Press.

Hobson, R. (1997). Individual voice on the shop floor: The role of unions. *Social Forces*, *75* (4), 1183–1212.

Judd, L. R. (1989). Credibility, public relations and social responsibility. *Public Relations Review*, *15*, 34–40.

Kierkegaard, S. (1941). *Concluding unscientific postscript* (D. F. Swenson & W. Lowrie, Trans.). Princeton, NJ: Princeton University Press. (Original work published 1846).

Kierkegaard, S. (1983). *Fear and trembling: Repetition* (H.V. Hong & E. H. Hong, Trans.). Princeton, NJ: Princeton University Press. (Original work published 1843).

Kierkegaard, S. (1987). *Either/or* (H. V. Hong & E. H. Hong, Trans.). Princeton, NJ: Princeton University Press. (Original work published 1843).

Kruckeberg, D. & Starck, K. (1988). *Public relations and community: A reconstructed theory.* New York: Praeger.

Laabs, J. (1998, November). The new loyalty: Grasp it. Earn it. Keep it. *Workforce*, pp. 1–9.

Ladd, J. (1968). Loyalty. In P. Edwards (Ed.), *The encyclopedia of philosophy.* New York: Macmillan & Free Press.

Ledingham, J. A. & Bruning, S. D. (2000). A longitudinal study of organization-public relationship dimensions: Defining the role of communication in the practice of relationship management. In J. A. Ledingham & S. D. Bruning (Eds.), *Public relations as relationship management: A relational approach to the study and practice of public relations* (pp. 55–69). Mahwah, NJ: Lawrence Erlbaum Associates Publishers.

Leeper, K. (1996). Public relations ethics and communitarianism: A preliminary investigation. *Public Relations Review, 22* (2), 163–179.

Loyalty: Asset or liability? (1999, November 1). *Computerworld,* 52.

Martinson, D. L. (1995/1996). Client partiality and third parties: An ethical dilemma for public relations practitioners? *Public Relations Quarterly,* 40, 1–6. Retrieved March 4, 1999 from ABI Inform, proquest.com.

McCurry on McCurry: "I got into trouble because I didn't seek the truth." (1999, June 1). *Ragan's Media Relations Report,* 3.

Mieszkowski, K. (1998, April/May). The power of public relations. *Fast Company,* 182–196.

Mill, J. S. (2002). *The basic writings of John Stuart Mill: On liberty, the subjection of women, and utilitarianism.* New York: Modern Library. (Original works published: *On liberty,* 1859; *The subjection of women,* 1869; and *Utilitarianism,* 1863)

Murdock, P. K. (2017, December 28). The new reality of employee loyalty. *Forbes.* Retrieved September 3, 2019 from www.forbes.com.

Oldenquist, A. (1982). Loyalties. *Journal of Philosophy* [On-line], 79 (4), 173–193. Retrieved October 9, 1999 from www.jstor.org/.

Parsons, P. H. (1993). Framework for analysis of conflicting loyalties. *Public Relations Review, 19,* 49–57.

Pearson, R. (1989). Business ethics as communication ethics: Public relations practice and the idea of dialogue. In C. H. Botan & V. Hazelton, Jr. (Eds.), *Public relations theory* (pp. 111–131). Hillsdale, NJ: Lawrence Erlbaum Associates.

Peters, J. D. (1999). *Speaking into the air: A history of the idea of communication.* Chicago: University of Chicago Press.

Profits from loyalty. (1998, November 9). *Time,* 122.

Pruzan, P. (1998). From control to values-based management accountability. *Journal of Business Ethics,* 17 (13), 1379–1394. Retrieved September 9, 1999 from ABI/INFORM Global, proquest.com.

PRSA (n.d.). Code of ethics. Retrieved May 4, 2017 from www.prsa.org.

Reichheld, F. F. (1996). *The loyalty effect: The hidden force behind growth, profits, and lasting value.* Boston: Harvard Business School Press.

Royce, J. (1971). *The philosophy of loyalty.* New York: Hafner Publishing Company. Reprinted from Royce, J. (1908). *The philosophy of loyalty.* New York: Macmillan Company.

Simon, R. & Wylie, F. W. (1993). *Cases in public relations management.* Lincolnwood, IL: NTC Business Books.

Smith, W. K. & Lewis, M. W. (2011). Toward a theory of paradox: A dynamic equilibrium model of organizing. *Academy of Management Review, 36* (2), 381–403.

Stoker, K. (1995). Existential objectivity: Freeing journalists to be ethical. *Journal of Mass Media Ethics, 10,* 5–22.

"The 2019 Employee Engagement Report." (2019). Retrieved September 3, 2019 from www.tinypulse.com.

Sundaramurthy, C. & Lewis, M. (2003). Control and collaboration: Paradoxes in governance. *Academy of Management Review, 28,* 397–415.

Turnley, W. H. & Feldman, D. C. (1999). The impact of psychological contract violations on exit, voice, loyalty, and neglect. *Human Relations,* 52 (7), 895–897. Retrieved February 17, 2000 from http://web2.infotrac.galegroup.com/itw.

We aren't all free agents. (1999, June 14). *Newsweek,* 47.

White, J. & Dozier, D. M. (1992). Public relations and management decision making. In J. Grunig (Ed.), *Excellence in public relations and communication management* (pp. 31–64). Hillsdale, NJ: Lawrence Erlbaum Associates.

Weick, K. E. (1979). *The social psychology of organizing.* Reading, MA: Addison-Wesley.

Wilson, L. (2000). Building employee and community relationships through volunteerism: A case study. In J. A. Ledingham & S. D. Bruning (Eds.), *Public relations as relationship management: A relational approach to the study and practice of public relations* (pp. 137–144). Mahwah, NJ: Lawrence Erlbaum Associates.

7 The community paradox

The company eReleases serves small to medium-sized businesses and entrepreneurs by distributing press releases and offering writing services (eReleases, n.d.). It also provides tips to individuals and companies on how to improve their public relations. In a release that originally appeared in *PR Fuel*, Brown (2019) explained that community relations may be the most perplexing of all the subsets of public relations. "That's because the term encompasses so many different types of activities" (para. 1). She then offered some basic principles of community relations. First, practitioners should segment targeted communities and focus on those that "have the greatest potential to impact your success" (para. 2). These targeted groups are the ones who could enable or hinder an organization's success. After researching these communities and identifying opinion leaders, the organization should align its interests with the interests of these "priority" communities. This narrative sharply contrasts with the more politically correct approach of building relationships. A more established public relations consultant provided a more proper definition: "Community relations refers to the methods companies use to establish and maintain mutually beneficial relationships with the communities in which they operate" (How important is community relations to a company? 2016).

The community paradox for public relations emerges from these contradictory views of community relations and the very nature or our relationship with communities. Practitioners have traditionally viewed community relations as a strategic process for advancing organizational interests in their virtual and geographic communities. As Schriner (1997) bluntly described community relations, "Community involvement—what's in it for you?" A more positive interpretation was that corporations established community relations programs to "nurture the best possible climate in which the organization can operate" (Kruckeberg & Starck, 1988, p. 24). Even this more benign philosophy of community relations reflected a predominantly organization-centric approach in which corporations use community connections and relationships to promote organizational interests. Public relations educators have sought to move the field away from this kind of strategic use of community relationships. However, even their calls for the field to build community and establish mutually beneficial relationships creates some separation between organizations and the community.

Though communities may mutually benefit from the organization's success, the act of using these close relationships to serve self-interests may morally detach an organization from its community (Royce, 1916). Stated another way, community relations, when used to benefit an organization, can actually cost the organization its membership in a community. Thus, the paradox of connecting and disconnecting from community is not easily solved by just saying that the community benefits as well. According to Group Theory, community exists at a higher level of abstraction than the individuals and social units that reside in it. Community is the name of the thing but not the thing itself (Korzybski, 1933[2000]). By treating the community as a key public or even a stakeholder, public relations begins to sever that connection. Would we strategically identify our family, friends, and neighbors as targets for relationships? The paradox of connections and disconnection can produce tension and overcoming these tensions requires reframing the relationship. In our relations with communities, we need to move to a higher level of abstraction to embrace values and ideals associated with community membership. We can then reinterpret community relations as interpersonal, integral, and ontological. The gentle act of reframing embraces community members as family, friends, neighbors, and colleagues.

This chapter lays the groundwork for this reframing by further exploring organization-community paradoxes. First, I will discuss the concept of community, its meaning, evolution, and paradoxes. Second, I examine the public relations literature regarding community and the role of public relations in promoting and building community. Third, I propose incorporating the community philosophy of Josiah Royce as the first step to resolving the public relations-community paradox, particularly the role public relations can play in creating communities of inquiry and interpretation. Finally, I will propose that public relations adopt an existential watchfulness that emphasizes listening, truth seeking, interpretation, and inquiry.

Community

Citing Korzybski (1933[2000]), Elson (2010) noted that "we categorize things by how we respond to them" (p. 164). Thus, the classification of a community can elicit a myriad of interpretations and responses. In denotative terms, a community constitutes a group of people living in a contiguous location or a group of people connected through common characteristics and interests. Community can refer to a geographic location with members living in close proximity, or it can represent a virtual community made up of members spread throughout the world. We talk about the scientific community, global community, and music community, each with multiple sub communities. Our responses to community depend on the context, situation, and even the way we use the term in a sentence. In other words, there are multiple levels of abstraction represented in the classification of a community, and the discontinuity between levels produces a number of paradoxes. Fowler (1995) claimed that "any community is fraught with paradox…" (p. 94), and the emergence of the digital community has simply created a new set of paradoxes. These paradoxes are apparent in the philosophical and political debate over what community actually means.

Community traditionally referred to a geographic locality or a "universal community in which all human beings participate" (Delanty, 2003, p. 12). Communitarian scholar Amitai Etzioni (1995) defined communities as "webs of social relations that encompass shared meanings and above all shared values" (p. 24). A family, village, or neighborhood could qualify as a community as well as a group of people bound by a common faith tradition. "People are at one and the same time members of several communities such as those at work and at home" (p. 25). Those communities range in scope from one's family and neighborhood to one's city, state, and country. Each smaller community is nested in a larger community, and community members can shift their moral commitments from the local community to more expansive and encompassing communities. At each level, shared values play a critical role in promoting a common cause and sense of community. These shared values and ideals help to tie individuals to their communities.

Contemporary conceptions of community have been influenced by the ancient Greeks and early Christian theologians (Delanty, 2003). Aristotle was one of the first political philosophers to provide a definition of community (Friedrich, 1959). He defined the teleological goal of community as achieving something good. People were bound to their communities by the things they had in common. Members of a community were diverse, distinct, and self-sufficient, but they also were unified by their complementary goals and ideals. Aristotle associated society with friendship and, thus, did not distinguish between the social and communal (Delanty, 2003). More modern evaluations of community considered "the advent of society" as undercutting the eighteenth century "golden age of community" (p. 8).

Aristotle's view of people being bound by what they had in common influenced subsequent conceptions of community. The Stoics promoted an elite community of the wise; the Christians envisioned a universal community of the faithful. Christian philosophers viewed community as a group of people bound together by love, a common cause, and the pursuit of the common good. Friedrich (1959) noted that the Christian writer Aquinas espoused "the idea that community had a personal existence apart from the members composing it" (p. 11). This approach reflects communitarian philosophies that emerged in sociology and philosophy during the twentieth century.

Other conceptions focused on the polis or political community, which consisted of people living in the same locality, interacting face to face, looking out for each other, and acting with a common purpose and goal (Delanty, 2003). Thus, large cities with highly diverse populations failed to qualify as true communities because they lacked the required proximity and interdependence. As cities have grown larger and community life has become more impersonal, the ideal community has become incoherent and indistinct in the face of mass society, industrialization, and technology. Most important, cities have lost some of the humanity associated with small communities. Instead of viewing each other as neighbors and friends, community members are pitted against each other in competition over scare resources. Large cities and nation states allow the powerful to exploit community members. Machiavelli viewed community as a resource for advancing, gaining, and maintaining power and control. Political leaders (or companies for that matter) used the community as a propaganda device for increasing power (Friedrich, 1959) and advancing economic self-interests. As with loyalty, community has this dark side. The very trust and interdependence that exists in communities enables Machiavellians to exploit their fellow community members. The fox can wreak havoc in the hen house. Furthermore, the very structure of communities, their borders, membership, and classifications can contribute to exclusion and oppression (Blackshaw, 2009).

The growth of modern nation states inspired natural law thinkers to look to civil society and the state to establish communities of law based on values and beliefs of the broader cultural community. French philosopher Jean-Jacques Rousseau viewed community as a moralizing agent representing the highest moral values. His conception of the *general will* embodied the personality of a community and the need for organic social groups to assure their survival. Community was "an organic, personalized whole" (Friedrich, 1959, p. 20). While Aristotle and even contemporary philosophers reject the notion that larger communities can be considered true communities, Rousseau viewed emerging cities as an essential expression of community.

Enlightenment thinkers believed "community expressed the bonds of commonality and sociality" (Delanty, 2003, p. 8). Distinct from the state and society, communities were directly experienced by community members. Delanty argued that this separation of state and community inspired the idea of community as a utopian concept, "a quest for a perfect society" (p. 9). Thus, as cities grew larger and more industrialized, political philosophers, such as Karl Marx, warned about alienation and the loss of community (Friedrich, 1959). The debate over community continues. The questions raised by Friedrich in 1959—whether community exists or is willed into existence and whether community is organic or a purposive community of law or love—remain relevant today. Writing in the same edited volume as Friedrich, Ladd (1959) argued that rather than asking what a community stands for and how it should be defined, the most important questions are what kind of thing a community is and what is its function and use. In an age of geographic, global, and virtual communities, the answer to these questions are especially relevant to public relations, a field engaged in interpreting and communicating the social and moral obligations of individuals and organizations to their various communities.

Ladd (1959) contended that one's obligation to a community differs from obligations to a formal organization, which imposes certain expectations and obligations. Membership in communities implies informal and indefinite obligations and rights. In other words, the expectations of community membership are typically not requisite or mandatory. We may have well-defined civic obligations or business responsibilities, but our communal obligations are less formal and not well defined. Formal obligations require us to perform while informal obligations do not require specific actions. They "instead call for certain attitudes and interests" (p. 286). Thus, community obligations, like Royce's loyalty, are a matter of choice and reflect what members ought to do, who they ought to be, and what they should value. Formal organizational obligations may not provide the same kind of freedom of choice. However, if we take seriously our social contract, even communal obligations could be considered strict and obligatory. The concept of community reveals the facts and ideals espoused by its members and the "facts about their actual conduct and attitudes" (Ladd, 1959, p. 295). In other words, we both define our communities and are defined by them. The answer to Ladd's question regarding what a community is may be best answered by asking who we are. The paradox of community arises from the fact that communities exist separately from their members while at the same time embodying the ideals and values of their members. Indeed, in many respects, the community is an extension of its members, and the quality of a community depends on the balance between the individual member and the community (Etzioni, 1995).

Individuals have an identity independent of their communities and often try to change their communities to align with their own personal values and ideals. At the same time, the community influences individuals and tries to bring them in line with community values and ideals. In contrast to Buber's (1970) I and Thou relationship, Etzioni (1995) proposed the *I&We* relationship to describe "the tense but close bond between individuals and communities" (p. 19). Communitarians believe the United States has shifted too far toward individualism and advocate a "return to community" and a restoration of the balance between I and We (p. 19). In Western liberal societies, the balance has shifted too far toward the isolated, self-interested individual who "imagines himself absolutely free, unencumbered, and on his own and enters society, accepting its obligations only in order to minimize his risks" (Walzer, 1995, p. 54). Separated from society, the individual considers only private interests and connects only when necessary to fulfill those self-interests. Walzer noted that this communitarian criticism of liberalism depends on a "vulgar" Marxist theory of reflection. In a vague reference to Hirschman (1970), Walzer contended that this conception of isolated selves had more to do with exit than voice. A second communitarian critique of liberalism argues that it "misrepresents real life" (p. 56). Liberalism overemphasizes our capacity as individuals to invent ourselves and truly develop our identities outside "patterns of relationship, networks of power, and communities of meaning" (p. 56). Walzer (1995) found both criticisms false and inconsistent and misrepresentative of everyday life. Communities and traditions could not exist if the first criticism were true and the second critique belies the fact that communal invention is ongoing and continuous.

It is a matter of principle that communities must always be at risk. And the great paradox of a liberal society is that one cannot set oneself against this principle without also setting oneself against the traditional practices and shared understandings of the society. Here, respect for tradition requires the precariousness of traditionalism.

(Walzer, 1995, p. 68)

Communitarians also question the morality of economics because the market shifts the balance toward self-interest and individualism (van Staveren, 2009). This criticism has created a paradox in which economists invoke communitarianism to create a more morally defensible view of the economy while rejecting the market's morality. van Staveren contended that communitarians fail to consider more expansive definitions of economic theory encompassing more than just markets. The economy, van Staveren explained, is embedded in society and "economic behavior is part of social behavior" (p. 40). Those agents participating in the economy share values and meanings that "develop, sustain, challenge, and institutionalize morality through the value of internal goods and the standards for excellence that these internal goods set in practice" (p. 43). van Staveren's resolution of the paradox showed that sometimes communitarian perceptions of community can themselves be out of balance. For example, communitarians, like modernists, believe the modern world has destroyed community (Delanty, 2003). They also contend that people in industrial societies have a weakened sense of obligation and commitment to each other and their communities (Wolfe, 1995). Public relations scholars have adapted this view of imperiled communities and have re-envisioned community relations as rebuilding and restoring community (Kruckeberg & Starck, 1988).

Public relations and community

In the field's most significant work on community, Kruckeberg and Starck (1988) claimed that community, in the context of community relations, is a misnomer (p. 26). The traditional definition of community relations has been "an organization's planned, active and continuing participation with and within a community to maintain and enhance its environment to the benefit of both the institution and the community" (p. 24). In this context, community should be more accurately called a "geographic public" (p. 26). Instead, the appropriate use of the term "community relations" describes an attempt to "restore and maintain a sense of community which has been lost in contemporary society" (p. 26) Basing their ideas on the Chicago School of Social Thought, Kruckeberg and Starck proposed public relations take the lead in helping organizations revive community. Chicago School scholars John Dewey, Herbert Mead, Louis Wirth, and others lamented the loss of community and called for its return (Kruckeberg & Starck, 1988). They blamed the loss of community on the development of mass communication, transportation, industrialization, and urbanization. Mass communication allowed for greater homogenization of larger social units and weakened the reliance on communities to teach and reinforce values, ideas, and behaviors. Mass transportation provided the means to ship goods to other parts of the country and world, and communities began to produce goods that were sold to strangers rather than neighbors. Therefore, communities became more dependent on the unknown rather than self-sufficient with the familiar. "With this interdependence came a homogenization of America and Americans. The nationalization of communication and transportation systems was largely responsible for mass culture" (p. 39).

With industrialization came urbanization. In the city, the sense of community continued to lose ground. The urban lifestyle revolved around work opportunities, and those vocations became identities. "People in cities lived together not because they were alike, but because they were useful to another" (Kruckeberg & Starck, 1988, p. 46). Citing the work of various communication scholars, Kruckeberg and Starck claimed that a society's preoccupation with individual pursuits weakened community. "The common notion today is of an impersonal, even hostile, society—a society in which all actions and motives seem to have equal value and to be perversely detached from human direction" (p. 48). Their premise is that modern public relations grew in importance as communities became more fragmented and focused on self-interests. Hence the need for persuasion and advocacy grew beyond the political and expanded into the social and economic sectors of society.

Kruckeberg and Starck (1988) advocated using public relations to help build communities with common values and a solidarity of purpose. Through communication, public relations practitioners inform community members about common goals.

> Practitioners can help various publics and the organizations they represent become conscious of common interests that are the bases for both their contentions and their solutions. With conscientious thought and an appropriate theoretical base, practitioners can help individuals in the community maintain their existence as individuals and promote their worth as persons.
>
> (pp. 65–66)

The restoration and maintenance of community, however, often lies outside "the purview of contemporary public relations thought" (p. 71). Because of the strong relationship between community and effective communication, Kruckeberg and Starck (1988) argued that many of the problems that public relations practitioners face stem from a loss of community. Therefore,

> being a facilitator of communication in the traditional sense—that is, seeking out and promoting discourse along all avenues—is a role of critical importance today, which can help to build a sense of community among organizations and their geographic publics.
>
> (p. 112)

Culbertson and Chen (1997) claimed that Kruckeberg and Starck's analysis of community relations sounds a lot like communitarianism. Leeper (1996) identified communitarianism as the appropriate approach to public relations ethics. The communitarian principle that community members "must recognize and fulfill certain responsibilities for the communities and societies of which they are a part" (p. 164) is essential to corporate social responsibility (CSR). She cited Etzioni's (1993) contention that no society can tolerate taking without giving. It's amoral and self-centered. "Rights presume responsibilities" (p. 9). The moral approach is for organizations to become truly involved in giving back to their communities.

Organizations can begin by making positive contributions to the community and their community relationships (Culbertson & Chen, 1997). The people involved must care genuinely about each other's welfare. "So long as self-centered adversaryism [sic] dominates the public realm, the quality of relationships seems bound to decline" (p. 37). The second is that community requires a sense of interconnectedness and social cohesion. "In this view, people must feel they are part of something larger than themselves. In some measure, they must be willing to sacrifice for the welfare of others—and for society as a whole" (p. 38). The third is identification of and firm commitment to core values and beliefs essential to a sense of community. Community members must feel that they share something worthy of their sacrifice. "Otherwise, they will not look beyond narrow, partisan interests as needed for a meaningful social contract" (p. 38). Culbertson and Chen advocated appealing to basic ideals and values, including decency and respect. Finally, all citizens must feel empowered to make and implement decisions that affect their lives. "Of course, relationship building with a hidden agenda of persuasion may lead to reduced credibility and charges of hypocrisy" (p. 41). Culbertson and Chen make valid points regarding caring, interconnectedness, and shared values, but they appear to ask organizations and the public relations professionals to totally disregard the organization's self-interests. In other words, as Walzer (1995) explained, this interpretation of communitarianism ignores real life.

The reality is that much of what passes as community relations in the corporate environment emerges from a strategic agenda to enhance the bottom line. Having an agenda, however, does not necessarily make an organization's community building efforts unethical. In eschewing an enlightened self-interested approach to community relations, public relations scholars paint themselves into a corner. They advocate mutual benefit, trust, respect, and cooperation while at the same time describing their goal as the development of strategic cooperative communities (Wilson, 1996). Strategy implies agenda. The public will always perceive an organization's cooperative efforts as serving an organization's interests and goals. Leeper (1996) acknowledged that "what is best for the community is ultimately in the best interest of the organization" (p. 165). The paradoxical nature of community relations may help explain why most contemporary public relations textbooks all but ignore the concept, noting that it is just one of several strategic services offered by public relations agencies.

In 1988, Baskin and Aronoff (1988) devoted an entire chapter to community relations, arguing that "good community relations is derived from understanding the nature of a community" (p. 220). They quoted William Gilbert's definition of community as "A place of interacting social institutions which produce in the residents an attitude and practice of interdependence, cooperation, collaboration, and unification ..." (Gilbert, 1975, p. 103). Gilbert's book dealt with public relations in local government, and his description of community reflected a localized view of the relationship between social organizations and individuals. This contrasts with today's virtual communities in which some businesses do business online, with customers and suppliers spread across the globe. The local community, however, does remain important. "As a company, we recognize that now, more than ever, it is crucial to build a lasting and tangible connection within the community where you've chosen to grow your roots ... it's true what they say: There is no replacement for the human connection" (Oliveira, 2017, para. 1).

There is, however, a replacement for community relations. Contemporary public relations textbooks adopt community building as a more acceptable term. They also focus on public support for an organization's actions (Wilcox, Cameron, Reber, & Shin, 2013) and the need to create good will between the organization and the community in which it resides (Wahl & Maresh-Fuehrer, 2016). Community relations is embedded in corporate social responsibility (Wahl & Maresh-Fuehrer, 2016) or public affairs and relationship management (Broom, 2009). Community relations ensure local community support (Types of PR, 2019), especially in times of crisis (Wahl & Maresh-Fuehrer, 2016). Professionals credit community relations with increasing employee morale and loyalty (Bollier, 1996; Hein, 1997; Autodesk focuses on volunteerism, 2000;), inspiring consumer confidence and product loyalty (Cashing in on teen spirit, 2000; Randels, 2001), and enhancing trust (Monroe, 1998). It contributes to the quality of the workforce (Mason, 1991; Goldstein, 1993; Greenberg, 1993), promotes a better image (Himmelstein, 1997; Mack, 1999) and improves the local political and economic environment (Schriner, 1997; Nassutti, 1999; Regout, 2001). All of these community relations goals smack of a strategic self-interest, including CSR and public affairs.

After reviewing the contemporary literature on community relations, Valentini, Kruckeberg, and Starck (2012) complained that it focused too much on publics and organizations and not enough on issues or problems as John Dewey (1927) advocated in his philosophy of publics. By its very nature, segmentation of publics based on common interests and impact on organization favors the organization, not necessarily its stakeholders or the public. Valentini et al. (2012) rejected the idea that publics can be managed or controlled and suggested viewing publics and stakeholders as part of a community of which the organization also claims membership. They argued that relationships are difficult to manage, especially online relationships. The field needs to move away from these kinds of organization-centric solutions, and instead focus on community building and creating space for dialog and mutual understanding.

By interacting with community members through community involvement and service, public relations can build friendships and promote understanding of organizational goals (Vujnovic & Kruckeberg, 2011).

In addition, Valentini et al. (2012) contended that globalism has altered conceptions of the public as well as what constitutes common interests and concerns. Publics could be anyone in the world, with direct or indirect effects on an organization. Interests and concerns can vary. Thus the need for public relations to shift its focus to issues and problems. This means adopting an approach consistent with Etzioni's *I&We*, which places the individual and the community at equivalent levels of abstraction. At this level, public relations serves as interpreter and facilitator, bringing the oppositional forces together in what Harvard philosopher and idealist Josiah Royce called a community of inquiry.

Communities of inquiry and interpretation

American idealist Josiah Royce is best known for his book on *The Philosophy of Loyalty*, published in 1908, but he also pioneered a perspective of community in two lesser-known books, *The Problem of Christianity* (1913) and *The Hope of the Great Community* (1916). Royce taught at Harvard from 1885 to 1915 and was a close friend of the pragmatist William James. George Herbert Mead of the Chicago School of Social Thought studied under Royce and wrote about his mentor's love of community. In 1930, he wrote that Royce's philosophy belonged "to culture and to a culture which did not spring from controlling habits and attitudes of American society …. It was part of the escape from the crudity of American life, not an interpretation of it" (Mead, 1930, p. 223). For Royce (1916), the community served as the source of happiness and salvation. Individual experience is meaningless, he argued, without the social experience shared by the community. "We are saved, if at all, by devotion to the Community," Royce wrote. "This is what I mean by loyalty …. I now say that by loyalty I mean the practically devoted love of an individual for a community" (Royce, 1913, pp. xvi-xvii). Royce believed that love for and devotion to a community united disparate individuals in a common cause that produced infinite moral value. Royce defined love as "a very positive and active and heroic attitude towards [a] life" filled with "unsolved certain practical problems" (Royce, 1908, 1971, p. 229). In public relations terms, this implies that practitioners champion their communities and community issues. As with other objects of loyalty, practitioners subordinate personal will to identify with the common will of the community. This way the individual and the social group unite to achieve happiness. As practitioners show loyalty to higher causes, they strengthen the loyalty of others who then unite in infinitely larger communities of interconnected individuals. Thus, an individual or for that matter an organization maintains private interests but subordinates those interests to the community to achieve common goals and solve community problems.

According to Royce (1908), genuine communities can offset the mainstreaming effect of modern communication and civilization that stifles individual spirit and independence. He called this mainstreaming a "leveling" tendency that discouraged individuality and promoted mediocrity.

> For a man is in large measure what his social consciousness makes him. Give him the local community that he loves and cherishes, that he is proud to honor and serve,—make his ideal of that community lofty,—give him faith in the dignity of his province,—and you have given him the power to counteract the leveling tendencies of modern civilization.
>
> (Royce, 1908, p. 79; quoted in Brown, 1948, p. 19)

When people are treated as a mass audience or a market, they lose a share of their liberty and dignity as individuals. The community preserves and enhances these social ideals of freedom and democracy, allowing individual variety and pluralism to flourish (Brown, 1948, p. 24). George Herbert Mead felt Royce expressed the "American democratic ideal of a plurality of diverse persons united in devotion and loyalty to the construction of an ideal community in which every individual's differences would be preserved and would contribute to the richness of the whole" (Randall, 1966, p. 73). In other words, the ideal community balanced the I and the We, allowing both to exist as a part of a pluralistic whole.

The global community consists of a variety of nations. These nations are made up of a variety of provinces, and inside these provinces are a variety of communities. Though these communities consist of a finite number of individuals, they represent more than just an aggregate of their individual members. The genuine community is the outward expression of the ideals and values of its individual members (Brown, 1948, p. 26). Royce saw the genuine community as a collection of individuals, distinct in their natures, but common in purpose and ideals. "The infinity of intercommunicating selves constitutes one body, one community, the Absolute Self" (Randall, 1966, p. 62). Randall said Royce viewed connectedness as the key to comprehending reality. Indeed, Royce believed that individuals could only realize their purposes through knowing their position in the order of things.

However, the relationship between an individual and a community is not so reciprocal, reflexive, or symmetrical but asymmetrical. In other words, the individual may belong to the community, but the community does not belong to the individual. "Royce notes that if I am a member of a community, however I may stand related to it, it does not stand related to me in the same way" (Smith, 1969, p. xvi). Royce explained that "no entity stands in relation to itself" (p. xvi). A company may belong to a community, but the community never belongs to the company because a company is the community. In this sense, a company may own a town, but it cannot own the community. The company and the community are cut from the same cloth and should share the same values and ideals. Loyalty and devotion to a common cause and common ideals brings people together in a community.

This begs the question as to what act or process binds people together in a community. Borrowing from Charles S. Pierce, who was known for his theory of signs, Royce explained that individuals gain a sense of place and meaning through interpretation. Pierce defined signs as symbols "invested with meaning by the experience of community. When any object acquires meaning, it is 'interpreted'" (Randall, 1966, p. 63). The process of interpretation consists of the sign, the interpreter, and the interpretee. For Royce, interpretation linked one individual to another, the individual to his or her community, and the community to society.

> The process of interpretation involves, of necessity, an infinite sequence of acts of interpretation. It also admits of an endless variety within all the selves which are thus mutually interpreted. These selves, in all their variety, constitute the life of a single Community of Interpretation, whose central member is that spirit of the community whose essential function we know ….The history of the universe, the whole order of time, is the history and the order and the expression of this Universal Community.
>
> (Royce II, 1968, p. 340; quoted in Randall, 1966, p. 64)

Our experiences are never consigned to just dyadic relations of perception or conception but also consist of triadic relations of interpretation (McDermott, 2005). Interpretation is a social process that starts with self-interpretation or reflection and continues with social interactions that mold and shape who we are as individuals and social beings. Individuals are not really completed and do not really get a complete picture of who they are until recognized by another. "Recognition enables humanity," wrote John Durham Peters (1999) paraphrasing Augustine. "Self-consciousness exists only as it is recognized. The internal loop of self-recognition must pass through the external loop of being recognized by another self-consciousness … to be is to be recognized" (pp. 114–115). The process of recognition and interpretation results in the creation of community. Neither the individual nor the community exists without "the creative articulation that is embodied in loyal interpretation" (Kaag, 2009, p. 98). We develop our sense of self through our communal commitments, and our fidelity to those commitments are also interpreted by the community.

When an organization creates a communication campaign to enhance community relations, it initiates the process of interpretation. The very campaign process reflects an act of interpretation in regards to what the problem is and how it might be resolved through communication. If the campaign conflicts with what the organization actually is and what it stands for, its impact and influence will be finite or short lived because the community will see through the charade. Public relations campaigns are finite, they have a beginning and end. The interpretation of the community, however, is infinite. Unless the communicated messages reflect the organization's authentic identity, the community's interpretation will outlast the finite messages of the campaign. In a community of interacting and interconnecting individuals, the infinite process of interpretation will expose the individual's or an organization's disconnect from the ideals and values of the community. The most effective public relations campaign serves as an interpretation of the relationship between the organization, the community, and their shared values and ideals.

Business organizations do not operate in a vacuum. They operate in a social sphere in which their actions impact the lives of organizational members and outsiders. Once an individual or an organization begins to participate in a community, the act of interpretation begins. It is not enough to just be a member of a community. Moral attachment means to go a step further and actively contribute to the moral health of the community. Brown (1948), citing Dewey and Royce, noted that social processes consist of an interaction between individuals and groups.

> But the individual is more than a mere reflection of social qualities, and the community is more than the mere aggregate of its members. When a social group is simply an organization without ideal ends and purposes, it cannot command the ideal loyalty of its members and so is not a true community of the faithful in either Paul's or Royce's sense, and an individual who is merely a member of an organization cannot be ethically loyal and hence a truly free man.
>
> (Brown, 1948, p. 25)

Stated another way, to be a part of a community requires more than just owning a physical location within a defined geographic area, it demands loyalty to the ideal ends and purposes of the community. Like the loyal individual, an organization subordinates its interests to the interests of the community. Paradoxically, those interests exist at the same level of abstraction because they are based on higher ideals, such as freedom and democracy. The organization simply subordinates its interest to its own ideal purposes and ends. Loyalty to community enhances the freedom and democracy of those inside and outside the organization. By enabling a community of inquiry, public relations augments and implements individual freedom and democracy, regardless of place in the community. The resulting relationships are more complementary than mutually beneficial because they share in each other's success. The goal is not so much building mutually beneficial relationships as it is to find solutions to the problems that put communities at risk. The primary goal is to build united and resilient communities.

Social organizations that lack these kinds of ideal ends and purposes fail to earn the deeper loyalties of their members. Instead they try to buy loyalty through philanthropy or corporate giving. The results of such efforts, however, are finite and fleeting because they have conditioned the community's loyalty on a reciprocal exchange rather than asymmetric loyalty of a common cause. No loyalty or freedom exists beyond the purse. Royce's analysis also calls into question the ability of an organization to demand loyalty from its members or its community if the organization disregards its loyalties to the national and international community. The organization, like the individual, only has meaning and content "in the light of the community or purposes and ends all men ought to share" (Randall, 1966, p. 67).

Social organizations that are uninformed by shared ideals do not contribute to the overall welfare of the community and inevitably become morally detached. The detached individual poses the biggest threat to the development of a great and beloved community (McDermott, 1985). "That person who lacks loyalty and concern is fair game for seduction of those nefarious movements which seek to wreck the community on behalf of some political, social, or religious ideology, all of them self-aggrandizing" (McDermott, 1985, p. 164). The only hope to build genuine communities is to show loyalty to the community through "sacrifice in the name of shared ideals ..." (Royce, quoted in Brown, 1948, p. 26). Royce's loyalists must base their decisions on whether their choices promote the ideals of freedom and democracy. Today, he might add equity, diversity, and justice to those ideals. Loyalty binds ethics to social practice. "It is loyalty which forms a bridge between any individual and any group, and it is loyalty to the ideals of freedom and democracy which forms the bridge between the free individual and the provinces of democracy" (Brown, 1948, p. 23).

Royce (1916) described the detached individual as "essentially a lost being" (p. 46). Detached individuals hate restraint and oppose the spirit of loyalty. They are free riders in the community (Walzer, 1995), longing for bliss, enjoyment, and desire. Organizations that exploit their communities create conflict and tension because they are paradoxically exploiting themselves. The only thing that can save the detached individual or social organization "at any level of human social life is union" (Royce, 1916, p. 52). Communities only exist as long as people belong to them.

> The value of community in all its instances is twofold: by showing the individual a supreme value which introduces some harmony among his conflicting inclinations it helps him toward self-realization, and by interpreting all its members to all its other members through a common past and a common future it brings about a unity and a harmony among persons such as would not otherwise be possible.
>
> (Smith, 1969, pp. 9–10)

Royce defined community as "a group of selves who interpret certain specific past events and certain expected future events as important parts of their lives" (Trotter, 2001, p. 82). The individual self is a community, and the community is a self, meaning that every experience and expectation integrated into who we are is also integrated into individual members of the larger community. Sure, we are distinctly different, but we are also very much the same. As interpreters, we seek truth and "all communities are communities of inquiry"

(p. 83). The success of a community of inquiry depends on being directed toward the truth, whether absolute truths or intersubjective truths. As with interpretation and inquiry, the search requires a constant striving for truth and knowledge. Interpretation is the act of inquiry and the pursuit of truth.

> The will to interpret, then, is not merely a wish for truth. It is the germ of truth within each inquirer, seeking to actualize itself through a fundamentally social process of interpretation. Understood in this way, Royce's theory of inquiry is an account of self-discovery in community.
>
> (Trotter, 2001, p. 77)

This self-discovery is of critical importance to individuals and organizations. It reflects a form of public relations that listens and communicates in an effort to better understand how one's organization's actions and goals fit within the broader framework of the community. By self-discovery, the organization orients its actions to conform with community expectations and goals. The purpose of two-way communication is not just to find agreement or establish relationships but to better understand ourselves, our organizations, and our communities. Conflicts, crises, and miscommunication lead to insight, renewal, and re-engineering (Ulmer, Sellnow, & Seeger, 2019). In other words, we interpret, we inquire so that we might improve ourselves, our organizations, and our communities.

After a spending his lifetime advocating idealism and moral absolutism, Royce's embrace of community marked an important shift toward the development of dynamic community of interpretation or learning community (McDermott, 1985). His embrace of Charles W. Pierce's doctrine of signs helped him incorporate third-term mediation into his philosophy of community.

> For every A in relationship to B, there is needed a third interpretive term C. Royce converts this triadic logic into a doctrine of interpretation, wherein protagonists in an otherwise communal setting take it upon themselves to listen to a third party, one who has the sense of both missions, both allegedly viable and praiseworthy, so as to render a *vade mecum* [manual], for purpose of amelioration.
>
> (p. 174)

Public relations practitioners possess this unique set of skills that enables them to serve as interpreters, facilitating communication and understanding among individuals, organizations, and community. They interpret "the fragmentary and dissatisfying conflicts, antitheses, and problems of our present ideas..." (174). Seeing the world for what it is lays the groundwork for discovering self and community.

Building community, according to Royce, required three basic conditions. First, individual selves must have the power to extend their lives back into the past and forward into the future without definable limits. Second, the community needed a social world filled with distinct individuals capable of communication and willing to engage in communication. Finally, among those past and future extended selves, there must exist some events that all selves view as identical (Royce, 1913; McDermott, 1985). The transcendent thread in Royce's conditions for building community is that we must reach beyond our "jealously guarded turf, beliefs, commitments and assertions … [and] at the very least, subject to the viewpoint of another, distant, although concerned participant" (McDermott, 1985, p. 175). This means reframing community to see ourselves and others wearing the same shoes, breathing the same air, and sharing the same ideals and values. The community of interpretation is about integrating our life's plan with the plans of others in our social sphere. "In the highest stages of moral life," wrote Royce scholar Griffin Trotter (2001), "individuals develop, through empathy and other powers of social communication, a deeper moral insight and an ability to interpret the ideals of ever wider cross sections of humanity. Narrow loyalties are expanded" (p. 84). We creatively mediate community risk and differences. We interpret our "specific loyalties in terms of an overarching loyalty to humanity" (p. 84).

Public relations as community interpretation and inquiry

Public relations overcomes the paradox of community by serving as an interpreter, integrating the I and the We to strengthen and build community. This approach allows practitioners to move to a higher level of abstraction and begin to see individual interests and community interests as one and the same. This act of reframing changes the perception of community relations in public relations. The individual and organization are integrated into the same community, and thus community relations represent an organization's efforts to serve common interests and resolve common problems. The solution to the paradox of community is much the same as resolving the Prisoner's Dilemma. The best of all possible outcomes occurs if the prisoners move to a higher level of abstraction and choose to cooperate with each other and not with the authorities. This option, however, is not without its risks because success depends on both choosing to cooperate. "Curiously, despite the numerous situations represented by the Prisoner's Dilemma in which it would be rational to defect, society nevertheless seems to be based on cooperation" (Elson, 2010, p. 54). The effectiveness of a society depends on mutual cooperation, and the paradox arises from the fact that people do cooperate. Elson surmised that the explanation for this kind of behavior stems not just from societal sanctions against non-cooperation but from repeated interactions with close associates or even strangers that confirm that non-cooperation produces undesirable consequences. Since the Prisoner's Dilemma is a nonzero sum game, both prisoners or players stand to benefit from cooperation and ultimately collaboration. The conflict between the rational choice and the moral choice presents an especially challenging paradox because the most advantageous choice is not the rational one but the empathetic one, the one that reflects a "collective rationality" (Rapoport, 1974; Elson, 2010, p. 56).

The community of interpretation and inquiry calls for public relations to help their organizations see the advantage of empathy and collective rationality. By reframing the individual and the organization as neighbors, friends, and family in the same community, public relations moves organizational strategy to a higher level of abstraction in which empathy and cooperation serves the interests of all members. As noted, Valentini et al. (2012) warned that public relations' public outreach needs to focus more on promoting private and public inquiry to solve community issues and problems. Royce's community of interpretation advocates a more holistic, paradoxical approach that centers on the individual, the organization, and the community. The interpreter helps organizations recognize that the community's problems are the organization's problems.

If communities are always at risk, as Walzer (1995) alleged, then individuals and organizations are constantly at risk. For public relations, this means that the fate of the organization and the community are inextricably linked. It does not matter if the community is geographical or virtual, there are certain ideals and goals that all members have in common. Through interpretation and inquiry, practitioners actively listen, communicate, and collaborate with the goal of discovering how they and their organizations can together build better communities. Unlike communitarian theory that "requires submission to the authority of tradition" and hierarchy (Cohen, 2000, p. 259), Royce's philosophy entrusts that power to individuals, who extend their lives from past to future, looking for shared events, common causes, and ideal ends and purposes. They also serve as interpreters, adopting an "existential watchfulness" that nurtures and seeks out community while at the same time staying vigilant to its complex and elusive nature (Fowler, 1995, p. 94). This existential watchfulness reflects paradoxical thinking and requires a deeper loyalty to community than simply the claim of membership. It demands that practitioners actively maintain bridges between the I and the We and enable individuals, organizations, and communities to risk cooperation and together thrive.

Dr. Bradley L. Rawlins contributed to some earlier iterations of this chapter.

Works cited

Autodesk Focuses on volunteerism and community involvement. (2000, March 21). *PR Newswire*, 1–2.

Baskin, O. W. & Aronoff, C. E. (1988). *Public relations: The profession and the practice* (2nd Ed.). Dubuque, Iowa: Wm. C. Brown Publishers.

Blackshaw, T. (2009). *Key concepts in community studies*. London: Sage. Retrieved October 12, 2019 from http://ezproxy.library.unlv.edu.

Bollier, D. (1996). Building corporate loyalty while rebuilding the community. *Management Review, 85* (10), 17–23.

Broom, G. (2009). *Cutlip & Center's Effective Public Relations*. Upper Saddle River, NJ: Prentice Hall.

Brown, S. G. (1948). From provincialism to the Great Community: The social philosophy of Josiah Royce. *Ethics, 59*, 14–34.

Brown, L. (2019, June 11). PR basics: Taking the mystery out of community relations. *eReleases*. Retrieved October 12, 2019 from ereleases.com.

Buber, M. (1970). *I and thou*. (W. Kaufman, Trans.). New York: Charles Scribner's Sons.

Cashing in on teen spirit: Companies that support causes win teen loyalty and dollars. (2000, August 22). *Business Wire*, 1–3.

Cohen, A. J. (2000). Liberalism, communitarianism, and asocialism. *The Journal of Value Inquiry, 34*, 249–261.

Culbertson, H. M. & Chen, N. (1997). Communitarianism: A foundation for communication symmetry. *Public Relations Quarterly, Summer*, 36–41.

Delanty, G. (2003). *Community*. London: Routledge.

Dewey, J. (1927). *The public and its problems*. New York: Holt.

Elson, L. G. (2010). *Paradox lost*. Cresskill, NJ: Hampton Press.

eReleases (n.d.). Retrieved October 8, 2019 from ereleases.com.

Etzioni, A. (1993). *The spirit of community: The reinvention of American society*. New York: Simon and Schuster.

Etzioni, A. (1995). Old chestnuts and new spurs. In A. Etzioni (Ed.), *New communitarian thinking: Persons, virtues, institutions, and communities* (pp. 16–36). Charlottesville, VA: University Press of Virginia.

Fowler, R. B. (1995). Community: Reflections on definition. In A. Etzioni (Ed.), *New communitarian thinking: Persons, virtues, institutions, and communities* (pp. 88–95). Charlottesville, VA: University Press of Virginia.

Friedrich, C. J. (1959). The concept of community in the history or political and legal philosophy. In C. J. Friedrich (Ed.), *Community* (pp. 3–24). New York: The Liberal Arts Press.

Gilbert, W. H. (1975). Public relations in local government. Washington, DC: International Management Association.

Goldstein, L. J. (1993, April-May). Business and education: The power of productive partnership. *Executive Speeches*, 1–4.

Greenberg, L. (1993, November). The new education agenda for the '90s: Business moves to reform the system. *Public Relations Journal*, 31–33.

Hein, K. (1997, January). Corporate conscience: Volunteer programs create goodwill within the community—and in the workplace. *Incentive*, 30–31.

Himmelstein, J. L. (1997). *Looking good and doing good: Corporate philanthropy and corporate power*. Bloomington, Indiana: Indiana University Press.

Hirschman, A. O. (1970). *Exit, Voice, and Loyalty: Responses to decline in firms, organizations, and states*. Cambridge, MA: Harvard University Press.

How important is community relations to a company? (2016, May 3). PRMR Public Relations Consultants. Retrieved October 8, 2019 from www.prmrinc.com.

Kaag, J. (2009). American interpretations of Hegel: Josiah Royce's philosophy of loyalty. *History of Philosophy Quarterly, 26*, 83–101.

Korzybski, A. (2000). *Science and sanity: An introduction to non-Aristotelian systems of general semantics*. Brooklyn, NY: International Non-Aristotelian Library Publishing Company. (Original work published 1933).

Kruckeberg, D. & Starck, K. (1988). *Public relations and community: A reconstructed theory*. New York: Praeger.

Ladd, J. (1959). The concept of community: A logical analysis. In C. J. Friedrich (Ed.), *Community* (pp. 269–293). New York: The Liberal Arts Press.

Leeper, K. (1996). Public relations ethics and communitarianism: a preliminary investigation. *Public Relations Review, 22*, 161–170

Mack, R. (1999, July). Event sponsorship: An exploratory study of small business objectives, practices, and perceptions. *Journal of Small Business Management*, 25–30.

Mason, J. C. (1991, October). Business steps up to the blackboard. *Management Review*, 23–27.

McDermott, J. J. (1985). Josiah Royce's philosophy of the community: Danger of the detached individual. *Royal Instituted of Philosophy Supplements, 19*, 153–176. Retrieved October 31, 2019 from www.cambridge.org.

McDermott, J. J. (2005). Introduction. In J. J. McDermott, D. R. Anderson, & J. Jones (Eds.), *The basic writings of Josiah Royce, Volume 1: Culture, philosophy, and religion* (pp. 3–18). New York: Fordham University Press.

Mead, G. H. (1930). The philosophies of Royce, James, and Dewey in their American setting. *International Journal of Ethics, 40*, 211–231.

Monroe, S. (1998, October 12). Duke and Durham: A matter of trust. *Time*, 84.

Nassutti, C. P. (1999, August 31). Doing well by doing good. *Journal of Accountancy*. Retrieved October 8, 2019 from www.journalofaccountancy.com.

Oliveira, A. (2017, March 31). The digital age: How to stay connected in your community. *Forbes*. Retrieved October 12, 2019 from www.forbes.com.

Peters, J. D. (1999). *Speaking into the air: A history of the idea of communication*. University of Chicago Press: Chicago.

Rapoport, A. (1974). *Game theory as a theory of conflict resolution*. Boston: D. Reidel.

Randall, Jr., J. H. (1966). Josiah Royce and American Idealism. *Journal of Philosophy, 63*, 57–83.

Randels, Jr., G. D. (2001). Loyalty, corporations, and community. *Business Ethics Quarterly, 11* (1), 27–40.

Regout, P. (2001, January). Get on with your community. *Management Training*, 72.

Royce, J. (1908). *Race questions, provincialism, and other American problems*. New York: Macmillan.

Royce, J. (1913). *The problem of Christianity*. New York: Macmillan.

Royce, J. (1916). *The hope of the great community*. New York: Macmillan.

Royce, J. (1971). *The philosophy of loyalty*. New York: Hafner. *The philosophy of loyalty*. New York: Macmillan. (Original work published 1908).

Schriner, J. (1997, Sept. 1). Community involvement—what's in it for you? *Industry Week*, 70.

Smith, J. E. (1969). *Royce's social infinite: The community of interpretation*. Hamden, CT: Archon Books.

Trotter, G. (2001). *On Royce*. Belmont, CA: Wadsworth.

Types of PR: The five you need to know. (2019, October 8). Retrieved October 8, 2019 from www.mediaupdate.co.za.

Ulmer, R. R., Sellnow, T. L., & Seeger, M. W. (2019). *Effective crisis communication: Moving from crisis to opportunity* (4th Ed). Los Angeles: Sage.

van Staveren, I. (2009). Communitarianism and the market: A paradox. *Review of Social Economy, 67*, 25–47. doi:10.1080/00346760802431306.

Valentini, C., Kruckeberg, D., & Starck, K. (2012). Public relations and community: A persistent covenant. *Public Relations Review, 38*, 873–879.

Vujnovic, M. & Kruckeberg, D. (2011). Managing global public relations in the new media environment. In M. Deuze (Ed.), *Managing media work*. Thousand Oaks, CA: Sage.

Wahl, S. T. & Maresh-Fuehrer, M. M. (2016). *Public relations principles*. Dubuque, Iowa: Kendall Hunt.

Walzer, M. (1995). The communitarian critique of liberalism. In A. Etzioni (Ed.), *New communitarian thinking: Persons, virtues, institutions, and communities* (pp. 52–70). Charlottesville, VA: University Press of Virginia.

Wilcox, D. L., Cameron, G. L., Reber, B. H., & Shin, J. H. (2013). *Think public relations*. Boston: Pearson.

Wilson, L. J. (1996). Strategic cooperative communities: A synthesis of strategic, issue management and relationship-building approaches in public relations. In H. M. Culbertson & N. Chen (Eds.), *International public relations: A comparative analysis* (pp. 67–80). Mahwah, NJ: Lawrence Earlbaum Associates.

Wolfe, A. (1995). Human nature and the quest for community. In A. Etzioni (Ed.), *New communitarian thinking: Persons, virtues, institutions, and communities* (pp. 126–140). Charlottesville: University of Virginia Press.

Index

abstraction, levels of 6, 16, 22, 47, 48, 55–57
accountability 97–98; agent- 110–112; art of reframing and 98–100, 116; ideal 113–116; liability as 101–102; performative model of 101; principal-agency theory of 106; PR professionals' perspectives of 110; in public relations 108–110; relational aspects of 105–106; sense of responsibility and 103–104; social 102–103, 109, 112–113; social contingency theory of 106; three paradoxes of 107; as virtue and mechanism 104–105
Adams, H. C. 28
aesthetic consciousness 127
agent-accountability 110–112
Angoco, V. 101
Apple 14–16
Aquinas, T. 143
Aristotle 143, 144
Aronoff, C. E. 149

Baktin, M. 61
Baskin, O. W. 149
Bateson, G. 16, 19–21, 55–56, 121
Baxter, L. A. 61, 68
Bernays, E. 33–35, 40–41
Biden, J. 124
Bishop, C. 28, 30
Bivins, T. 44, 48, 132
blind obedience 126
Bloch, H. 127
Bok, S. 124
Boroff, K. E. 125
Botan, C. 17
Bovens, M. 104–105, 106
Bozeman, B. 27, 36

Broom, G. M. 63, 65, 89
Brown, L. 141
Brown, R. E. 44–45, 83
Brown, S. G. 151, 153
Brownell, A. 31
Bruning, S. D. 60, 64–65, 66–67
Buber, M. 83, 86, 145

Cahuc, P. 124
Cameron, K. S. 2
Canary, D. J. 60
Canfield, B. R. 40
capitalism 38
Casey, S. 65
Cassinelli, C. W. 27
Center, A. H. 63
Chapman, K. 20
Chen, N. 147–148
Cheng, Y. 67
Chicago School of Social Thought 150
Clinton, B. 134
Cochran, C. E. 27
communal model of public interest 27
communal relationships 64–65
communication, dualism of 88–93
community: communitarians and 145–146, 157; definitions of 142–143; of inquiry and interpretation 150–156; obligation to 144–145; paradox of 141–142; public relations and 146–150, 156–157
contingency theory 82
control mutuality 60, 64
Coombs, W. T. 108
Copleston, F. 127
corporate social responsibility (CSR) 19, 45–46, 97, 108–109, 148
Cox, M. 101
Creel, G. 30–31

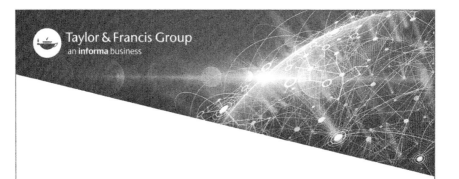